Prostitution in Medieval Society

Women in Culture and Society
A Series Edited by
Catharine R. Stimpson

Prostitution in Medieval Society

The History of an Urban Institution in Languedoc

❧ Leah Lydia Otis

The University of Chicago Press
Chicago and London

LEAH LYDIA OTIS currently lectures in economic history at the University of Montpellier I, and in southern French history and civilization for the University of Minnesota's Montpellier Program.

The University of Chicago Press, Chicago 60637
The University of Chicago Press, Ltd., London
© 1985 by The University of Chicago
All rights reserved. Published 1985
Printed in the United States of America
94 93 92 91 90 89 88 87 86 85   54321

LIBRARY OF CONGRESS CATALOGING IN PUBLICATION DATA

Otis, Leah Lydia.
    Prostitution in medieval society.

    (Women in culture and society)
    An adaptation of the author's thesis (Ph.D.)—Columbia
University, 1980.
    Bibliography: p.
    Includes index.
    1. Prostitution—Europe—History.   2. Social history—
Medieval, 500–1500.   3. Prostitution—France—Languedoc—
History.   I. Title.   II. Series.
HQ184.A5085   1985   306.7'4'094   84-16184
ISBN 0-226-64032-9

To my brother,
and to the memory of our mother and father

Il faut que l'histoire cesse de vous apparaître comme une nécropole endormie, où passent seules des ombres dépouillées de substance. Il faut que dans le vieux palais silencieux où elle sommeille, vous pénétriez, tout animés de la lutte, tout couverts de la poussière du combat, du sang coagulé du monstre vaincu—et qu'ouvrant les fenêtres toutes grandes, ranimant les lumières et rappelant le bruit, vous réveilliez de votre vie à vous, de votre vie chaude et jeune, la vie glacée de la Princesse endormie.

Lucien Febvre, Combats pour l'histoire

❧ Contents

Contents

❧ Foreword

Prostitution in Medieval Society, a monograph about Languedoc between the twelfth and sixteenth centuries, is also much more than that: it is a compelling narrative about the social construction of sexuality.

Leah Lydia Otis uses the implements of scholarship to reveal profound changes in prostitution, that trade in women's bodies. At first more or less tolerated, prostitution later became institutionalized. Various authorities sought to regulate, and to profit from, brothels. In so doing, such powers distinguished legal houses from illegal competition. Arguments against competition became models for a more general assault on prostitution that characterized a third stage: active repression by an increasingly misogynistic sixteenth century. During this period the prostitute became the marginal, criminal figure that haunts the modern imagination.

Dr. Otis reminds us of the limits of her evidence. Preferring silence to heedless speculation, she judiciously refuses to say more than the leavings of history permit her to say. Her archives are too mute to give us more than shadowy outlines of the prostitutes themselves. "Property," she writes, "in this case was far better documented than people."

Despite this, *Prostitution in Medieval Society* weaves the history of women with the histories of several vast phenomena: sexuality; the growth of urban economies; the contest among municipal, state, and religious authorities for the power to define public morality and order; and the struggle within Christianity between Catholicism and an emerging Protestantism. Although this story of the prostitute can be little more than an outline, it is bold enough, in its telling here, to picture that of early modern history itself.

Catharine R. Stimpson

᪉ *Preface*

This book is an adaptation of a doctoral thesis in medieval history presented at Columbia University in 1980. It was originally conceived in 1975, first as an article, then—at the urging of my friend Danièle Neirinck, who knew well the archival potential involved—as a thesis. The book, like the thesis, has a dual orientation. It is both a regional study of medieval prostitution and an attempt to place this regional example in the context of the development of prostitution in western Europe as a whole. As the regional study is based on original archival research, the "case history" of Languedocian prostitution forms the nucleus of the book. The comparative material, gleaned largely from bibliographical research, assumes a secondary role, complementing, confirming, or qualifying the regional study. Hence, a word of advice to the general reader: You may wish to keep an eye on the notes. Although they often contain scholarly apparatus for the use of specialists, many are devoted to comparing Languedocian prostitution with its Italian, German, and English counterparts and are therefore of as much potential interest to the general reader as is the text itself.

A second *caveat* may be added for nonmedievalists. Some of the chapters, especially those dealing with the earlier centuries, proceed by a careful analysis of a series of individual documents, conclusions and generalizations being kept to a minimum. This method has been adopted not out of love of pedantry but out of the concern not to deform, by "filling in the blanks" between existing documents, what little we know of the truth—and our knowledge is limited indeed. Errors in past studies of the history of prostitution have often been due to a rather too wild extrapolation from one or two documents. Hypotheses are presented in this book, but always cautiously, with the awareness that they are subject to confirmation or invalidation in the light of future regional studies. This process is sometimes a frustrating one, for author as well as reader, but it is the only valid approach in a domain suffering from scant documentation, where the discovery of just one new document can lay to rest even the most plausible and seductive of theories.

To the medievalist, I should like to specify that all translations of original texts are mine unless otherwise indicated. From you I must beg indulgence for any lacunae you may discover. This book was written entirely in France, and I have not always been able to consult the best critical edition of the non-Languedocian texts cited and may well be ignorant of some recent relevant article in an English-language periodical.

Vocabulary is often a stumbling block for writers on prostitution; one cannot use a varied and colorful vocabulary without employing terms generally considered to be vulgar or, from the point of view of the prostitute, insulting. If the words used in this book are measured and neutral, it is not only to avoid a pejorative connotation, however, but also to reflect the vocabulary used in medieval legislative and administrative texts; hence, *public women* and *public house* are used frequently, not out of prudery but because they are direct translations of medieval Latin, Occitanian, and French terms. *Prostitute* is usually a more appropriate translation of *meretrix* than *whore*; *whore*, on the other hand, is probably the best translation of *bagassa*, *putain*, *garce*, and other pejorative epithets used in the late Middle Ages. Similarly, when I use the term *"honest"* *women* to refer to nonprostitutes, I do not intend to imply that prostitutes are dishonest, nor to indicate skepticism, via quotation marks, about the honesty of nonprostitutes, but simply to render the term used in medieval texts, more evocative and less cumbersome than any contemporary circumlocutional equivalent.

Indispensable to the realization of this book were the efforts of many people—professors, colleagues, archivists, librarians, and others—whom I thank collectively for their contribution.

I am particularly grateful to Professor André Gouron, who made it possible for me to research and write this essay during an extended stay in France as a lecturer at the Faculté de Droit de Montpellier and its branch campus in Nîmes, and to the municipality of Nîmes for its generosity.

Special thanks go to Mlle Galceran and Mme Siraudin of the Inter-Library Loan Service in Montpellier for procuring much of the bibliography and to Barbara Beckerman Davis, who provided an indispensable lifeline with the archives of Toulouse. I am also grateful to Ian Dengler, to Professors Jean-Marie Carbasse, Michel Lacave, and Kathryn Reyerson, and to Alison Klairmont Lingo for sharing their knowledge and advice with me; to Gerry Moran for his wise counsel and moral support; and to my husband, Patrice Cour, who provided a confidence and enthusiasm that I myself often lacked.

Some contributions are nonetheless important for having been indirect. I am grateful to Andrej Kaminsky, whose courses sensitized me to the problem of "marginality"; to Betty Nassif, who taught so many of us that history can be a passion as well as a discipline; and to Robert Somerville, without whose example and constant encouragement I should never have undertaken doctoral studies in history.

Finally, my greatest debts of gratitude are to my mentor, Professor John H. Mundy, who has had faith in this project since its conception and who gave earlier drafts of this essay the most exhaustive critical commentaries, and to Danièle Neirinck, *archiviste-paléographe*, without whose inspiration, guidance, and friendship this book would never have seen the light of day.

🍁 Abbreviations

The reader is asked to consult the bibliography for complete references.

AD	Archives départementales
AM	Archives municipales
AN	Archives nationales
An-ESC	*Annales: économies, sociétés, civilisations*
BEC	*Bibliothèque de l'Ecole des Chartes*
BM	Bibliothèque municipale
BSABéz	*Bulletin de la Société archéologique de Béziers*
BSFHMéd	*Bulletin de la Société française de l'histoire de la médecine*
FCM	Fonds des coutumes méridionales
FHL	*Fédération historique du Languedoc méditerranéen et du Roussillon*
HGL	Devic and Vaissete, *Histoire générale de Languedoc*
Inv.	Inventaire
Le Pileur, *Documents*	Le Pileur, *La prostitution du XIIIᵉ siècle* . . .
l., s., d.	livres, sous, deniers (tournois)
MANî	*Mémoires de l'Académie de Nîmes*
MSAMtp	*Mémoires de la Société archéologique de Montpellier*
Ord	Laurière, *Ordonnances des roys de France*
PL	Migne, *Patrologiae, series latina*
RHD	*Revue historique de droit français et étranger*

RMT-SHD   *Recueil de mémoires et travaux* publié par la Société d'histoire du droit et des institutions des anciens pays de droit écrit (Montpellier)

ZSSR   *Zeitschrift der Savigny-Stiftung für Rechtsgeschichte*

Approximate Money Equivalences

Coins in circulation	Value in accounting terms
1 franc	= 1 l.
1 mouton d'or	= 20 s.
1 ducat	= 40 s.
1 écu	= 37 s.
1 florin de Provence	= 13 s. 9 d.
1 gros	= 15 d.
1 dobla de Savoie	= 10 d.
1 blanc	= 5 d.
1 ardit	= 3 d.
1 liard	= 3 d.

NOTE: 1 l(ivre) = 20 s(ous)
     1 s. = 12 d(eniers)

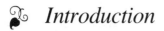 *Introduction*

A History of Medieval Prostitution: Framework and Assumptions

It is no longer necessary—thankfully—to preface a historical investigation of prostitution with an apology for the choice of topic. A growing number of studies of prostitution is making up for the years of neglect, or rather of avoidance, of what had seemed to some historians a scandalous, and to others a frivolous, topic of research.[1] From these recent studies is slowly emerging a sketch of the evolution of prostitution in the Western world.

The period for which this sketch is the haziest is the Middle Ages. On the one hand, the general histories of prostitution include chapters on the Middle Ages that are inadequate and notoriously contradictory.[2] Recent studies of medieval prostitution, on the other hand, while contributing enormously to a better understanding of the phenomenon, have been limited to one town or to a short period of time or to one aspect of the problem. The aim of this essay is to attempt to clarify and refine our understanding of medieval prostitution by means of a *regional study*—a framework limited enough to allow a careful, detailed archival study, yet broad enough, geographically and temporally, to permit generalizations and a sense of the evolution of what was a very dynamic phenomenon.[3]

The new interest in the history of prostitution owes much to the growing popularity of three greater topics of investigation: the history of marginal social groups, the history of women, and the history of sexuality. This study touches on all three domains but has not adopted any of the three as a predominant orientation. Its goal is to present a global description and analysis of *all* aspects of medieval prostitution: the attitude of government and society

I

toward prostitution and prostitutes, the material structures and human dynamics of the phenomenon, and its function in, and relation to, Languedocian society. The sources available have made it perforce institutional in orientation;[4] if it must be seen as part of a larger history, then it is a chapter in the history of urban institutions.

It is not possible in undertaking a study of the history of prostitution to rely to any great measure on the social sciences for a set of assumptions or constructs. There is, in fact, no single model for the analysis of prostitution, as it is a phenomenon of psychological, social, commercial, and moral dimensions. Given its commercial importance, it could be studied from the economic point of view, but in fact it has attracted little attention from economists or economic historians, as it is a "nonproductive" activity and is often illegal or semilegal. The sociological literature devoted to prostitution, on the other hand, is considerable. Defining the prostitute as a type of deviant, sociologists have tended to concentrate their studies on the sociological and psychological factors that determine recruitment. The usefulness of this type of model for the medievalist is limited: first, because it analyzes information (vocational motivation, socioeconomic backgrounds, psychological profiles) that is generally not available for the medieval period; and, second, because it is based on the assumption that prostitutes are "marginal" people, which, while valid enough for the early modern and modern periods, does not apply well to the Middle Ages, when prostitution was a recognized, if not particularly respected, profession.[5] Nor have anthropologists provided an analytic model, since, dealing principally with preliterate and pre-exchange societies, they have little to say on the subject.[6] The rudimentary tools for an analysis of prostitution, a multidimensional cultural problem, have been forged essentially by those interdisciplinary social scientists with an interest in the cultural history of sexuality, whether they be sociologists, historians, or philosophers.[7]

Often more descriptive than analytic, this study rests on few theoretical assumptions. Fundamental to it is a definition of the prostitute, that of the Roman jurist Ulpian, as a person engaging in sexual activity with a large number of customers for money or other material remuneration.[8] Accepting this definition of the prostitute, I define prostitution, for the purposes of this study, as a phenomenon in which *a socially identifiable group of women earn their living principally or exclusively from the commerce of their bodies.*[9] Thus strictly defined, prostitution appears as an essentially urban phenomenon: only in towns is the demand for sexual services large enough to justify the existence of a professional category to satisfy it.[10] The amplitude of the demand comes from the nature of the social groups there (communities of traveling merchants, large groups of unmarried young men) as well as from the scale of the population,[11] and payment is facilitated by cash flow, characteristic of urban exchange economies.[12] These conditions are, of course, not sufficient unless there is a greater tolerance for male than for female sexual activity, but this condition would seem to be characteristic of all cultures in which cities have appeared.[13] Only in an urban environment do we find the social and professional phenomenon of prostitution, and only when a society is confronted with such a phenomenon and is aware of the necessity of reconciling it to the common good do we find a consciously expressed attitude, if not policy, toward it.

Also underlying this essay is the assumption that a study of prostitution cannot be limited to that of just prostitute, procurer, and brothel. Viewed in economic terms, these factors are but the "supply side" of the phenomenon, meaningless without a consideration of demand in the person of the customer and, more globally, of society and its mores. Changes in attitude toward prostitution reflect changes—qualitative or quantitative—in supply and demand, and these in turn are determined by economic, social, and cultural factors. Changes in social structure, changes in cultural values—these are the factors that determine and transform the shape of prostitution in a given society. The growth and transformation of prostitution in the modern period, for instance, cannot be comprehended without an awareness of the rapid industrialization and urbanization of the nineteenth century; the demographic boom; the vagaries of female employment, unemployment, and exploitation; the emphasis on romantic love in middle-class marriages; the growing tolerance of male premarital sexual activity in the twentieth century; and so on. So medieval prostitution was shaped by demographic, economic, social, and cultural forces. In order to understand the prostitution of medieval Languedoc, we must consider the institutional and cultural context in which it developed.

Languedocian Urban Life in the High and Late Middle Ages

Languedoc (*Langue d'oc*) originally meant the language of the southern half of what we now call France, a tongue bearing more similarity to other Mediterranean languages than to that spoken in the north of France (*Langue d'oeil*). But the term *Languedoc* soon came to stand for the land itself—all that lies south of an imaginary line undulating from Bordeaux to the Italian border. Nowadays the French refer quite simply to the Midi (South) or sometimes to Occitania, although the latter grates on almost all but the medievalist's ear, because of its popular association with regionalist and autonomist movements. *Occitania* is so convenient a term for the land, however, and *Occitanian* so unambiguous a name for the language (as opposed to the misleading *Provençal*, which makes one think of that one region rather than the whole of the Midi) that these words will be used consistently throughout this book.[14]

Languedoc in the title of this book is a large region in the center of southern

Occitania. Stretching from Toulouse in the west, along the Mediterranean coast to the Rhone River, and up the right bank to Le Puy, Languedoc, its boundaries fixed in the fourteenth century, was the largest and one of the most varied of the old French provinces, comprising the fertile, rolling Lauragais plains, the sun-baked Mediterranean coast, and the often rugged and infertile southern and eastern slopes of the Massif Central.[15]

Far from constituting a political unit in the High Middle Ages, Languedoc was a mosaic of seigneuries—some ecclesiastical, especially in the mountains, but most lay seigneuries—the largest of which was the county of Toulouse, covering most of western Languedoc.[16] By the early thirteenth century, most of the major urban centers in the region had succeeded in winning a certain degree of autonomy from their lords (such a politically and administratively active municipality was called a *consulat*, and its executive officers *consuls*), but the Languedocian towns were never to achieve that sovereignty characteristic of the Italian city-republics.[17] From the close of the Albigensian wars to the middle of the fourteenth century, the Capetian monarchy assimilated the lands of Languedoc into the kingdom of France, some by direct conquest, others by insinuation into the system of collegial lordship typical of medieval Occitania.[18] Although the towns retained a large degree of administrative autonomy, they recognized, as did the rest of the population, the sovereignty of the French crown and found themselves increasingly monitored in the late Middle Ages by the expanding royal administration.

Languedoc had no great international capital of the dimensions of Paris or Florence, but it boasted two large towns—Toulouse, with a population of about 35,000 in the early fourteenth century, and Montpellier, with somewhat fewer inhabitants—which played important roles in international commerce, and a dense network (at least in the lowlands) of medium-sized and small towns which were centers of some industry and considerable commercial activity.[19] These Languedocian towns experienced a cycle of economic and demographic development similar to that of most western European towns in the Middle Ages: the uninterrupted, often spectacular growth of commerce, industry, and urban population in the eleventh, twelfth, and thirteenth centuries; a "flattening of the curve" in the early fourteenth century, then the catastrophic demographic and economic decline of the second half of the fourteenth century (exacerbated in many parts of Languedoc by the ravages of the Hundred Years' War); the slow rise of commerce and population in the fifteenth century, culminating in the demographic and commercial boom of the early sixteenth century.[20]

At the head of this urban society were the great *burgenses*, mainly important merchants and moneylenders, and the petty nobles, who, in Languedoc as in Italy, often resided in the town. Smaller merchants, craftsmen, and numerous agricultural workers accounted for most of the population of the towns, which also included important enclaves of secular and regular clergy.

The relatively harmonious coexistence of these classes was interrupted periodically by disputes and occasionally by uprisings. In the second half of the fourteenth century, violent insurrection plagued Languedoc, as it did other European regions in the same period.[21]

The cultural values of medieval society, in Languedoc as elsewhere, were dictated to a great extent by the Church, which by the thirteenth century had developed a particularly coherent system of sexual morality based on the restriction of all sexual activity within the bonds of marriage and the decision that the only acceptable form of Christian marriage was perpetual monogamy. Yet, despite the Church's effort to impose its moral framework on the lay population by means of preaching and pastoral care as well as the Inquisition (both of particular importance in heresy-inclined Languedoc), secular customs and attitudes continued largely to define popular notions of sexual morality.[22] Particularly tenacious was a considerable tolerance of male premarital and extramarital sexual activity. Condoned in Germanic custom, this double standard was reinforced in Languedoc by the spread of Roman law in the twelfth and thirteenth centuries via notarial practice and the teaching of law in small-town schools and in the universities of Montpellier and Toulouse.[23]

There are, unfortunately, significant gaps in our knowledge of the cultural and social context in which this study is set; these lacunae must be filled as best they can with comparative material from other regions. Our knowledge of Languedocian family structure, for example, is limited by the nature of the Languedocian tax registers (the *compoix*), which contain much less information of demographic interest than their Italian counterparts, and by the scarcity of family narrative comparable to the *ricordi* (personal diaries) left by numerous Italian merchants. To have some idea of the proportion of unmarried men and women in the population, the average age at marriage, and other factors relevant to a study of prostitution, it is to studies of Italian towns— especially that vast panorama of Tuscan society recently sketched by D. Herlihy and C. Klapisch-Zuber—that we must turn.[24]

The literary lacunae are equally important. Rich as medieval Languedocian literature was in matters of love, it deigned not to deal with the amorous activities of the lower classes, unlike the northern French *fabliaux* and the bawdy tales of Italy, in which prostitutes play such prominent roles.[25] Here, too, comparison is our only option, and, rather than rely on the cultural context to help us appreciate the subject at hand, we are obliged, on the contrary, to seek in a study of prostitution elements that may be propitious to a better understanding of that context.

PART ONE

Prostitution and Public Authority: An Evolution

Toward a Chronology of Medieval Prostitution

Methodological Problems

The study of medieval history is riddled with methodological problems: some documents are undated, others misdated; some are later copies or translations of a lost original, others are veritable fakes; some are anonymous, others the products of biased authors. For the medievalist, a healthy skepticism is necessary, and checking and verifying a constant preoccupation.

Skepticism and prudence are nowhere more necessary than in the study of those aspects of medieval society that have left sparse documentation, such as prostitution. Uncritical acceptance of all surviving documents can only lead to what we see in the popular histories of prostitution—an incoherent and sometimes flatly contradictory account of the attitude of public authorities toward prostitution in the Middle Ages.

Generally speaking, three policies on prostitution are possible in a given society: repression (defining prostitution as a punishable offense), tolerance, or institutionalization.[1] There are medieval documents testifying—or seeming to testify—to all three policies. To find some order in this chaos, one must analyze each text carefully, checking its authenticity and taking into consideration the circumstances of its production and its historical context. Care must also be taken to distinguish between the attitudes of different public authorities (seigneurial, royal, municipal, ecclesiastical) in different countries and towns and in different periods of time. Making this chronological distinction is especially important; many of the seeming contradictions can be explained by the evolution, from the twelfth to the sixteenth century, of very different attitudes toward prostitution. An attempt to label the Middle Ages a

globally "repressive" period or a period of "institutionalization" often reflects inadequate attention to the importance of this chronological evolution. The opinion that medieval society favored the repression of prostitution, found principally but not exclusively in the works of nonhistorians, is a fundamentally anachronistic view. Some justification for this interpretation would seem to be found in the Church's hostility toward illicit sex, in a capitulary attributed to Charlemagne, and in an ordinance of Saint Louis,[2] but this view is based principally on a methodological error—the tendency to "read back" to the Middle Ages punishments for prostitution current in the late sixteenth and seventeenth centuries. A classic example is the case of "dunking," a form
- of punishment in which the convicted person is placed in a cage and lowered several times into a river or pond. Used in the southwest of France in late medieval times principally to punish blasphemers,[3] dunking may indeed have been a punishment for prostitutes in this region in the late sixteenth and seventeenth centuries, but there are no grounds for concluding, as some writers have, from later evidence and from the antiquity of the punishment, that it had been used against prostitutes in the Middle Ages and, hence, that prostitution was then considered a punishable offense.[4] Reading back to the Middle Ages the punishment of prostitutes and the general hostility toward prostitution characteristic of the Reformation and Counter-Reformation can only lead to a distorted view of medieval attitudes toward prostitution.

The majority of historians, however, have generally agreed that prostitution was tolerated in the Middle Ages. Some have gone so far, moreover, as to imply that institutionalized prostitution, which was indeed the rule in fifteenth-century Languedoc, had been an integral part of medieval society from the High Middle Ages onward.[5] Such a view is also anachronistic. It is based to some extent on reading back to an earlier period attitudes and institutions current in the fifteenth century, much as advocates of the repressive theory read back punishments of early modern times to the Middle Ages. A good example is the case of the well-known medieval fair of Beaucaire, celebrated annually on the feast day of Saint Mary Magdalene (22 July). It was customary at this fair for the municipality to sponsor a series of games and competitive events, including a race for prostitutes.[6] An officially sponsored race for prostitutes, while a vivid illustration of the integration of public women into the customs of Languedocian society in the fifteenth century, cannot, however, be considered, as has been assumed by several authors, to represent the place of the prostitute in the society of the High Middle Ages: first, because the oldest text attesting to such a custom is from the 1490s; second, and conclusively, because the fair of Beaucaire, believed in the past to have existed since the twelfth century, has in recent years been proved to have been itself a creation of the 1460s.[7]

Another example of reading back institutions of the fifteenth century to the High Middle Ages is seen in the history of a certain charter from Toulouse dated 1201. Paraphrased, beginning in the seventeenth century, to give the impression that it provided for the creation of an authorized red-light district in that town, this charter is in fact merely an order for the expulsion of prostitutes from the center of town—hardly a proof of institutionalization at that period.[8]

Some medieval documents actually encourage the historian to read back. In a safeguard for the municipal brothel of Toulouse dated 1425, for example, it is stated that the consuls had owned such a house "for a long time before." In a somewhat later royal document, it is declared that maintaining such a house was "a custom of great antiquity" in Languedoc.[9] Yet we know for a fact from other sources that the municipally owned brothel was a creation of the 1360s and 1370s, not an ancient custom whose origins were lost in the mists of time. These fifteenth-century documents were not intended to give an accurate picture of the situation in the thirteenth or even the mid–fourteenth century, but rather to enhance the legitimacy of a contemporary institution, with a solemn evocation of its supposed antiquity.[10]

Even when dealing with strictly contemporary documents, one often faces a problem in interpreting the vocabulary used. The words cannot be taken out of context and given a meaning alien to the intention of the author. This is a particular problem when dealing with Latin texts in which the author is often struggling for Latin equivalents of vernacular expressions. Thus, the word *meretrix*, which in Roman times signified unambiguously a public prostitute, may be used in early-medieval texts to evoke generally a "loose" woman.[11] Similarly, when William of Malmsbury relates in his *Gesta Regum Anglorum* that William IX, duke of Aquitaine (fl. 1100–1127), established a *prostibulum*, he is not, as some authors have inferred, announcing the chartering of a public brothel but rather attempting to convey in Latin the idea of a sort of harem kept by the duke, fuel to stoke the fire of his diatribe against William's lubricious nature.[12]

Yet another kind of methodological problem is presented by the charter granted to the town of Villefranche-de-Lauragais by Philip III in 1280.[13] The last article of this document, granting the townspeople authority to establish an official house of prostitution, has been cited as evidence of the institutionalization of prostitution in the thirteenth century.[14] Unimpeachable as this evidence would seem at first to be, it must be called into question in light of the fact that the extant document is not the original thirteenth-century charter but a sixteenth-century copy, which includes later revisions and additions (e.g., references to towns founded in the fourteenth century). An analysis of the language and content of the article on the public brothel proves that it is, in fact, an interpolation from the late fourteenth or fifteenth century.[15]

A last example shows to what extent the path to a better understanding of medieval prostitution may be strewn with red herrings. The eminent eighteenth-century Doctor J. Astruc, in his *De morbis venereis*, published a document that he believed to come from the archives of Avignon. Bearing the date 1347, "The Statutes of the Queen Jeanne for a Public House in Avignon," a list of regulations for the running of a brothel, has been accepted as authentic by many authors of general histories of prostitution.[16] Yet two successive studies by P. Pansier have proved beyond any doubt that the document is a fake, concocted by some mischievous residents of Avignon as a hoax on Astruc.[17] Most of the articles are loosely based on authentic documents from the fifteenth century, but the language (the text is in Occitanian) and handwriting are, as Pansier shows, purely eighteenth-century. The patronage of a brothel by a queen, moreover, is inappropriate for the mid–fourteenth century, as is the provision for a weekly sanitary inspection of the women.[18]

Once these and other methodological problems are solved, it becomes possible to determine that the period from the twelfth to the sixteenth century witnessed a considerable evolution in public policies on prostitution. A primitive attitude of tolerance had evolved into a policy of institutionalization in the late Middle Ages, only to be replaced in the sixteenth century by an active repression of prostitution. Before examining this evolution in detail, however, let us consider briefly how prostitution was regarded in the period preceding the twelfth century.

Prostitution before the Twelfth Century: The Roman and Christian Heritage and the Early Middle Ages

Prostitution, like concubinage, was a fully accepted part of life in the Roman Empire, viewed as a practical means of dissuading young men from intriguing with married women.[19] Houses of prostitution were tolerated, although the owner of such a house was considered infamous; that is, he was deprived of his civic rights because of the nature of his business. Prostitutes were supposed to register with the authorities; a state tax on these registered prostitutes was introduced in the first century A.D. A woman who had once registered as a prostitute retained that stigma for the rest of her life, even if she ceased all professional activity.

Although the Church fathers fulminated against the commerce of the body with the same ferocity as against other sins of the flesh rampant in the Roman world, prostitution, being a social phenomenon rather than a personal sin (such as fornication), did not, strictly speaking, lie within the spiritual jurisdiction of the Church. Despite its condemnation of all premarital and extramarital sexual activity, the Church recognized prostitution to be an inevitable feature of worldly society, which it had no hope or ambition to reform. Saint Augustine even warned that the abolition of prostitution, were it possible, would have disastrous consequences for society; the practice, he believed, was a necessary evil in an inevitably imperfect world.[20] Canonical wrath was focused, rather, on those who profited from this commerce, for, while pros-titution was regarded as a social phenomenon distinct from the sin of fornica-tion, procuring was considered by the Church to be synonymous with the sin-ful act of encouraging debauch (since the latter is usually associated with a pecuniary motive, whereas fornication can be committed out of passion as well as out of desire for money). Procuring was therefore considered to be a matter of spiritual jurisdiction, and strong measures were taken against it at the Council of Elvira (c. 300), whose canons were included in most of the major canon-law collections of the Middle Ages.[21]

The Church firmly rejected, of course, the Roman notion of a permanent stigma attached to women who had once been prostitutes. Because all people were considered sinners who must repent to be saved, prostitutes found them-selves in no especially stigmatized category but were accepted, like all other sinners, provided they abandoned their former life. Indeed, several of the fe-male saints of the early Church were former prostitutes.[22] Thus, the Church's position on prostitution, crystallized by the fourth century, consisted of these three elements: acceptance of prostitution as an inevitable social fact, con-demnation of those profiting from this commerce, and encouragement for the prostitute to repent.

The teachings of the Church were reflected in the legislation of the Chris-tian emperors, which directed its sanctions against those profiting from pros-titution. The clause forbidding prostitution of slaves became mandatory in contracts of sale; fathers and guardians who tried to force their daughters and wards into prostitution lost all power over them.[23] Justinian eventually out-lawed procuring and brothel keeping in Constantinople, providing severe penalties for offenders (Novella 14).

Little has been written on prostitution in the early Middle Ages, and, in-deed, there is but a scant documentary basis for such a study. The general histories have mostly labeled the early Middle Ages a "repressive" period, relying for evidence almost exclusively on a Carolingian capitulary that in-veighs against *meretrices*.[24] As neither the Roman nor the Christian tradition provides a precedent for punishing prostitutes which might account for this measure, a closer analysis of the document is called for.

Although E. Baluze attributed the capitulary to Charlemagne, A. Boretius, relying on internal evidence, has proved it to be from the reign of Louis the Pious, thus placing it in the context of moral reform characteristic of the son of Charlemagne. The specific object of reform in this capitulary, however, as we see from its very title (*De disciplina palatii Aquisgranensis*), was the royal palace, not society at large.[25] The author of the text, far from envisaging a campaign to rid the villages of their occasional common prostitutes, was surely aiming this measure at any women of questionable sexual conduct re-siding within the royal palace. The term *meretrix* is, after all, merely an at-tempt at a Latin equivalent of an original Frankish expression.[26] In this rural society of little commercial activity, where prostitution had dwindled to a marginal phenomenon, the word *meretrix* had ceased to designate the professional prostitute and had become instead a general term for any woman of questionable sexual conduct.[27] It is indeed in this way that the word is used in its only appearance in *Lex Salica*—as a simple insult devoid of any specific meaning.[28]

The unspecific nature of the word *meretrix* in this period is well illustrated by a passage from *De institutio laicali* by Jonas of Orleans, bishop of that city in the first half of the ninth century. In a section on sexual morality, Jonas warns young men not to have sexual relations "secretly with 'prostitutes' [*meretrices*], nor openly with handmaidens [*ancillae*]."[29] This text was addressed to the *potentes* (powerful people) of society, for whom extramarital relations consisted largely in concubinage with social inferiors.[30] Concubinage of the *potentes*, although called into question by contemporary ecclesiastics, was a generally accepted secular institution and therefore did not need to be hidden.[31] Amorous adventures with women of a higher social status, on the other hand, had to be carried on with more discretion, as they compromised the woman's position in society. There was no place in this system for the professional prostitute; the *ancilla* of the text is a concubine, and the *meretrix* simply an "immoral" woman, not a professional prostitute.

The specific meaning of the word *meretrix*, pertinent to the urban culture of the Roman Empire, had little relevance in this rural, clan-oriented society. Prostitution, insofar as it existed in Carolingian times, was surely an occasional and marginal aspect of village life. The word *meretrix* did not signify a professional prostitute, but rather a woman whose sexual conduct betrayed and brought shame on her husband or family. The capitulary of Louis the Pious calling for the punishment of such women has nothing to do with prostitution, strictly speaking.

A "policy" on prostitution became even less of a comprehensible notion in the ensuing feudal period, when the idea of the state and of public order faded from consciousness; legislation in the interest of the commonweal was inconceivable once public power had been reduced to a private possession. The social phenomenon of prostitution, impossible outside the context of flourishing commerce, became once again an object of reflexion and regulation only when a new urban society began to evolve out of the rural, feudal legacy of the Frankish world.

℘ *Chapter One*

The Twelfth and Thirteenth Centuries: Prostitution Accepted

What historians refer to as the "renaissance of the twelfth century"—that burgeoning of European society and culture in the High Middle Ages, characterized by a great demographic surge, the expansion and technological improvement of agriculture, the growth of industry and commerce, the religious and intellectual ferment associated with a renewed papacy, and the spread of schools and universities—was felt in Languedoc, as elsewhere in western Europe, and was manifested most visibly by the growth and multiplication of that region's urban centers. Whether a traditional center of the ancient Roman world, such as Toulouse, Narbonne, and Nîmes, or a creation of the feudal period, such as Castres, Alès, and, most spectacularly, Montpellier, the towns of Languedoc experienced considerable demographic, commercial, and political growth in the High Middle Ages.

Although one might expect such urban growth to have been propitious to the development of prostitution, the archival documents of these towns, rare and almost all political in nature at the turn of the eleventh to the twelfth century, are mute on this subject. To touch at the roots of the development of prostitution in these first decades of urban growth, one is obliged to rely on extra-archival sources.

In his *Summa Codicis*, Placentinus included among those people inapt to testify "[a woman] who openly does commerce with her body" (*"qui palam corpore quaestum fecerit,"* 4:20). A native of Italy and a teacher of Roman law in Montpellier, Placentinus was not presenting an original formula in his *Summa* but rather paraphrasing the definition of the prostitute given by the third-century Roman jurist Ulpian in the Digest.[1] Roman law, the rediscovery and renewal of which was the keystone of the intellectual developments of the "twelfth-century renaissance," provided its students with the vocabulary and concepts necessary to discuss and comprehend the social phenomenon of prostitution. The twelfth-century civilians' interest in this vocabulary and these concepts seems to indicate their relevance to an actual growth of prostitution in the towns of this period.[2]

Like the Roman jurists, the medieval civilians accepted without question the fact of prostitution. Placentinus and the author of *Lo Codi*, moreover, kept the Roman argument for the justification of the salary of the prostitute.[3] The twelfth-century jurists also accepted the Roman notion of the stigma attached to the prostitute. All three authors refused the validity of testimony by a prostitute.[4] The author of the *Exceptiones* refused, in addition, the validity of marriage between "noble and honest men and public prostitutes [*meretrices publicas*] and their daughters."[5]

The last passage shows that the twelfth-century civilians were not merely copying out by rote the provisions of the Roman jurists. Not only is the content original,[6] but the term used—*meretrix publica*—is not a Roman one. This term would have been redundant in Roman times, a *meretrix* being by definition a public person who earned money (*merere*) from her activities, not a privately "immoral" woman. The word *meretrix* continued to be used in the West after the decline of Roman cities, but it had lost, as we have seen in the Prologue, its precise and specific meaning and had come to be used as a general insult implying illicit sexual conduct. The addition of the adjective *publica* was therefore necessary, in a period of rising prostitution, to distinguish the professional public woman from the private amateur.

The renaissance of the study of Roman law was closely associated with the commercial and urban expansion of the twelfth century. The schools in which Roman law was taught were located in the towns, and the professors of Roman law often acted as legal advisers to the town council or to local merchants, since the material of Roman law brought much that was relevant to the government, business, and family relations of the day. It is therefore not unreasonable to suppose that the use of the new term *meretrix publica* by the twelfth-century civilians and their interest in defining the position of the prostitute in society testify to the "renaissance" of prostitution in this period and the concern of urban society with the problems it posed. Such a supposition is supported by the fact that the same vocabulary and a similar attitude toward the prostitute are found in the earliest relevant archival documents.

One of the most important attributes of certain Languedocian town consulates of the twelfth and thirteenth centuries was the power to determine the laws and legislation of the municipality. These laws, usually referred to as customs or statutes, and the administrative acts concerning their enforcement were recorded, with other significant documents, into cartularies (registers) kept in the newly developed town archives. It is in such archival documents that one finds the first indications of a municipal policy concerning prostitution in the western Languedocian towns of Carcassonne and Toulouse.

The 105th article of the customs of Carcassonne, dating probably from the very beginning of the thirteenth century,[7] reads, "Public prostitutes [*meretrices publice*] are to be put outside the walls of Carcassonne."[8] An example of the actual enforcement of a similar municipal law is found in a cartulary of the city of Toulouse.[9] Dated 31 August 1201, it concerns the complaint of a certain Bernard Raymond of Toulouse and of the "good men" (*probi homines*) living in the street of Comminges about prostitutes (*meretrices publice*) living there, causing "great evil and damage" (*magnum malum et dampnum*), day and night, to all the residents. The good men request the consuls of the city to rule that no prostitute shall live in that street, basing their demand on an extant law (*constitutio*) of the city which states that no prostitute should live within the city walls. The consuls comply, ruling "that no public prostitute shall stay nor live in any way or for any time within the walls of the city of Toulouse or in its suburbs."[10] In case of infraction, the good men of the neighborhood are to complain to the vicar. If he does not immediately remove the prostitutes, the good citizens themselves may eject the women without fear of punishment.[11]

This Toulousan charter, along with the laconic custom from Carcassonne, indicates that professional prostitutes were indeed recognized as a specific social group in these towns in the early thirteenth century; the term *meretrix publica*, the same as in the Roman law texts (and perhaps inspired by them), is unambiguous. The rudimentary policy on prostitution presented in the documents is negative in tenor, consisting simply in the refusal to allow prostitutes to stay within the city walls, removing them in this way from the areas in which "honest" citizens resided and most commercial activity was carried on.[12] One can assume, moreover, that this "negative" policy was already in effect in the twelfth century. The statute of Carcassonne, being a part of the customary law of that town, had presumably a relative antiquity. Even more persuasive is the reference in the Toulousan charter to an already existing law (*constitutio*) barring prostitutes from the center of town, the text of which was presented to the consuls as precedent for a new ruling.

Neither text, it must be emphasized, mentions an official red-light district where prostitutes should reside, despite the fact that the Toulousan charter of 1201 has been paraphrased in such a distorted manner as to suggest just that.[13] The earliest public policy on prostitution in Languedoc was a negative one, simply forbidding prostitutes from residing within the city walls, not, as was later to be the case, assigning them an official residence.[14]

The customs and charters of eastern Languedoc from the early thirteenth century are mute on the subject of prostitution. One must look farther east, to Arles and Avignon, two great commercial centers of the lower Rhone River valley, to find other statutes regulating prostitution in this period. Published and enforced since the towns were raised to the rank of consulate in the early twelfth century, these statutes have survived in their last revised form, published in the 1240s, shortly before the loss of the extensive municipal liberties of these towns to Charles of Anjou.

The relevant statute from Arles, no. 49, reads:

We statute that no public prostitute [*meretrix publica*] or procurer dare stay in Arles in a street of "good men," and if by chance they be found in such places, that anyone of that area or neighborhood have the power to expel them from the neighborhood, on his own authority, without punishment or contradiction of the court.[15]

Article 116 of the statutes of Avignon contains many of the same elements as the Arlesian text,[16] and both are similar to the documents from Carcassonne and Toulouse, in that they describe an essentially negative policy concerning the residence of the *meretrix publica*. Barring prostitutes from honest neighborhoods came more or less to the same thing as relegating them to places outside the city walls, although it was a custom that was less precise and perhaps less categorical than its western Languedocian counterpart.

A clearly different element in these Rhodanian texts, on the other hand, is the reference to procurers (*leno* in the Arlesian document and *ruffiane seu destrales* in the Avignonese statute).[17] Arles and Avignon, unlike Carcassonne and Toulouse, explicitly tolerated procuring as well as prostitution and applied to procurers the same legislation as to prostitutes.

There are important distinctions to be made, moreover, between the Arlesian and Avignonese legislation on prostitution. In Arles, prostitutes found living in respectable neighborhoods could be expelled by any of the residents of that neighborhood (a procedure that was licit in Toulouse only after resort to a responsible public officer proved ineffective). In Avignon, on the other hand, such procedure was not allowed; punishment of offending prostitutes there was firmly in the hands of the public authorities. The Avignonese statutes include, moreover, a rudimentary code of conduct for prostitutes: article 116 deals with their manner of dressing[18] and prohibits married *meretrices* from practicing within the city; article 137 forbids prostitutes to touch food products on the market;[19] and article 77, concerning gaming, prohibits such activity after curfew in "brothels and prostitutes' houses," as well as in inns, gaming houses, and taverns.[20] This last statute amounts to an acceptance and recognition of places of prostitution as well as prostitutes. Its significance can be appreciated when one notices that in an otherwise identical article concerning gaming in the statutes of Arles,[21] no such mention of brothels is made. The statutes of Avignon represent a first, primitive step toward the development of a policy regulating places of prostitution, as well as prostitutes, in Occitania.

The revision of the statutes of Arles and Avignon marked the end in Provence of a period of relative municipal liberty, an emulation of the Italian city-states. The succession of Charles of Anjou to the county of Provence in 1246 and his consequent crushing of municipal liberties was, in fact, only one phase in the development of Capetian hegemony in the south of France, which had begun with Louis VIII's intervention in the Albigensian conflict in 1226. In the treaty of Meaux-Paris of 1229, Raymond VII of Toulouse had ceded the eastern half of his Languedocian territories to the throne of France. The western half of his lands passed, on Raymond's death in 1249, to his daughter, Jeanne, and her husband, Alphonse of Poitiers, the king's brother, then to the Crown in 1271, when Alphonse and Jeanne died without heirs.

The initiatives of the king of France had, therefore, a relevance for the south of France during the reign of Louis IX that they had lacked at the beginning of the thirteenth century. Influenced by the developments in law and in ecclesiastical government, inspired by the model of Charlemagne, Saint Louis launched a program of administrative and moral reform that marked the reestablishment of royal legislative initiative.[22] While the primary aim of the first great monument of Capetian legislation, the ordinance of 1254,[23] was to reform the administration of royal bailiffs, the ordinance also includes measures intended to insure public morality: prohibitions of gaming, blasphemy, and usury, and an unambiguous condemnation of prostitution.

> Public prostitutes are to be expelled from the fields [*de campis*] as well as from the towns, and once these warnings or prohibitions made, their goods are to be seized by the judges of the localities, or taken, by their authority, by anyone else, unto the tunic and robe. Who knowingly rents a house to a public prostitute, we wish that that house fall to the lord [king], by whom it is to be held in feudal commission.[24]

It is this text which has been used to support the theory that, in the Middle Ages, public authorities favored a repressive policy on prostitution.[25] The document indeed calls for repression of prostitution and punishment of prostitutes, but in doing so, far from characterizing contemporary policies on prostitution, it flies in the face of established custom of the south of France, and perhaps that of the north, as well. The very formula "expelled from the 'fields' as well as from the towns" is an explicit refusal of the custom established in Carcassonne and Toulouse of relegating prostitutes to the area outside the town walls, and in Avignon and Arles of barring them from neighborhoods of honest citizens. This text should be seen, not as typical of medieval legislation on prostitution, but as a purposeful reversal of the traditional policy of tolerance. Such reversals of traditional law were imposed by the king of France, especially Louis IX, in an effort to suppress what they considered to be bad customs and to replace them with a legislation esteemed to be more rational and just.[26] Just as Saint Louis prohibited traditional trial by battle and opposed many other "irrational" aspects of criminal procedure, so he attempted to extirpate the "bad custom" of tolerance of prostitution.

The traditional policy of tolerance of prostitution seems to have been tenacious, however. Just two years after the declaration of 1254, a second ordinance of Louis IX admitted tacitly the unenforceability of the earlier text.[27] While it retains some elements of the first document, such as the punishment of those renting houses to prostitutes, the ordinance of 1256 differs from it on its most fundamental point: prostitutes were no longer to be expelled "from the fields as well as the towns," but simply from the center (*cuer*) of towns, and were to be "put outside the walls," thus marking a return to established custom—the tolerance of prostitution in areas far from honest neighborhoods, outside the center of town.[28] The text adds that prostitutes should be placed "far from all holy places, such as churches and cemeteries." This provision, found in none of the municipal customs of the early thirteenth century, may have been imposed by the king in the light of his special role as protector and guardian of churches.[29]

In a last text concerning prostitution, Saint Louis returned to the spirit of the ordinance of 1254. In a letter to Matthew, abbot of Saint Denis, and to Simon of Neste, written in 1269 on the eve of his second departure on crusade, the king ordered "notorious and manifest brothels . . . to be exterminated, in towns as well as outside them."[30] The terms *notorious* and *manifest* come from canon law, where they were used to describe an irregular act or situation that was so well known to the community that normal criminal procedure could be waived in their case and a condemnation pronounced forthwith.[31] Brothels were designated by Louis as targets of an expeditive justice that could "exterminate" them effectively. The letter does not repeat, however, the punishment of prostitutes prescribed in the ordinance of 1254. The shift from an attack on prostitutes to an initiative against brothel keepers may well have been due to the growing influence of Roman law in the *curia regis*.[32]

No texts from royal Languedoc inform us of the effort of Louis IX's officers to enforce his legislation on prostitution, nor do we have any evidence of the influence of this legislation as a model for municipal policy. The few southern French documents referring to prostitution in this period come from Poitevin Toulouse and Angevin Provence. A list of complaints presented in 1256 by the residents of Arles to two commissioners sent by Charles of Anjou contains two articles on prostitution. In the first the residents request that accusations brought by prostitutes no longer be accepted.[33] In the second they demand the expulsion from Arles of a certain Robin of Lis, who had been extorting money from the city's prostitutes.[34] Although there is no proof that this complaint was inspired by Capetian and Angevin legislation, we can observe simply that it shows a similar hostility toward procuring or profiteering from prostitution and therefore marks a departure from the acknowledgment of the procurer present in the statutes of this town.[35]

A more explicit link to Capetian legislation on prostitution is seen in the statutes of Marseille, revised for the last time between 1253 and 1257, when Charles of Anjou had already installed a bailiff and a judge in that town.[36] The long section on prostitution in these statutes[37] includes a very complete sumptuary law and a detailed list of places where prostitutes were not allowed to work, followed by two general principles: that prostitutes must not stay among good men (inter probos homines et honestos), as was the rule in Arles and Avignon; and that these women must not stay near churches (prope alias ecclesias). A church and a monastery are included, moreover, in the detailed list of forbidden places. These provisions recall those of the ordinance of 1256, as does the punishment of people renting houses in forbidden areas to prostitutes, set at a year's rent in both texts.[38] Roman law also influenced the writing of these statutes, as we know from internal evidence[39] as well as external (the eminent civilian John Blanc was an apparently influential member of the committee in charge of revising the statutes). But Roman influence cannot account for the specific punishment of a year's rent imposed on people housing prostitutes, nor does it provide any precedent for banning prostitutes from the neighborhood of churches. When we learn that John Blanc and other Marseille jurists formed the nucleus of a "French party" favorable to the hegemony being established over Marseille by Charles of Anjou,[40] there seems little doubt that these statutes were directly influenced by Louis IX's "moderate" ordinance of 1256.

An echo of the ordinance of 1254 is discernible in a document from Toulouse dated 1271, which relates the expulsion of prostitutes from a neighborhood where their behavior had scandalized the residents.[41] Although similar in some respects to the Toulousan charter of 1201, this document deals with a neighborhood well outside the center of town, and the procedure outlined is different.[42] The most significant aspect of this text, besides its redundant explicitness, is its violent tone and its provision for the punishment of prostitutes who had been plying their trade outside the city walls. The neighbors were authorized to expel the prostitutes from the neighborhood, to strip them and lead them to the vicar, where they would be punished according to the judgment of the vicar.[43] The conditions of expulsion here are reminiscent of the passage in the ordinance of 1254 that states that prostitutes' goods may be seized "unto the tunic and robe."[44]

The influence of the rigoristic ordinance of 1254 was short-lived, however. The moderate ordinance of 1256 was more in keeping with the spirit of the times, and, despite the loyalty of Alphonse de Poitiers and Louis IX's son Philip III to the moralism of the strictures of 1254 and 1269,[45] it was the spirit of the more moderate legislation that was eventually to be consecrated by later generations of royal officers.[46]

The tacit acknowledgment by Saint Louis himself in the ordinance of 1256 of the inevitability of prostitution may lead one to believe that, in the north of France as well as in the south, prostitution was normally tolerated. This impression is corroborated by an earlier document, the statutes of Pamiers, issued by Simon of Montfort on 1 December 1212 after his victory over the Albigensians, in an attempt to impose the customary law of the Ile-de-France on the lands he had conquered. Article 39, which reads, "Public prostitutes are to be placed outside the walls in all towns,"[47] may well be the application to all of the lands conquered by Simon of the custom of Carcassonne, rather than a custom of the Ile-de-France.[48] But, even if the text is Carcassonnese in origin, there is no reason that a northern conqueror should have respected it, had the provision contradicted his own principles, given the totality of his victory at this point in the conflict. As Simon's activities had the blessing of the Church (one of the principal beneficiaries of the statutes of Pamiers), one may assume that the principle of tolerated prostitution outside the city walls shocked neither the northern French nor the ecclesiastics in the early thirteenth century.

Although there would seem to have been no equivalent in northern French customary law of the thirteenth-century Occitanian customs regulating prostitution,[49] some texts from north of the Loire indicate indirectly that prostitution was tolerated. The *Très ancien coutume* of Normandy, written down about 1200, sanctions the rape of the prostitute, thus implying an acknowledgment of the activity of prostitutes.[50] Although a register of justice from Abbeville indicates that several prostitutes were banished from that town at the end of the thirteenth century, they were accused, not simply of being prostitutes, but of engaging in procuring (*houlerie* or *ribaudie*).[51]

Ecclesiastics, too, seem to have accepted with more or less equanimity the inevitability of prostitution in urban society. Prostitution was, in fact, a frequent topic of discussion in Parisian ecclesiastic circles at the turn of the twelfth to the thirteenth century. Particularly interested in the subject was the circle of the theologian Peter the Chanter, who seems to have been at the origin of a new concern with the spiritual fate of the prostitutes. One of the Chanter's students, Fulk of Neuilly, made the conversion of prostitutes to the married or religious life the main goal of his illustrious preaching career, an effort continued by clergy and laymen alike throughout the Middle Ages.[52] What distinguished the circle from subsequent as well as former theologians, as J. Baldwin has observed, was its concern with practical questions of everyday life. Thus, the interest evinced by its members in prostitution extended beyond the state of the public woman's soul to such questions as how to define a prostitute; whether her earnings could be kept, even in case of fraud; whether prostitutes could offer alms from their earnings; whether they should be excommunicated.

A variety of answers to these questions were proposed within the Chanter's own circle.[53] Sympathetic to the prostitute, Thomas of Chobham devoted several passages of his *Summa Confessorum* to a definition of the prostitute, to a justification for the Church's tolerance of prostitution, and to the practical problems concerning these women, defending their right to keep their earnings, to offer alms, and to go to church, though not to commune.[54] Robert of Coursson, on the other hand, while admitting that prostitutes could keep their earnings, was of the opinion that the Church should not accept alms from public prostitutes and urged bishops not only to excommunicate such women but to expel them from the town so that they would not scandalize others.[55] Raised to the dignity of cardinal, legate at a series of councils held throughout France from 1213 to 1215, Robert published this canon at the Council of Paris of 1213:[56]

> We prohibit public prostitutes (frequent cohabitation with whom is more effective than the plague for bringing harm) from being permitted to live in the city or bourg, but rather [they] should be set apart, as is the custom with lepers. If, once warned, they do not wish to comply, they shall be struck with the sentence of excommunication.

Robert went further than most of his contemporaries—or followers—in advocating a policy on prostitution, a matter more of secular jurisdiction than of ecclesiastical concern.[57] The policy advocated—relegating them to areas outside the town—was in harmony with the provisions of the statutes of Pamiers.[58]

Although there is evidence that prostitutes were prosecuted in certain ecclesiastic jurisdictions,[59] there seems to have been no general ecclesiastic movement to attempt the elimination of prostitution from society. As in so many other domains, it was Saint Thomas Aquinas who crystallized the Church's position on prostitution in the late thirteenth century by paraphrasing the Augustinian warning that an elimination of prostitution would result in the pullulation of sexual passions and abuses.[60]

Given the acceptance of prostitution by most secular and ecclesiastical northern French authorities, Saint Louis's ordinance of 1254, ordering the abolition of prostitution, seems like a lone voice calling in the wilderness, more reminiscent of Old Testament strictures than of contemporary mores. It is not his hostility toward prostitution that distinguished him from contemporaries—such hostility can be seen in the sermons of preachers, in certain registers of justice, even, one might argue, in the abrogation of the "civil rights" of prostitutes in the southern French customs—but rather his active attempt to extirpate the phenomenon from his kingdom. Most contemporaries recognized that prostitution was inevitable, even if they did not go so far as Saint Thomas in underlining the value of such women in an inevitably imperfect world.

The moderate ordinance of 1256 was far more in keeping with the spirit of the day, and Louis's legislation is important, not for its lonely and generally unheeded call for the extirpation of prostitution from the kingdom of France, but for its tendency in its more moderate form to treat prostitution, not simply as a natural and inevitable human phenomenon, but as a social matter to be regulated by the protectors of the commonweal. The global trend of the thirteenth century, represented by the statutes of Avignon and Marseille, as well as by the ordinance of 1256, was toward the development of a positive policy on prostitution[61] and increasing "governmental intervention" in a realm that had previously been left to function on its own. It is this "interventionism" that laid the foundation of the institutionalized prostitution characteristic of the late Middle Ages, a key element in the development of which was the establishment and protection of official red-light districts in the late thirteenth and early fourteenth centuries.

🎐 *Chapter Two*

The Fourteenth and Fifteenth Centuries: Prostitution Institutionalized

No precedent for establishing authorized areas of prostitution can be found in the ancient customary law of Languedoc, whose provisions, as we have seen, were rudimentary and negative in tenor. The creation of official red-light districts in the late thirteenth and early fourteenth centuries was a conscious innovation on the part of certain municipal authorities in that period and can be seen as the logical culmination of the gradual transformation, in the public mind, of prostitution from a private concern or natural phenomenon to a social matter requiring public intervention and supervision.

The oldest document attesting to the creation of an authorized red-light district in Languedoc is found in the archives of the town of Montpellier,[1] whose residents were subjects of the king of Majorca.[2] It is perhaps not by chance that this first example of a vigorous, positive policy on places of prostitution came from the most important Mediterranean Languedocian town in which the king of France did not have a firm foothold at the end of the reign of Louis IX.[3]

Dated 1285, the document is the decision of the bailiff (*baylus*) of the king of Majorca to assign, on advice of a commission of citizens, a particular street in the suburbs of Montpellier as the official residence of the city's prostitutes and may be summarized as follows: For a long while this question had been debated before the bailiff, the king's lieutenant, and the consuls of the town. Various places had been assigned to prostitutes in the past (*diversa loca eis olim fuerint assignata*), but the women had been subsequently ejected from these areas by the residents, some citizens (*burgenses*) and members of the regular clergy (*religiosi*) having obtained letters from the king ordering expulsion. Finally, after much consultation, the bailiff created a commission consisting of two good men (*probi viri*) under oath from each of the six administrative units of the city (*seizein*) to determine the most suitable place for the prostitutes. After visiting many places and after much discussion among themselves and with others, the commission unanimously recommended two streets. Having heard their recommendations, the bailiff declared that the women should stay in the second street recommended, the "Hot Street" (*Carreria Calida*), located in the suburb Villanova.[4] They could not be expelled unless the bailiff or his successors decided to move them to the first street recommended. This declaration was made in the presence of the advocate John of Lunel, representing Guirauda of Béziers and Elys of Le Puy and all other prostitutes residing or wishing later to reside in Montpellier. The bailiff promised that the women might there reside without opposition from any person, under the protection of the king and the court.

The great interest of this document is, of course, its significance as a first indication of a positive policy concerning the residence of prostitutes.[5] Far from repeating the early-thirteenth-century Occitanian customs barring prostitutes from the center of town or from respectable neighborhoods, the Montpellier authorities innovated in creating one official red-light district in which the public women were obliged (*debeant*) to live, abandoning all other places in the city (*aliis omnibus locis derelectis*). Residence in the Hot Street was, moreover, a privilege; the women had not only the duty but the right to live there unmolested by their neighbors. The prostitutes could not be expelled (*expelli non debeant sive possint*); they were to reside in that area without objection from anyone (*sine contradictione alcujus persone*). As a guarantee of this right to reside peacefully in Villanova, the women were placed under the protection of the king and his court (*sub protectione dicti domini regis et sue curiae*).

Red-light districts, it is true, had already been assigned in the past, but none of those past assignments had had the force and moral authority of the document of 1285. In the past it was the king who ordered the expulsion of prostitutes from the streets to which they had been assigned, whereas in the document of 1285 it was the king himself who guaranteed the right of prostitutes to reside permanently in Villanova with his royal protection. Montpellier seems to have been, moreover, the avant-garde in the development of this new policy of authorization; there is no evidence that other Languedocian or even Italian towns instituted a similar policy in the thirteenth century.[6] One cannot help wondering whether the precocity of authorized prostitution in Montpellier may not be related to that town's privileged link to the Iberian peninsula.[7] The cosmopolitan culture of medieval Spain had profoundly influenced the civilization of Languedoc, and that of Montpellier in particular, in other domains.[8] Perhaps the institutionalization of prostitution, like other aspects of the cultural and social life in medieval Languedoc, can be traced, at least in part, ultimately to Arabic influence.[9]

One could hardly imagine, at any rate, such an initiative having been taken in a town under Capetian hegemony in this period. Louis IX's son and successor, Philip III, showed early in his reign (1270–85) a continuing concern with the moral reform initiated by his father. A surviving fragment of his ordinance of 1272 includes instructions to the royal bailiffs to prohibit blasphemy, gaming, and brothels (*bordeaux communs*).[10] Evidence of Philip's intention to enforce this prohibition actively is found in a passage from the charter he granted to the town of Cordes (Tarn) in 1282, which stipulates that those found guilty of procuring (*lenoscinium*) should have their houses seized or, if they were not house owners, should pay a fine of 20 l.[11] These two texts, aimed at brothel keepers rather than prostitutes, but bearing no mention of possible tolerated prostitution outside city walls, reflect Louis IX's last expressed opinion on the matter—his letter of 1269.[12] In the light of Philip's continuing concern with his father's moral reform, it is clear that the passage granting the right to establish a brothel in the town of Villefranche-de-Lauragais, found in the charter granted to the town by this king in 1280, cannot be attributed to Philip III; it must be a later interpolation.[13]

Capetian ardor for moral reform seems to have cooled considerably during the reign of Louis's grandson, Philip IV (1285–1314). None of the ordinances or charters of Philip the Fair include strictures against prostitution or brothel keeping. All we know of his policy on prostitution is that his officers in Languedoc were sometimes put at the disposal of citizens there requesting the expulsion of prostitutes from town or neighborhood. A seventeenth-century inventory of the municipal archives of Beaucaire summarizes a document, since lost, that describes such an expulsion.[14]

A small charter . . . of the year 1304, ordinance of Messrs. the reformers sent by the King. By which at the request of Father ——— of the Franciscans and the nobles and burghers of Beaucaire, the whores [*putains*] who resided and made their home in Beaucaire, in a certain street called at the time La Laguque, are thrown out and "disinhabited" from the street. The said ordinance executed on order of the lieutenant of the vicar, by the subvicar of the said town.

A similar entry is found in a sixteenth-century inventory of the municipal archives of Alès. There the king had ordered the seneschal of Beaucaire to oversee the expulsion, probably in response to a request by the citizens of Alès.[15]

There is no evidence, however, of a royal initiative having been taken to abolish a red-light district established by municipal authorities. The Hot

Street of Montpellier was apparently left as it had been created.[16] French royal policy on prostitution at the turn of thirteenth to the fourteenth century seems to have been, as in other matters, to allow the municipalities to run their lives much as they pleased, provided that the towns recognized the authority of the king of France.[17]

Even without the intervention of the king of France, other towns of Languedoc were still expelling prostitutes in this period. In July 1299 a proclamation issued by the archbishop, viscount, and council of *prud'hommes* of Narbonne warned prostitutes and procurers to leave that town within ten days, under pain of corporal punishment.[18] The syndics (*rectores*) of the town of Bourg-Saint-Andéol (Ardèche) were guaranteed, in privileges confirmed by the bishop of Vivier, that they might expel prostitutes if the bailiffs of the bishop were negligent in this matter.[19] But the charter of Bourg-Saint-Andéol, dated 1321, is the last mention in Languedocian sources of the simple expulsion of prostitutes from a town. The tide was turning rapidly in favor of the recognition of districts reserved for prostitutes.

By the end of the thirteenth century, a house of prostitution was operating openly in the heart of Toulouse. Its existence is revealed in the commentary on the customs of Toulouse, completed in 1296, in the context of a discussion on adultery.[20]

> Item, it is asked, if a married man enters a house where commonly are found women for money (as, for example, in the house of Madame Cagarafes in Bertrand David Street), believing to have relations with an unmarried woman, when in fact it was a married woman, whether he commits adultery. I respond "No," since the place excuses the same.

This Toulousan brothel, even if it were *de facto* rather than *de jure* (there is no extant document attesting to an official creation), was clearly so well established and accepted that it could be used in this legal argument exonerating a hypothetical fornicator from the crime of adultery.

A more official document, an undated set of police regulations (probably from the late thirteenth or early fourteenth century), testifies to the existence of an authorized red-light district in Nîmes.[21]

> Item, it is mandated by the said court that no woman who gives herself for money should be so bold as to stay within the city of Nîmes nor outside, unless in the public *postribulum* of Nîmes . . . under pain of losing her dress and being beaten throughout the town.

Authorized districts of prostitution existed not only in the large towns of the plain of Languedoc, but also in the smaller hill towns. An early register of municipal deliberations from the town of Uzès (Gard), although damaged by humidity, retains enough legible passages to reveal the existence, in June 1326, of an authorized brothel in that town.[22]

> . . . that all frivolous women [illegible] give themselves for money to men, from now in the future [illegible] and stay in the house of Peter Rascacii, situated outside the Gate Stephan in the street called Naquintuna.

The document specifies that the women were not to circulate or install themselves (*ire nec se ponare*) in any other place, under pain of confiscation of their clothing and corporal punishment.

Even the tiny mountain town of Lacaune (Tarn) had a red-light district by this time, as is shown in a document dated January 1337, preserved in a cartulary.[23] The bailiff and the constable of Lacaune, officers of the countess Eleanor of Montfort, acting on orders from the seneschal of the countess, ordered three women accused of being immoral women (*avols femnas e vida deshonesta menans*) no longer to live in the town "unless among the public immoral women in the street called the street of France" (*sino solamen e tan solamen entre las publicas avols femnas et en la carrieyra apelada de Fransa*), under pain of a fine of 60 s. This document is in many ways analogous to the Toulousan charter of 1201: women of questionable morals were to be expelled from the town. The difference here, of course, is that the women of Lacaune had the choice between expulsion and compulsory residence in the local red-light district.

The examples of areas of authorized prostitution begin to multiply at this time.[24] The residents of Narbonne, who as recently as 1299 joined with the archbishop and viscount of their city in expelling prostitutes and procurers from its limits, had changed their point of view by 1335. In a series of documents concerning the privileges granted the new consulate by their lord, the viscount Aymeric, one of the major articles deals with a proposal for a red-light district similar to the one in Montpellier, finally officially granted by Aymeric on 23 May 1335.[25]

> We, the said Aymeric . . . give . . . and liberally concede to you, the said consuls, . . . in order that the several scandals and evils which are said to touch the town of Narbonne should be avoided, that there be and can be henceforth a *postribulum*, *lupanar* or "Hot Street" in some suitable place in Narbonne . . . with the same modalities, forms, privileges, uses and customs with which the *postribulum* of Montpellier exists and has been the custom to exist, that is, that in the said *postribulum* . . . no one can be arrested by the subvicar or sergeants of our court or by others of our men, by day or by night, for adultery.

The initiative for creating the red-light district, as the text makes clear, came from the consuls. In an earlier paragraph of the same document, Aymeric had promised that his officers should no longer abusively arrest citizens for adultery, nor extort outrageous fines, thus limiting his seigneurial rights of justice.[26] The establishment of the Hot Street was a further concession on the part of the viscount, a means of guaranteeing the terms of the earlier article, for within its limits none of his officers could make adultery arrests. The argument of the author of the commentary on the customs of Toulouse—that a man who had intercourse with a married woman in a brothel was exonerated from adultery charges—received official recognition in this document. The immunity from adultery arrest was even vaster in Narbonne than that recommended by the author of the Toulousan commentary: a document from 1337 specifies that men were exempt from such arrests, not only within the Hot Street, but anywhere in Narbonne, if found with a prostitute from the *postribulum* (*cum mulieribus in dicta carreria comorantibus*).[27]

The establishment of a *postribulum* with its consequent privileges was, moreover, not unique to Narbonne. The consuls were, in fact, copying, so the document of 1335 explains, a situation that existed already in Montpellier. The creation of the Hot Street of Montpellier in 1285, too, had been conceived as a guarantee against arbitrary adultery arrest as well as a solution to the problems of public order.[28]

It has been suggested several times in this essay that the burghers of Languedoc were in favor of a positive policy on prostitution which was frustrated by the policy of the king of France and possibly other regional lords. The document of Narbonne is the most solid justification for such a hypothesis. The reasons for this conflict in Languedoc between citizen and king, burgher and lord, were, however, more conjunctural than ideological. If the *bourgeoisie* was inevitably the vanguard of a positive policy on prostitution, one would expect to have seen the earliest evidence of such a policy in Toulouse, with its city-state tradition, or, better yet, in the city-republics of Italy. Such was clearly not the case. One might argue that the city-states of Italy had, in fact, no need for such centers in the thirteenth century precisely because of their very municipal liberties. It was, on the contrary, in towns circumscribed by royal or seigneurial authority that defining an official red-light district became a major concern for the residents, not only in the interest of public order, but also in an effort to limit the king's or lord's prerogative to make adultery arrests. Jurisdiction in cases of morals charges was a powerful means of reinforcing authority over a population;[29] defining an official Hot Street, within which town residents could not be arrested for adultery, was one way of struggling against that reinforcement of authority.

But royal opposition to official red-light districts was of short duration. By the end of the fourteenth century, municipality and throne were united in their efforts to realize a positive policy on prostitution in the interest of public order. The burgher contribution to this policy was the establishment of municipally owned brothels; the French kings' contribution was the granting of royal protection to such institutions.

There is no more eloquent testimony to the integration of prostitution into the institutional framework of Languedocian urban society than the popularity in the late medieval period of the municipally owned brothel. Impressed with the symbolic and real value of this institution, many historians and popular writers have seen it as typical of the "medieval" attitude toward prostitution. Yet a study of the documents from three western Languedocian towns— Toulouse, Castres, and Albi—proves conclusively that the municipally owned brothel, far from being a traditional institution in that region, was an innovation of the last third of the fourteenth century, troubled decades of plague, war, and social disorder.

The best-known example of a municipally owned brothel in Languedoc is that of Toulouse, the region's largest town. Although Lafaille, in his *Annales de la ville de Toulouse*, interpreted a document of 1201 to mean that there was at that time a municipal brothel in the street of Comminges, the text, as we have seen, makes no mention of a brothel; it merely restates the principle that prostitutes should stay outside the town walls.[30] The first reference to an actual house of prostitution in Toulouse is in the commentary to the customs, written in 1296.[31] A document from 1357 seems to indicate that the red-light district of Toulouse continued at this date to be unofficial and of a private nature.[32] The Toulousan historian M. Chalande, in his article on the public house of Toulouse, concluded that the municipal brothel was established there sometime in the second half of the fourteenth century.[33]

A study of the financial documents from the fourteenth century, unexploited by Chalande, makes it possible to determine the moment of the creation of this house with somewhat more precision. The account books of the consuls appear for the first time in the 1330s and continue erratically throughout the fourteenth century. In each complete account book, there is a list of municipal properties farmed out to individuals.[34] The first appearance of the municipal brothel in such a list of farms is in the account book of 1372–73, which also includes an entry concerning expenses for the repair of the house.[35] There is, unfortunately, a lacuna in the account books covering most of the decade preceding 1372, the book of 1363–65 being a mere fragment, with no list of farms. The book of 1362–63,[36] on the other hand, does have such a list; all the farms are detailed, and there is no mention of the brothel. The *termini*, then, are from 1363 to 1372; sometime within these nine years, Toulouse had acquired its municipal brothel.

There is, unfortunately, no narrative source to accompany these laconic financial documents from Toulouse.[37] The deliberations of the municipal council of Castres are somewhat more informative about the creation of a municipal brothel in that small town in a slightly later period. The business of prostitution had previously been limited in Castres to its suburban red-light district, according to police regulations issued in 1373 and 1375:[38] "No one dare keep a brothel in any place outside Bela Cela, under pain of a 10 s. fine or running the town." Bela Cela was a thinly populated suburb in which several churches and hospitals were located. The nature of the area had begun to change, however, with the population decline in the wake of the plagues and with the vicissitudes of the Hundred Years' War. The Trinitarians, for example, moved their convent and hospital from Bela Cela to within the fortified part of town near the Gate Toulouse in 1364.[39]

A similar fate was to befall the prostitutes in the last decade of the fourteenth century. On 11 March 1391 it was proposed to the municipal council that a brothel be built near the Gate Toulouse. After discussion, the council voted against the proposal, deciding instead to purchase the house already existing in Bela Cela, where the women would continue to live,[40] a decision that received further confirmation on 13 May.[41] At the end of the same year, the consuls agreed to the publication of an ordinance concerning the prostitutes.[42] The proposal to move the women to the center of town was considered once again, however, on 2 September 1398, and this time the council decided in favor of a municipal brothel within the city walls, concluding that prostitutes wanting to reside within the town might do so in a house to be assigned to them, to be financed by the residents of the house.[43]

There is no parallel in the Castres archives to the rich fifteenth-century documentation on municipal prostitution that has been preserved in Toulouse.[44] The municipal brothel of Castres does not reappear in the documents until 11 January 1511 in an *arrêt* of the Parlement of Toulouse concluding an action brought by the Franciscans of Castres against the consuls of the town because of the proximity of the municipal brothel (*maison des filles de vie*) to their convent.[45] One is inclined to see continuity here, for the convent of the friars was located not far from the Portal Nau (New Gate), in the same northwestern section of the center of town where the Trinitarians had been relocated and the original brothel proposed in 1391. One may therefore presume that a municipal house existed in Castres, as was the case in Toulouse, from the end of the fourteenth to the sixteenth century.

A livelier account of the municipalization of a local place of prostitution in this period is found in the archives of the small hill town of Albi, which furnish sometimes surprising details concerning the circumstances surrounding the establishment of the municipal brothel there. Suffering, like all western Languedocian towns of this era, from the population loss due to repeated plagues, economic depression, and social turmoil, and the ravages of the Hundred Years' War and its mercenaries,[46] Albi was further tried in this period by a conflict of power between the lord of the town, the bishop of Albi, and the town consuls.[47] The two parties clashed not only over the defense and police of the community but also over the control of the district of prostitution, which the bishop claimed as one of his prerogatives.[48]

It pertains and should pertain to the said lord bishop, by reason of the said jurisdiction which he has in the said city and possessions, to assign the place, streets and houses in which the public prostitutes living in the said city and suburbs should have to stay, and to move them from one street to another, according to the exigencies of necessity and public utility.

But the consuls were not willing to accept with equanimity the bishop's acclaimed right to move the town prostitutes to a different street, a right that he had apparently acted on in the spring of 1366. The consuls protested to the lieutenant governor of the king of France, Louis, duke of Anjou, who accordingly ordered the seneschal of Carcassonne and the vicar and judge of Albi to remove the prostitutes from the place where the bishop had transferred them. In this order, dated 3 May 1366,[49] we see that there was already a customary red-light district in Albi in this period (*loco seu carreria in quibus morabantur et morari consueverant*). The bishop had moved the prostitutes from this district to an unfortunate location, opposite the abbey church of Saint Anthony, near the Gate le Vigan, a place where there was a constant flow of people entering and leaving the town and where, according to the consuls, many terrible sins (*orribilia peccata*) took place because of the presence of prostitutes. The consuls, in their appeal for help to the lieutenant governor, claimed that the situation was offensive and dangerous, not only for Albi but for all of Languedoc, because of the security (*custodia*) of this town, a key to the three seneschalsies. The lieutenant governor ordered the prostitutes to be expelled from the place where the bishop had put them and placed in an area more suitable to the security of the town and the honor of Saint Anthony (*in alio loco magis condecenti ad securitatem dicte ville et honorem dicti gloriosissimi confessoris Sancti Antonii*).

The problem of the control of prostitution in Albi seems to have been settled shortly after the intervention of Louis of Anjou, for, in the agreement reached by the consuls and the bishop in 1368 and in a further agreement concluded in 1374, no mention was made of the problem of prostitution.[50] The first reference to an actual brothel in the town is found in the consular account book of 1380–81.[51] In November 1380 the brothel appeared in a dispute between the bishop and the consuls. During a meeting of the town council, the bishop complained that the town was badly run and defended (*que la vila se gardava mal e se regis mal*).[52] He proposed to change the captains of defense, repair the walls and moats of the town, rearm the militia, and relocate the

33

brothel outside the town walls (*e que hom mudes lo bordel deforas la vila*). The council accepted all his suggestions except the one concerning the captains.

Although accepted by the council, the proposal concerning the brothel must not have been acted on, for in July 1383 the bishop made a similar suggestion. This time, however, he proposed two brothels—one outside the walls for working hours and one inside the walls where the prostitutes could be housed at night.[53] Again, the primary concern seems to have been security. A double brothel was indeed the ideal solution, as it allowed the municipality to keep customers, who might include undesirable, suspect persons,[54] well away from the walled town and yet, at the same time, to keep the women under safe protection at night.

It was probably too costly an endeavor, however, for the town to undertake, for, while the council agreed to follow the bishop's advice, the project for a double brothel was never completed. The first recorded expenditure by the town for housing the prostitutes is found in an account-book entry six years later (July 1389): the consuls paid William Rossinhol rent for sheltering the public women for an undefined period of time.[55] Four years later a series of entries record the expenses incurred by the municipality in constructing a brothel or in reconstructing a house as a brothel.[56] This piece of municipal property was officially recognized by a royal officer, John of Clermont, who was commissioned to collect payments due to the king on *franc-fiefs* and new acquisitions in Languedoc; in a document dated 30 September 1393 it is recorded that the town paid 74 s. for property recently acquired, which included the new municipal brothel: ". . . for a certain garden, acquired by their predecessors for perpetual use of the said city, in which is a lupanar or brothel [*bordellum*] . . . situated outside New Gate of the said city."[57] By the end of the fourteenth century, in Albi as in Toulouse and Castres, the municipally owned brothel had become an accepted feature of the urban landscape.[58]

The municipalization of formerly privately owned places of prostitution continued throughout the fifteenth century in Languedoc. In January 1399 the new owner of the brothel of Pézenas, its madam, Raynalda of Melus, made a donation of her recent acquisition to the Great and Small Charities of Pézenas, charitable institutions of the municipality.[59] The creation of a municipal house of prostitution in Castelnaudary was proposed by the consuls in 1445, but financial difficulties seem to have impeded them from realizing their plans, and it was left to an individual to undertake the construction of the brothel in 1452. The municipality eventually took over the house sometime toward the end of the fifteenth century.[60] As in Pézenas, a donation was the cause of the municipalization of the brothel of Lodève. When Bernard Hugues gave the house to the town in 1455, the structure was in ruins; the municipality had it repaired and restored to its former function.[61] The acquisition by municipalities of formerly private houses of prostitution continued into the sixteenth century: Alès seems to have acquired its brothel in about 1510,[62] and in 1520 the town of Montpellier bought the formerly private town brothel.[63]

Not all municipalities had a population sufficiently large or tolerant to justify the establishment of a municipal brothel, however. A solution often settled on was the observation of the custom of "once a week" (*semel in septimana*): prostitutes might stay no longer than one night a week in a given municipality. Thus, prostitution was regulated temporally rather than geographically; the scandal and expense of a permanent residence were avoided, while allowance was nonetheless made for a certain activity. The first explicit reference to such a custom is in a document from Narbonne dated 1299.[64] A police regulation of Castelnaudary dated 1333 also includes such a provision.[65]

While the custom of once a week came to be a solution to the problem of the police of public morals in many small villages in the fifteenth century,[66] it appears often to have been, in the fourteenth century, a halfway step between the relegation of prostitutes outside the town walls and the establishment of an authorized red-light district or municipal brothel. Thus, in Narbonne the custom of once a week, proclaimed in 1299, was superseded by the creation of the Hot Street in 1335. An article of the customs of Lunel, published by E. Bondurand, presents the seemingly paradoxical juxtaposition of the custom of once a week and the existence of a *postribulum*.[67] A study of the archival document shows that the passage originally dealt only with the custom of once a week; the reference to the *postribulum* was added at a later date.[68]

An illustration of the custom of once a week as a phase between a period of expulsion of prostitutes and that of the establishment of a municipal brothel is found in a text from the tiny town of Saint-Quentin-la-Poterie (Gard). The document, dated 1377, is an appeal of the consuls to the royal judge and vicar of Uzès protesting against the proclamation of the royal bailiff and bailiff of the other lords of the town forbidding prostitutes to stay in Saint-Quentin and its territory more than one night. The consuls objected to the continuation of this temporal limitation of prostitution in view of the fact "that there is in this place a house suitable for vagabond women, and it is everywhere the custom of the land, in order to avoid greater evil, that there be a *postribulum* in these places."[69] The result of the appeal is not known, but one may venture to guess that Saint-Quentin, like so many other towns in Languedoc and elsewhere, was allowed to maintain a municipal house of prostitution.[70]

There is no reason to suppose that French royal officers would have firmly opposed the creation of a municipal brothel at this time, in Saint-Quentin or elsewhere. The fervor of Saint Louis's campaign for moral reform had, as we have seen, dissipated by the reign of Philip IV, who, while willing to order his officers to expel prostitutes on request of town residents, made no effort to suppress the Hot Street established in Montpellier in 1285.[71] Nor did his successors impede the creation of such red-light districts in one Languedocian town after another.[72] The French crown issued no directives on prostitution for almost a century after the ordinance of Philip III, until the reign of Charles V (1364–80), when a vigorous new policy on prostitution was adopted.

In 1367, a year after the king's lieutenant governor of Languedoc, Louis of Anjou, intervened in Albi, as we have seen, in a case of disputed jurisdiction over prostitution, Hugh Aubriot, appointed provost of Paris by Charles V, put into effect an ambitious plan for the amelioration (*assainissement*) of Paris, which was in many ways similar to the more modest proposals of the bishop of Albi in the same period.[73] Aubriot sought to restore internal order to Paris in the wake of the political and social turmoil resulting from the war by repairing the town fortifications, reorganizing the prisons, and controlling marginal elements and activities in the town. The unemployed were to engage in public works projects on the fortifications; gambling houses, cabarets, and hotels were placed under strict control; and prostitution was limited to certain areas. An ordinance of 1367 lists the streets designated as suitable for the residence of prostitutes; public women found elsewhere were to be put in prison on simple complaint of two neighbors and banished on conviction for their offense.[74]

The policy of authorizing centers of prostitution, initiated by Aubriot, was to remain that of the monarchy and its officers for more than a century and a half. It was legitimized, ironically enough, by invoking the legislation of Saint Louis. Rather than citing Louis's moderate ordinance of 1256, which tolerated prostitution outside city centers, however, the king and his officers chose to invoke the ordinance of 1254—perhaps because it was more famous than the later text.[75] Although the ordinance of 1254 was cited integrally in a letter of Charles VI dated 1381, expelling prostitutes from certain streets of Paris,[76] it became usual to change the wording of Saint Louis's law, either by omission or by transformation, in an effort to render it more compatible with contemporary policies. Omission was a simple and effective means of changing the sense of the ordinance; elimination of the phrase *de campis* resulted in the impression that Louis had intended to relegate prostitutes to outlying parts of town. This expurgated version of the ordinance of 1254 was first cited in a letter of Charles V in 1368[77] and was consecrated in the *Grand coutumier de France* at the end of the Middle Ages.[78] A transformed version of the ordinance of 1254 is found in a royal letter confirming a monopoly on prostitution to certain residents of Montpellier in 1469,[79] in which *de campis* had been changed to *de castris*; once again, the effect is to suggest that Louis prohibited prostitution only within town centers, by implication allowing it elsewhere. It was implied, moreover, in Aubriot's ordinance of 1367, that Louis, like Aubriot, had actually assigned certain streets to prostitutes,[80] an implication that was not lost on contemporaries. A lawyer defending prostitutes who had been threatened with expulsion from Baillehoc Street (a district authorized by Aubriot in 1367) argued before the Parlement of Paris in 1388 that his clients had the right to stay there because "Saint Louis ordered that there be brothels in . . . Baillehoc Street."[81]

The new royal policy of authorizing centers of prostitution was pursued in Languedoc as well as in Paris. Favoring municipally controlled prostitution as early as in the Albi conflict of the 1360s, the king's officers in Languedoc seem to have actively encouraged its maintenance during the difficult years of the early fifteenth century. According to a brief entry in the account books of Albi, the seneschal of Carcassonne ordered the consuls of that town, in 1419, to build a brothel (actually, as we know, to rebuild it, for it had existed already in the late fourteenth century) and to take care to staff it![82] Six years later, apparently in an effort to assure the smooth functioning of the municipal brothel of Toulouse, Charles VII placed that house under his personal safeguard.[83] The consuls themselves had requested his intervention when the substantial profit realized on farming the house had diminished, due to attacks by procurers and other malevolent people (*ribaldi, lenones et malevoli*) who threatened and maltreated the occupants and damaged the house. Taking the brothel under his safeguard (*salvagardia*), Charles instructed his seneschal, his vicar, and their lieutenants to enforce his protection, which should be represented by the sign of the fleur-de-lis on the house; the consuls were allowed to hire royal sergeants to patrol the place without loss of their jurisdiction over it. Thus, the royal safeguard, whose beneficiaries in the earlier days of the monarchy were principally churches and abbeys, was extended to the Toulousan municipal brothel.

By the mid–fifteenth century, royal control of prostitution was so well established that Languedocian town consuls turned to the king for permission to create a municipal brothel. In 1445, for example, the consuls of Castelnaudary asked the king permission (*congie ou permission et licence*) to construct a municipal brothel.[84] In response to the consuls' request, the king sent a letter,[85] dated 9 November 1445, to the royal judge of the Lauragais, instructing him to choose, with the king's attorney general, a suitable place (*place ou lieu convenable*) for the brothel, to give permission to the consuls to build the house, and to oblige the town's prostitutes to reside there, expelling from the town those who continued to reside elsewhere. It had become the king's prerogative to authorize the establishment of a municipal brothel, and the task of his royal officers to supervise the realization of such a project, even in Castelnaudary, where the consuls had retained considerably greater consular powers than most other Languedocian towns in the same period.[86]

It is to this period that the famous article from the charter of Villefranche-de-Lauragais must be attributed.[87]

Lest dissolute and shameless women, prostituting themselves in various houses and lodgings of the said town, practice their debauch and lust to

the prejudice of the republic of the said town, and giving the worst example to many people, we grant the faculty to the said inhabitants, to
construct and build, in some part outside the said town, a house of prostitution in which the said women shall be received; and the profits from
this lupanar shall remain and pertain to those inhabitants for doing the
aforesaid repairs.

Although the charter is dated 1280, the passage in question does not reflect
the policy of Philip III, who, as we have seen, continued to observe the principles of Saint Louis's policy on public morals.[88] It is a later interpolation
dealing with an institution (the municipally owned brothel) and a custom
(royal authorization) typical of the fifteenth, not the thirteenth, century.[89]

Increasingly sensitive to the exigencies of public order, the consuls of Languedoc innovated, at the turn of the thirteenth to the fourteenth century, by
deciding to authorize licit centers of prostitution. The *ad hoc* practice of expelling prostitutes from neighborhoods where they had scandalized the residents was replaced by the more sophisticated, long-term policy of defining,
after collective consultation, an authorized red-light district where prostitutes
enjoyed the right to permanent residence. This policy was advantageous to the
burghers, not only in the interest of maintaining public order, but also, at least
in some towns, of protecting residents from abusive adultery arrests by the
local lord or the king.

Although prostitution was sometimes regulated temporally, by the mid–
fourteenth century most of even the smallest town of Languedoc boasted official centers of prostitution. These authorized places of prostitution changed
considerably in the second half of the fourteenth century, when they were in
most cases reduced from an entire street to a single house, sometimes moved
within the walls of the towns, and often appropriated by the municipality.
Smaller in scale and more intimately linked to the public authorities, the late-
fourteenth-century municipally owned public house was more easily policed
and controlled than a whole street of privately run brothels. Security was the
keyword in the process of municipalization during a period when brothels
were increasingly considered to be poles of attraction for suspect people.
Regulation of houses of prostitution, formerly considered desirable in the interest of public order, had, in the cauldron of the Hundred Years' War, become
vital to all notions of public security.

It was perhaps for reasons of security that the French crown, executing a
volte-face from the policy of the previous century, lent its approbation to this
tight municipal control of places of prostitution. Extending his safeguard to
such houses, encouraging their construction and the recruitment of personnel,
the king came eventually to be regarded as the sole authority capable of authorizing the creation of a municipal brothel. King and consul, formerly espous-

ing often divergent policies on prostitution, were now united in pursuing a consistent policy of protection of authorized prostitution.

Far from being limited to Languedoc, authorized prostitution was the rule in most regions of Europe in this period. Enjoying a virtually unquestioned legitimacy, the fifteenth-century public house seemed assured of a long and prosperous future. Yet, by the middle of the following century, the municipal brothel had all but disappeared from the Languedocian, and much of the European, urban landscape. King and consul had protected brothels in the fifteenth century, yet king and consul were to prohibit them in the sixteenth century.

The Sixteenth Century: The Institution Dismantled

The prohibition of all brothels was proclaimed in the 101st article of the ordinance of Orléans of 1561, which incorporated many of the demands for reform in justice and administration made by the Estates General.[1] Although some brothels had been abolished well before 1561 and others continued to function after that date, the ordinance was nonetheless a historical milestone, for it rang the official death knell of the late-medieval policy of authorized prostitution.

In Languedoc, a perusal of the municipal deliberations of the 1550s reveals that most of the municipal houses of prostitution had been closed definitively before 1561. Already in January 1553, the municipality of Alès announced the possibility of renting out "the common house where in the past was the public house of women, called the brothel of the said town."[2] On 13 January 1555, the consuls of Castelnaudary, describing to the municipal council the great evils that occurred daily because of the *maison de débauche*, proposed to sell the house or demolish it; the council voted to demolish the house and sell the ground on which it stood.[3] In its session of 25 July 1557, the council of Montpellier, which had previously agreed to close "the house in which used to be kept the public brothel," decided to sell the house to the highest bidder.[4] The brothel of Toulouse was not farmed out in 1557–58, and an entry in the list of farms for 1559–60 reads, "The house where used to be [the brothel] 'Green Castle.'"[5]

The factors that contributed to the widespread desire of public officials in the 1550s to close municipal brothels are numerous and complex. Within the context of this book, an exhaustive analysis of this topic is impossible; the following pages are simply an attempt to evoke the various factors that may have led to the dismantling of institutionalized prostitution in Languedoc in the 1550s.

It has often been suggested that the closing of brothels was a reaction to the spread of venereal disease, the first epidemic of which ravaged western Europe in the 1490s. This theory, although appealing, does not stand up to analysis. It does not, in the first place, explain the chronology of the closings. If fear of venereal disease were the real reason for dismantling institutionalized prostitution, brothels would have been shut during the period of intense epidemics of syphilis, from the late 1490s to the mid-1520s, rather than in the 1550s, a time when the more dramatic symptoms of the disease were diminishing.[6] Nor does the "syphilis theory" of the closing of the brothels take into account contemporary notions of disease and contagion. People of the fifteenth and sixteenth centuries understood well that certain illnesses could be communicated, but the exact mechanism by which the disease was transmitted was a mystery.[7] Many people thought that venereal disease could be communicated by a look as well as by intercourse. Others stressed the importance of intercourse in transmission and accused in particular the danger of prostitution,[8] but often for moral rather than scientific reasons.[9] Prostitutes had been accused of bringing on the plague, too, since it was often claimed to be God's punishment for the sin of fornication.[10]

It is, in fact, this association between prostitution and plague and contagion in general that emerges from early-sixteenth-century sources, rather than a special relation between prostitution and venereal disease.[11] Already in the fifteenth century, it was common to close brothels during epidemics of plague.[12] In time of plague, residents who were able to do so often fled the town for the countryside; even prostitutes may well have avoided cities where the plague raged.[13] Toward the end of the fifteenth and the beginning of the sixteenth centuries, documents witness to official closings, imposed by royal and municipal authorities. Beginning in the 1470s, the Parlement of Toulouse ordered bathhouses closed and prohibited dances during the plague.[14] The consuls of Toulouse ordered the municipal brothel closed in times of plague and prohibited the women of the house from circulating and spreading infection in town.[15] The privately owned brothel of Nîmes was ordered closed by the consuls of that town because of the plague in 1521 and 1531.[16] The consuls of Castelnaudary even included a clause in their yearly contracts with the brothel farmer providing for the closing of the house and a reduction of the farm due to the municipality in times of plague.[17] This close association between prostitutes and disease may explain why disaffected brothels were often used as hospitals (as in the case of an illicit brothel in Montpellier, closed by order of Parlement in 1498 and converted to a hospital for plague victims),[18] and why the money from the brothel farm in Toulouse was attributed, from 1529 to the closing of the house, to the town hospitals.[19]

Another factor that may have influenced the changing attitude toward prostitution in the sixteenth century was the growing repression of crime characteristic of this period. Those responsible for this repression were the secular authorities, especially the monarchs, who saw in the monopolization of criminal justice and its strict enforcement an effective means of consolidating their power. The kings of France published a series of ordinances throughout the sixteenth century that permitted a more rigorous enforcement of criminal law.[20] New punishments were introduced and the sentences handed down increased in severity.[21] Emperor Charles V promulgated a comprehensive codification of criminal law, the *Nemesis Carolina*, in 1532, and similar initiatives were taken in the Low Countries.[22] Much of this legislation was concerned with defining and strengthening measures against morals offenses.[23] Ferdinand I of Austria, for instance, issued a series of edicts against morals offenses, culminating in the creation of a "Chastity Committee" (*Keuschheitscommission*) in 1560.[24] Outlawing brothel keeping and prostitution was part of a comprehensive program for strengthening the criminal law undertaken by the secular rulers of the sixteenth century.

Often the victims of this penal repression, especially those laws against vagabondage and idleness, were the poor.[25] The demographic increase of the early sixteenth century had led to the pauperization of a large part of the population.[26] It is probably from this poorer class that most prostitutes were recruited in this period of cheap labor and low salaries. Prostitutes were numerous, poor, and associated in the popular mind with vagabonds and other suspect people. Demographic factors contributed to the devalorization of prostitution in the sixteenth century.[27]

It was a difficult time not just for prostitutes and poor women but for women in general, the capacity of women in French law tracing a steady decline throughout the sixteenth century. This deterioration of the legal status of women was, to a large extent, due to a conscious movement, a reaction against the "femininist" literature of the late Middle Ages and the Renaissance.[28] The misogynous attack was first led by Tiraqueau in his *De legibus connubialibus* of 1522–24, in which he gave a clear definition of the legal incapacity of women, prohibiting them from making contracts and acting in justice. The other jurists of the sixteenth century followed suit, and such measures passed even into the reformed customs of the day.[29] It was in this period, also, that in criminal law women were considered irresponsible because of their inferiority (*imbecilitas sexus*) and that the rape of a prostitute was no longer considered to be a crime.[30] This intense misogyny is reflected in much of the literature of the French Renaissance[31] and is found in another form in Protestant literature. Although most Reformation leaders encouraged women to learn to read and to participate in religious services and revalorized the role of wife and mother, they limited women's activities strictly to the home and emphasized the subordination of women to their husbands' will.[32] Thus, hostility toward prostitutes was but one manifestation of the misogynous spirit of the sixteenth century.

The topic of Protestantism has already arisen several times in the course of this investigation of possible causes for the dismantling of institutionalized prostitution in the sixteenth century, and it is indeed the influence of this movement that seems to provide the most satisfactory explanation for the closing of brothels in Languedoc in the 1550s. The great leaders of the Reformation were, in fact, vigorous opponents of institutionalized prostitution, and their views seem to have been adopted wholeheartedly by the Languedocian Protestant communities.

Fundamental to Luther's program for reform, based on deep theological divergences from the Roman church, was a rejection of the morals of the church and of contemporary society. Luther proposed a new image of man and society, at the heart of which was a new sexual morality. The extremes of sexual conduct found in sixteenth-century society—the asceticism of the monastic world and the libertinage of many laymen and clergy—were rejected in favor of a single norm of sexual activity within marriage for laymen and clergy alike. Luther protested vigorously against the opinion of many contemporary schoolmen that, although adultery ought to be avoided, the premarital sexual activity of young men (simple fornication) was inevitable and natural. The fact that most unmarried men were indeed not chaste was no justification, felt Luther, for condoning such behavior.[33] The logical consequences of this firm stand against simple fornication was the opposition to municipally owned or authorized houses of prostitution. Luther's unambiguous stand against such houses is clear in his letter to Hieronymus Weller of 1540, written in response to a concrete situation in Freiberg in Saxony, where the municipal brothel had been closed by the Lutherans in 1537, only to be reopened in 1540. "Those who wish to reestablish such houses," stormed Luther, "should first deny Christ's name, and recognize that, rather than Christians, they are heathens, who know nothing of God's name."[34] Luther's letter convinced the municipality to close the institution definitively. Lutheran preachers were responsible for the closing of public houses in Augsburg in 1532, in Ulm in 1537, in Regensburg in 1553, and in Nürnberg in 1562.[35]

Calvin was even more rigorous in his opposition to prostitution and brothels; he maintained that nothing could be tolerated that encouraged lechery (paillardise), detested by God.[36] The relation between Calvin's opposition to tolerated houses and his doctrine on sexual relations has been clearly outlined by A. Biéler.[37] Just before Calvin's arrival in Geneva, the town council announced that prostitutes must repent or leave the town. Calvin enforced to the letter these and other laws against paillardise, prosecuting even sexual relations between fiancés.[38] The civil authorities also enforced this moral rigorism: a list of arrests and trials in Geneva in 1562 shows that twenty percent of the criminal cases there involved illicit sexual relations, most of them concerning simple fornication.[39]

Because the Protestant movement in France was obliged to remain essentially underground until the late 1550s, fewer sources have survived from Languedoc in this period than from Lutheran Germany or Calvin's Geneva. Some documents attest, nonetheless, to the connection between Protestant sympathies and a desire to enforce a stricter sexual morality, even in the pre-Calvinist era. In the late 1520s at the medical school in Montpellier, an attack on the student organization that traditionally led the newly enrolled students to the town brothel seems to have been inspired by the Protestant ideas of certain professors and students.[40] Once the Huguenots came to power in Montpellier, their extreme moral rigorism aroused indignant protest from non-Protestants.[41] During the Wars of Religion, the Protestant troops who seized Gaillac beat the prostitutes in that town and cut off their ears.[42] The Protestant consistories established in Languedoc were as severe in their punishment of prostitution and simple fornication as their central European counterparts.[43]

Although there is no direct reference to Protestantism in the texts dealing with the closing of municipal brothels in Languedoc in the 1550s, one can nonetheless suppose that Protestant ideas were directly or indirectly responsible for these closings, for several reasons. This was the decade when Calvinism penetrated the population in Languedoc; Romier estimates that the majority of the population in the present-day *départements* of the Hérault and the Gard were Protestant by the end of the 1550s.[44] Moreover, the deliberations of Castelnaudary show clearly that the brothel was closed there for reasons of public morality.[45] Finally, as has been shown above, both before and after the crucial decade of the 1550s, Languedocian Protestants showed a marked hostility toward prostitution.

Although Protestant sympathies seem indeed to have been the immediate cause for the closing of brothels in Languedoc in the 1550s, it is important to remember that the desire for reform of church and society was broader, and deeper, than its manifestation in the Reformation. Thus, the leaders of the Counter-Reformation, seeking to tighten lay and clerical discipline, also waged a struggle against sexual immorality, including priestly misconduct, concubinage, and the use by families of common beds.[46] Prostitution, too, was a target of Catholic reformers; the Jesuits were particularly zealous opponents of authorized brothels.[47]

The desire for reform of sexual morality was deeper, too, than the Reformation and Counter-Reformation; it existed already in the early sixteenth century and found its roots in the late medieval period. This may at first seem contradictory, since the system of authorized prostitution manifested a certain vitality in the early sixteenth century. Languedocian towns continued to invest a great deal of money and interest in behalf of municipal prostitution in this period. The consuls of Montpellier purchased the formerly privately owned brothel for 900 l. in 1520,[48] and the Toulousan council paid 360 l. for a new brothel, Green Castle, in 1526.[49] The municipality of Albi invested in a new house, White Castle, in 1534;[50] and, until the 1550s, Alès kept trying to improve the municipal brothel, attract suitable women, and apparently make a profit.[51] The Green Castle of Toulouse was bringing in a small fortune in farms shortly before its definitive closing in the late 1550s.[52] But these facts and statistics sometimes masked a certain malaise. The documents from Toulouse, for instance, indicate that, as early as the 1520s, a minority of council members recommended that the city no longer farm out the brothel. Although the council did not follow this suggestion, it was obliged by public pressure to channel the money from the brothel farm, considered to be of *male acquisition*, to the hospitals for the poor.[53] Even in the case of Italy, where prostitution continued to be tolerated in the early modern times,[54] P. Larivaille has warned that the image of the cultivated, revered courtesan, a familiar *leitmotif* of Renaissance literature, should not blind us to the very real hostility toward venal women then current in all but the most exceptional circles in Venice and Rome.[55] Already in fifteenth-century Languedoc, growing disapprobation of concubinage and increasingly strong legislation against procuring were signs of a heightened sensibility to sexual immorality.[56]

Protestant sympathies were probably the immediate cause of the closing of brothels in Languedoc in the 1550s, but it is clear that the desire for change in sexual morality had been growing since the late Middle Ages. The importance of the Protestant movement was that it expressed this desire consciously and integrated it rigorously into an ideology. It systematized and carried to their logical conclusions ideas and feelings existing already at the end of the Middle Ages. In this new Christian society, which was to adumbrate its paradisaical successor, there was no longer room for the role of social stabilizer granted to the prostitute in late medieval times. And prostitution ceases at this point to be in the domain of institutional history, but rather becomes a part of the history of criminality and marginality in the early modern period.

PART TWO

Structures and Dynamics of Institutionalized Prostitution

The Language of Prostitution

In any thematic study of medieval prostitution, it is important to keep in mind the chronological development outlined above. While part 2 focuses on the period of institutionalization—the documentation being much richer than that from the High Middle Ages—frequent reference is made to the previous and subsequent periods, as the system of ownership and exploitation of houses, the status of the prostitute, and the attitude toward procuring all changed considerably from the thirteenth to the sixteenth century. An evolution is perceptible over this period even in the very language of prostitution.

The earliest terms used to designate places of prostitution were *lupanar* and *domus meretricum* (house[s] of prostitutes).[1] In the fourteenth century, the word *postribulum*, a deformation of the classical Latin *prostibulum*, appears in Languedocian documents. Map 1 (p. 149) shows that this term was limited in southern France to the towns of the lower Rhone River valley and those of Mediterranean Languedoc. Given that the Italian word for brothel is *postribulo* and that these Mediterranean Languedocian and Rhodanian towns were in constant contact with Italian cities, it would seem that this word was an Italian importation.[2] The words *postribulum* and *lupanar* usually corresponded to an entire district of prostitution rather than to an individual house. It was also common in this period to refer simply to a street (*carreria*), often without further qualification.[3]

In the second half of the fourteenth century, except in the very largest towns of Occitania, places of prostitution were reduced from a district to a single house. This change is reflected in contemporary vocabulary. Thus, the place of prostitution in Nîmes was no longer called *postribulum*, but rather *domus postribularis*;[4] one also finds the term *domus lupanaris*.[5] The most common vernacular word, *bordel*, sometimes Latinized as *bordellum*, meant simply "little house."[6] Increasingly in the fifteenth century, brothels were referred to simply as "public houses" (*hostal publique*).[7] The French equivalent in the later texts is *maison publique* or sometimes *maison commune*. Another term used in the fifteenth century was *bon hostal*.[8]

Similar changes occurred in the terms used to designate prostitutes. The High Middle Ages, as we have seen, popularized the term *meretrix publica*, which underlined the professional quality of the prostitute[9] (the Occitanian equivalent of *meretrix* being *puta* or *bagassa*).[10] Another way of designating a prostitute in the thirteenth and early fourteenth centuries was to give a short definition, as in a Nîmes police regulation that refers to "women who offer themselves for money."[11] Describing a woman with deprecating adjectives was also a way of indicating that she was a prostitute. Thus, the municipal council of Uzès refers to prostitutes as "trifling and vulgar women";[12] the vernacular expression was *avols femnas*.[13]

New terms to designate the prostitute appear in the texts from the end of the fourteenth century. It became common in that period to refer to prostitutes as "public women" (*mulieres publice*). This plain, neutral phrase—no infamous *meretrix*, no pejorative adjective—was to become the conventional term for prostitutes in the fifteenth century. It appears in Castelnaudary in 1391, used as a title to describe the person in question, just as one mentioned the trade of a man after his name. The prostitute who bought the *bordel* of Pézenas at auction in 1399 was referred to in two different notarial acts as *mulier publica* and *mulier seculara*.[14] The Occitanian equivalent was *femnas publicas*, although *las femnas* or *las filhas* was often considered sufficient, and the word was sometimes rendered in the diminutive, *las filhetas*. One finds occasional references to *bona filha*, a term that became quite popular in the late fifteenth and sixteenth centuries.[15]

Analysis of new terms introduced in the late fifteenth and early sixteenth centuries is complicated by the linguistic changes that were taking place in Languedoc, the replacement of Latin and Occitanian by French in official documents.[16] Hence, it is difficult to know whether the blossoming of terms for the prostitute in this period, most of which are of a generally pejorative character, correspond to Occitanian equivalents or are French importations. Prostitutes were referred to as *cantonnières*, *paillardes*, *garces*, *femmes lubriques*, *femmes déshonnêtes*, and *femmes dissolues*.[17] It was also common to describe prostitutes as "poor" and as "sinners" or "lost" girls.[18]

What is striking, in reviewing these terms, is the correlation between the period of institutionalization of prostitution and the widespread use of a relatively neutral official vocabulary for the places and women involved.[19] The prostitute was no longer—in official documents, at any rate[20]—a *meretrix* or *bagassa* and not yet a *femme lubrique* or *fille perdue*. She was a "public woman," who, with a certain air of respectability, confined her activities to the "public house."

Chapter Three

Public Houses: Physical Plant, Ownership, and Exploitation

The keystone of institutionalized prostitution in late-medieval Languedoc was the progressive recognition and organization of authorized places of prostitution. The passive acceptance of prostitutes and their activity characteristic of the High Middle Ages had given way to a situation in which the public authorities played an active role in defining, protecting, and later owning and exploiting districts and houses in which such activity was carried on. Prostitution had been transformed from a mobile, free-lance affair with the prostitute the principal actress, barred from respectable neighborhoods and from streets where she tarried too long, to a stable, spatially defined business, with the brothel as its fundamental structure and the brothel owner and brothel farmer as its principal figures.

By the late fourteenth century, there were two types of brothels—those privately owned and those publicly owned. Private places of prostitution, chronologically the earlier of the two, were found in two different forms. First mentioned in the documents is the red-light district—in which many houses of prostitutes were located—such as the Hot Street established in Montpellier in 1285.[1] By the fifteenth century, however, most of these districts had been narrowed down to one house. Only Avignon and Arles seem to have retained entire streets inhabited by prostitutes, a model that remained typical of the great Italian urban centers in the fifteenth century.[2]

The official *postribulum* of Avignon was the street of Bourg Neuf, located in a former suburb, within the fourteenth-century walls. An act of sale of part of this district dated 1491 describes "a certain place, fifteen canes square, in which are found a well, five huts of 'postribular' women and some trees."[3] The red-light district of Arles, called the *lupanar*, was located near the Hospital of the Holy Spirit in the parish of the Holy Cross.[4]

In most fifteenth-century Languedocian towns, however, the red-light district consisted of just one brothel, either privately or publicly owned. The only detailed descriptions of medieval brothels that have survived are those of municipally owned houses, such as that of the town of Alès, described in a series of leases. From the terms of the contracts stipulating the repairs the farmer was to make, one sees the actual state of the house and the appearance that the consuls hoped it would eventually have.

The building was a small, simple structure, with room enough for two stories. On the ground floor was a *foginea* (a kind of living room or hall) and two bedrooms (*camerula*). The farmer was requested to finish the wall between the *foginea* and the two smaller rooms, to put in a floor above the *foginea*, to install a fireplace of plaster, and to build a staircase leading to the second story. He was also requested to bar the windows on the ground floor, to secure the doors, and to open several windows overlooking the gardens of two of the neighbors of the brothel.[5] The repairs seem to have been complete by about 1530. The contract of 1535 describes the house as having four bedrooms—two on the ground floor and two on the upper story.[6] The consuls had also requested in 1515 that the farmer construct baths, but, since there is no mention of them in later contracts, one may assume that the project was abandoned, probably for lack of money.[7]

The basic elements of the brothel of Alès—one large common room, several smaller bedrooms, the importance of securing doors and ground-floor windows, the interest in a garden or a view on gardens—give a picture of the brothel that is valid for other towns as well. A charter from the cartulary of Albi gives this description of the new brothel, White Castle, constructed by the town in 1534–35:[8]

> The house of the public and common women, called White Castle [*Castel Blanc*], was built in the town (from the Gate Revel to the end of the vines), with a living room and fireplace and five bedrooms, all enclosed by a wall, and a porch in the middle. The town also purchased the [neighboring] meadow.

A lengthy account book listing expenses incurred in the construction of White Castle includes entries for an impressive quantity of locks and for the construction, finally, of six bedrooms. In the middle of the porch was the main entrance to the brothel, a portal above which were carved the arms of the town of Albi.[9]

The brothels of the large towns of Languedoc followed the same pattern but included a greater number of bedrooms. The bill of sale of the brothel of Montpellier to the municipality lists seven main bedrooms and four smaller ones in an adjacent structure.[10] The consular account books include numerous references to the purchase of additional locks and repairs of the premises due to attacks by *gens d'armes*. Although the previous owners of the brothel had constructed baths to be used by the women of the house, these baths seem to have been abandoned by the time the municipality purchased the building.[11]

The public house of Toulouse was described in 1462 as "big and spacious, with several stories, rooms and other houses, all enclosed [by a wall.]"[12] We know that there was a garden attached to this house.[13] The repairs were largely made necessary by aggressions on the house, and locks were often at the top of the list of replaced material. A repair bill records that one of the women accidentally set fire to her bedroom in 1499; this may indicate that there were fireplaces, or at least braziers, in the bedrooms.[14] We learn from other repair bills that the women spent their days in a sort of common room and that lodgings for the farmer were provided within the public house.[15] The fifteenth-century brothel included twenty-two bedrooms, whereas the town's new brothel, Green Castle (Château Vert), purchased and reconstructed in 1526–27, boasted twenty-five bedrooms.[16]

An inventory of furniture drawn up for the privately owned brothel of Nîmes in 1505 includes three categories of very simple furnishing:[17] beds and bedding, the importance of which is obvious; tables and benches, illustrating the importance attached to the custom that the prostitutes eat and drink only in the brothel (clients also may have been served); and boxes and cupboards, used for storing clothing and food and also, as the number of locks indicate, money.

In a street *postribulum* there were usually several different owners of the numerous huts in which prostitutes worked and probably lived. In Avignon in the fifteenth century, owners of postribular huts included a money changer (Nicolas Verceidi, 1444), a spice merchant (John of Parisiaco, 1489), and the widow of a sergeant of the temporal court (Perreta, widow of Francis Merce), who sold five huts to the candlemaker Ludowic Borgoing in 1491.[18] L. Le Pileur has shown that members of the regular clergy were also among the owners of these postribular rooms. Antonia of Laon, abbess of the monastery of Saint Catherine of Avignon, rented out a "postribular hut situated in the street Bourg Neuf" to John Minhoti in 1468. A passage from the registers of *reconnaissances* owed to the college of Saint Nicolas in 1500 lists two houses located "in the street of Bourg Neuf, in which are some rooms of girls of the said street." The same property was mentioned again in 1542.[19]

Owners of the postribular huts of the Arlesian *lupanar* included at least one prostitute. On 12 October 1360 the Franciscans sold a "house in the parish of the Holy Cross in the *postribulum* of Arles" to Margaret of Lyon. The same woman, apparently, described as *mulier publica*, bought a second house in the *postribulum* from Anthony Faugridi in 1364. Other huts were owned by merchants.[20]

The earliest known example of the single-house type of private prostitution in Languedoc is found in Uzès, where in 1326 the consuls declared that all prostitutes were to stay in the house of Peter Rascas, located outside the gate of Saint Stephan,[21] thus granting to an individual citizen a monopoly on the commerce of prostitution. A clue as to why it was Peter Rascas who obtained this privilege is found in a document dated 1323,[22] which records that John Rascas (surely from the same family as Peter) gave the municipality permission to construct on his land a grainery for storing the charity bread to be distributed by the town at Pentecost; the land in question lay near the same gate of Saint Stephan as the future brothel. Although nothing explicitly connects the two documents, the fact remains that the monopoly on prostitution was granted to a family from whose generosity the town had benefited. Thirty years later the monopoly on prostitution was held by a different person, Raymond Martini, and the brothel located in a different part of town, in the center opposite the tower of the king.[23]

References to this one-house type of private prostitution multiply in the late fourteenth and early fifteenth centuries. A number of these private houses were in the hands of prostitutes in that period. Two women were co-owners of the brothel of Foix, according to a tax list (*taille*) dated 1387.[24] At the end of the fourteenth century, the brothel of Pézenas, which had belonged to the judge Simon of Gyzard, was sold on his death, along with other property, to pay off certain debts owed by Simon to Queen Blanche. The buyer was Raynauda of Melus, the madam of the brothel.[25] In 1401 the brothel of Lodève was the property of "Isabel, the abbess of the brothel"; its changing ownership from then to its municipalization in 1455 can be traced through the town tax records.[26] Similar information can be gleaned from tax records (*compoix*) concerning the brothel of Beaucaire in a later period. Before 1480 the brothel was the property of co-owners Girardin Mourel and a certain Julian. The heirs of Mourel and Julian then sold the property to Rostauch Raymond, who resold it shortly thereafter to the tailor Estève Armen.[27] The property is listed as being in the same hands in the *compoix* of 1520.[28]

By the end of the fifteenth century, however, brothel ownership seems no longer to have been an affair for prostitutes, and not always for craftsmen. The great *bourgeoisie* and the nobility had a hand in the affair, too, especially in larger towns.[29] Etienne Médicis records in his *Livre de Podio* that the brothel of Le Puy (*maison des filles joieuses*) was one of the *maisons nobles* that had been omitted from the *compoix* of 1544.[30] In 1482 the *domus postribularis* of Nîmes was the property of Perreta Rastula, widow of the noble Valernin of Fiennes, resident of Villeneuve-lèz-Avignon.[31] On 18 April 1498, Anthony de Fiennes and his brother John, the sons of Valernin, also residents of Villeneuve, sold *lo bordel de Nysmes* to the noble Gabriel de Laye, "doctor of both laws."[32] De Laye was one of Nîmes's most illustrious citizens, having been elected several times consul and having served as the town's ambassador to the Estates of Languedoc in 1492.[33]

Montpellier also had a single privately owned house of prostitution in the fifteenth century, of which the coproprietors in 1469, listed in Louis XI's letter guaranteeing them the monopoly on prostitution in Montpellier, were Aubert and William Pavais (heirs of Clare Pavais) and William de la Croix.[34] In the *compoix* of 1480, William de la Croix is listed as owner of "half of a house outside the town, the abbey of the good street."[35] By 1489 a third party had been added, Jacquette, the wife of Jacques Bucelli. In the final bill of purchase preserved in the municipal archives, it is recorded that the town paid 200 l. to Johanna Pavais, 200 l. to the heirs of Jacques Bucelli, and 500 l. to Louis de la Croix, baron of Castries.[36] All of the owners of the brothel were from the great *bourgeoisie* of Montpellier; most were money changers, and the de la Croix family were nobles of recent date.[37] In the case before the Parlement of Toulouse in 1498, a protest against the existence of two illicit centers of prostitution in Montpellier, one cannot be sure whether William de la Croix, William Pavais, and Jacques Bucelli were acting in their capacity as consuls or as offended monopoly holders.[38] In the late fifteenth and early sixteenth centuries, the line of demarcation between public and private houses of prostitution had begun to blur.

Publicly owned houses of prostitution, which appear in the documents for the first time in the third quarter of the fourteenth century,[39] were of three sorts. A first type is exemplified by the brothel of Toulouse, which, like all other municipal property (weights and measures, butchers' stands, and so forth), was farmed out at auction to the highest bidder once a year, on the feast day of Saint Lucy (13 December). The money from this farm was used to pay for repairs necessary to the house; any money remaining after repairs helped swell the coffers of the municipality.[40] The town was responsible for the police and security of the house. Brothels municipalized in the course of the fifteenth and sixteenth centuries were generally run in this way; such was the case in Lodève, Castelnaudary, and Montpellier.

A second kind of arrangement existed in Pézenas in the fifteenth century, where the brothel was the property, not of the town, but of the Great Charity, a municipal organization established in 1236 for the purpose of managing the distribution of alms on feast days, the most important of which was Ascension.[41] All profits from the farm went to this charitable organization, but the farmer was subject to approval by the consuls, and the house was under the police of the consulate.[42] A somewhat similar situation existed in Toulouse after 1529, when the town council decided that henceforth, while the brothel remained the property of the municipality, the proceeds from the farm of the house were to go exclusively to the service of the hospitals. This change was made in response to public rumor that the profits of the brothel had been used to furnish luxurious robes for the consuls. Although the farm of the brothel continued to appear on the list of the annual farms, municipal documents concerning the brothel from after 1529 are rare, as repairs of the house and other problems arising from its management seem to have been the affair of the directors of the hospital services.[43]

A last type of public house existed in Albi and Castres. Although the consular account books of Albi furnish numerous references to expenses paid for the municipal brothel (notably for construction and repairs), the brothel is not included in the list of municipal properties farmed annually. There seems to have been no middleman between the consuls and the prostitutes. Perhaps the minor repairs and general costs of running the house were taken care of by the prostitutes, the major repairs by the municipality. At any rate, unlike in Toulouse, the town seems not to have realized a net profit on the house but rather to have run it on a deficit, as a sort of subsidized municipal service. The information for Castres is even scantier, the account books showing neither any expenses for repairs of the brothel nor any indication of farming out. The municipal deliberations establishing the public house indicate that the consuls there were planning a system of dues paying, perhaps hoping that the house could be self-supporting.[44] Although there are no documents concerning the management of the brothel of Saint-Quentin-la-Poterie, one can assume that, as in Castres and Albi, it was a nonprofit public service. Since it was a "house suitable for vagabond women," the revenues were surely too meager and unstable to warrant a farmer.[45] Where brothels existed in very small towns and large villages, they were probably of this sort.

Map 2 (p. 150), which illustrates the geographical distribution of private and public houses of prostitution, shows that eastern Languedoc and the lower Rhone River valley witnessed the first tolerated districts, which were private. This area remained the bastion of private houses throughout the late Middle Ages, although in several towns (Tarascon, Saint-Quentin) a municipal brothel was established, and in several others a private house was eventually made municipal (Lodève, Alès, and Montpellier). The idea of authorized centers of prostitution penetrated later into western Languedoc, but here the establishment of municipal brothels seems to have taken place earlier and more generally than in the east.

It should be noted, finally, that many small towns and villages were unable or unwilling to undertake the expense of establishing and running a brothel. Lacking a house of prostitution, many of these small municipalities continued to observe the custom of once a week (*semel in septimana*—allowing a prostitute in town no more than once a week), thereby regulating prostitution temporally rather than geographically.[46]

In the late thirteenth and fourteenth centuries, most houses of prostitution were exploited directly. In Avignon and Arles, a prostitute simply bought or rented a room in the red-light district and exercised her profession. The monopoly holder of Uzès seems to have been the direct landlord of the women who lodged in his house, and there are several examples in the late fourteenth century of small brothels in which a prostitute was both owner and manager of the house. In many small towns with a public house, the municipality dealt directly with the prostitutes who resided in it.

In the fifteenth century, however, one increasingly finds an indirect system of exploitation, in which a middleman came between the owner of the brothel and its residents. This was the system of farming out the house (*arrentement*), in which the right to the profits coming from the house were granted to a middleman in exchange for a fixed sum. The earliest references to such farms and farmers are the Toulousan account books from the fifteenth century, but more interesting are the actual contracts concluded between owner and farmer, most surviving copies of which date from the last decade of the fifteenth century and from the sixteenth century, the majority being those between farmers and municipalities where the house was publicly owned. These contracts constitute the primary source of information concerning the relationship between owner and farmer and the conditions of exploitation and management of the brothel.[47]

The most important element, present in every contract and in most account-book entries, was the price of the farm. The range of prices for which brothels could be farmed was considerable and seems to have been determined principally by the size of the municipality, the business conducted in its brothel, and the year in which the house was rented. The brothels of small towns, often in the mountains or foothills, were farmed out—if indeed they had a middleman at all—for a very small fee. In Lodève the municipality farmed out the house in 1471 for the sum of 17 s. 7 d.;[48] in Alès the farmers paid no money whatsoever but were simply obliged to maintain and repair the house.[49] Brothel farms in medium-sized towns on important trade routes brought in a higher price in more competitive bidding. The brothels of Beaucaire and Nîmes, both privately owned, brought in about 18 l. a year at the end of the fifteenth century.[50] The public house of Pézenas, a town whose fair flourished throughout the late Middle Ages, was farmed out for 33 l. in 1455 and for 27 l. in 1481.[51] In the sixteenth century Castelnaudary's brothel farm ranged from 6 l. 15 s. (1547) to 34 l. (1526), the average for the years 1515–28 being slightly below 28 l. Only Montpellier and Toulouse were large towns with important brothels, and Montpellier, as we have seen, had a much smaller house than did Toulouse. The highest price paid for the farm of the brothel there was 80 l. (1536), the usual price being between 50 and 60 l. This was a paltry sum compared to the revenues derived from the large and profitable public house of Toulouse, where farms in the same period ranged from 150 to more than 1,000 l.

In Nîmes and Toulouse the town brothels seem to have been profitable investments. The purchase price of the Nîmes brothel in 1498 was 175 l. The house was then farmed out for about 18 l, yearly revenues thus being about ten percent of the purchase price, a solid return for the time. Profitability was even more impressive in Toulouse, where the new brothel purchased in 1526 cost only 360 l., while the annual farm came to at least half that amount, usually more. This contrasts with the situation in Montpellier, where the consuls had paid the enormous sum of 900 l. in 1520 for a house that brought in a farm averaging only 50 to 60 l., a return of about six percent. The venture was clearly a net loss for the municipality, considering the many repairs and the number of occasions when the house was closed because of the plague.

The income from the brothel farm in Montpellier was not only low but declined steadily from the high of 80 l. in 1536 until the closing of the house.[52] In Castelnaudary, too, the sixteenth century witnessed a decline in the value of the brothel farm; it fell from 34 l. in 1526 to 12 l. in 1533. The slump continued, except for a slight comeback in the early 1550s, until the brothel was closed. This decline in the value of brothel farms is especially significant when one adjusts for inflation; the revenues of the public houses of Montpellier and Castelnaudary were declining as other prices were doubling and tripling.[53] It would be tempting to conclude from these statistics that, as reforming hostility toward prostitution grew, profits from the municipal brothels dropped, if it were not for the stunning exception of Toulouse, where profits had quintupled from 1503 to 1551.[54]

Another important element in the contracts between owner and farmer was the length of time of the *arrentement*, which ranged from one to six years. The most common period of time was one year, especially in towns with a publicly owned brothel, since the house was rented out annually with the other municipal property. Even in towns favoring longer terms, often the full length of these terms was not realized, the farmer staying, in fact, only a year or two at a time.[55]

The moment of the year when the contract began and ended varied greatly from one town to another. Towns with municipally owned brothels usually farmed them out at the same time as other town property. In Toulouse this was on the feast of Saint Lucy (13 December), whereas in Castelnaudary the traditional date was the feast of Saint Luke (18 October). In Pézenas the farm began on Quasimodo Sunday, this date having less to do with the functioning of the brothel than with the fact that the revenues of the house were used to subsidize the traditional distribution of bread to the poor practiced at Ascension.[56] It is not surprising that the two contracts from Beaucaire are both dated mid-July, since the great fair of Beaucaire took place on the feast of Saint Mary Magdalene (22 July). In Alès the consuls seem to have farmed out the brothel whenever they could find someone willing to take it.

The contracts also stipulated the times of payment. It was rare for the farmers to pay what they owed in one lump sum, since it was out of future profits that they were to pay the amount they had bid. Most contracts provided for triannual or quarterly payments; in Castelnaudary, Maria Lanas paid the thirty livres due for the year 1515–16 in five installments.[57] The consuls of Montpellier apparently accepted monthly or even weekly payments for the farm of La Bonne Carrière.

Because the sum due was paid over a long period of time, a pledge of security on the farmer's property was usually required. The movable goods of Steven Vincedy were taken in pledge (*pignus*) of future payments on the brothel farm in Beaucaire. Peter Massot, a farmer of the Nîmes brothel, had been obliged to present four men willing to back his enterprise by serving as security. In Toulouse in 1529, Domenge de la Font promised mortgage (*obligation et hypotheca*) of his possessions as security; his predecessor, Peter du Val, had been put in jail until he was able to provide sufficient guarantees.[58]

Special clauses were often added to these contracts, the most usual of which dealt with the repairs and upkeep of the house. The responsibility for major repairs was often taken by the owner, as was usually the case in municipal brothels.[59] A clause stipulated this responsibility in the contract between the municipality of Castelnaudary and Maria Lanas in 1515. The exception was Alès, where the farmer made repairs in lieu of rent. In the contract of 1482 concerning the brothel of Nîmes, the responsibilities for the material upkeep of the house were divided between the two parties, the owner being responsible for major repairs, the farmer for the upkeep of the gutters and drain pipes.[60] An unusual condition of "upkeep" was stipulated in a clause in the contract made in Alès in 1537, requiring the farmer to "keep beautiful and pleasant girl whores in order to maintain the said brothel."[61] Other clauses dealt with the eventual closing of the house in case of plague and with the observation of certain standards of order and morality within the brothel.[62] Although such clauses are found in few contracts, this may be due to the abbreviated nature of these documents, which are mere copies, in which such clauses were covered by the common expression "with the usual agreements" (*cum pactis consuetis*).

The farming contracts always included, of course, the name of the farmer, but, as the principal profession of the farmer was only occasionally indicated, it is difficult to know from what social class the *arrenteurs* were drawn. They must have been property owners in order to satisfy the requirements concerning security and guarantee of payment of the farm. Most of the women who farmed out the houses seem, naturally enough, to have been prostitutes in the brothel. The only series of contracts to give regularly an indication of the profession of the male farmers is that of Alès, where they were usually propertied craftsmen. Among the sixteenth-century farmers there were a weaver, a barber, a carder, a stonecutter, and a hat maker;[63] a royal sergeant was the *arren-*

teur in 1518. The list of farmers for Toulouse includes a few indications of profession between 1541 and 1551, when we see a carder, a tailor, a baker, a painter, and a fisherman.

The contracts from Alès indicate, in addition, that four out of the nine farmers there were not natives of Alès. In Castelnaudary nine of the sixteen women who farmed the brothel in the sixteenth century were definitely from other towns, and four of the remaining seven may have been. In the 1540s and 1550s, most of these women came from considerable distances, from the north of France in particular. The archives of Toulouse and Montpellier, on the other hand, show fewer indications of "foreign" farmers.

Both men and women farmed brothels in late-medieval Languedoc; the sex of the *arrenteur* had much to do with local tradition, it would seem. The Alès farm, for instance, was resolutely male in the sixteenth century, whereas the Castelnaudary farm seems to have been exclusively female up to the closing of the house in 1555. The two contracts concerning the farm of the private brothel of Beaucaire indicate that a man was the farmer (1490, 1492).[64] For Nîmes one finds a woman (1498) and two men (1482, 1506). The three farmers mentioned for Pézenas were male.[65] The Montpellier archives mention both men and women.

It would seem that man-woman management teams were common, even if only one name appears in the farming contract. The account books of Nîmes, for example, refer to a certain Beatrix as the *abbesse* of the brothel, whereas a notarial document indicates that a man farmed the brothel that year.[66] In a letter of remission concerning events that took place in the brothel of Toulouse in 1448, one sees that, although an abbess was in charge of the house, a man by the name of John Sudre seems to have acted as a sort of bouncer.[67] At the beginning of the sixteenth century in Castelnaudary, although Maria Lanas had farmed the public house, a certain Anthony Teyseyre was referred to as *abat del public*.[68] In 1528 the widow of the *arrenteur* Peter du Val, shortly after his death, was obliged by the consistory of Toulouse to secure the service of a man for running the affairs of the brothel.[69] Husband-and-wife teams were were apparently not rare.[70]

It has been suggested that toward the end of the Middle Ages there was a tendency for men to replace women at the head of brothels.[71] This trend toward the "masculinization" of brothel management characterizes, in fact, the situation in Toulouse, if not elsewhere in Languedoc, as can be seen from the list of farmers there.[72] In 1404, 1420, and 1425 the brothel was farmed by one or more prostitutes of the house; in 1431, 1432, and 1433, by a prostitute and a man together; from 1450 to 1464, only by men; and in 1469, by a woman. From 1488 onward the list is increasingly male and is indeed exclusively so from 1533 to its closing. Of the three women listed between 1488 and 1532, the only one to farm for more than one year (Johana Dangiera, 1516–22) was

following her husband in that post. A passage from the municipal deliberations of 1419, moreover, states unambiguously that "it was the custom for the
house to be farmed by women."[73] The royal safeguard of 1425 indicates that
the profit made by the municipality on the brothel was paid by "the women, or
farmers."[74] In a later period the trend toward masculinization drew protest,
moreover, from critics of the abuses of the system. The king's attorney general, prosecuting before the Parlement of Toulouse in 1460 a notorious procurer who had installed himself for a while as the *abbé del bordel* there, complained, "It is not well that such ruffians should be the abbots of the girls, but,
rather, it should be one of the older prostitutes."[75]

The most vigorous protest against the presence of a male abbot, however,
was emitted by the women of the public house of Toulouse themselves. Bringing their complaint against the municipality before the Parlement of Toulouse
in 1462,[76] their plea was essentially an indictment of the system of brothel
farming as it was practiced in Toulouse in the mid–fifteenth century. The
women charged that, by farming out the house annually to a man, the consuls
were encouraging the proliferation of vice,[77] because the farmer, called "in
derision . . . the abbot of the brothel," was no more than a common procurer
(*ung roffien*) who tried to extort the maximum from the women, therefore encouraging illicit intercourse.[78] Auctioning the brothel farm to such a man was,
in the words of the women's lawyer, "a foolish custom, if in fact it should be
called a custom." The women had normally owed obedience to an abbess,
according to the document, and their lawyer claimed that the new system of
exploitative management would never have been tolerated in the past.[79] The
prostitutes presented an alternative plan of "government."[80] Although the
women may have been idealizing the advantages of a system in which one of
the prostitutes assumed the responsibilities of abbess, the so-called *Procès des
Fillettes* of 1462 seems to be an otherwise accurate testimony to the difficulties encountered in the transition from a system of direct exploitation, in-
volving only the proprietor and the prostitutes, to the system of a middleman
or brothel keeper, which seems to have encouraged a more efficient exploitation of the profitability of the authorized houses.

By the mid–fifteenth century, a period of renewed economic expansion,
the widely accepted role of the brothel in the maintenance of public order and
security was supplemented by the attractiveness of its commercial potential.
The interest in the financial gains possible in the exploitation of prostitution is
attested to by the virtual domination of private prostitution by the great *bourgeoisie* and the nobility in this period, and by the growing popularity of municipal brothels, which often aspired to, even if they did not always achieve,
profitability. The desire for maximally efficient exploitation of the financial
possibilities of prostitution is seen, also, in the increasing emphasis on the
role of the middleman or brothel farmer; the very masculinization of brothel
management in this period serves to underline the growing importance of the

middleman. The prostitutes of Toulouse were quick to grasp the logical and moral dilemma in which the consuls found themselves by profiting from prostitution through the *arrenteur*. The women's protest against exploitative brothel farming was echoed in the sixteenth century by the people of Toulouse, complaining that the consuls profited from ill-gotten gains (*male acquisition*), and by reforming leaders, who condemned a system that in effect encouraged the proliferation of fornication.[81]

Chapter Four

Public Women: Geographical Origins; Economic, Legal, and Social Status; and the Problem of Repentance/Retirement

From a sociological point of view, the study of late-medieval Languedocian prostitution is a frustrating endeavor, since there remains little archival information on the individual prostitutes themselves. The staples of contemporary studies of prostitution—analyses of the women's economic, social, and geographical background, their psychological profile and vocational motivation—are virtually impossible, given the lack of relevant documents.[1] Property, in this case, was far better documented than people; while a distinct image of the brothel—its size, layout, exploitation, and management—emerges from the archival documentation, the prostitute, by contrast, remains a shadowy, elusive figure, emerging briefly in a handful of occasional references, her name, or often only a nickname, appearing on a few remaining lists of brothel residents. Little, consequently, can be said of individuals, and a chapter on public women must therefore focus on a certain number of generalizations concerning prostitutes in medieval Languedoc: that is, their geographical origins; their economic, legal, and social status; and the solutions found by Languedocian society to the problems posed by the prostitute's repentance and/or retirement from professional activity.

Medieval prostitutes seem to have preferred to practice their trade outside their native towns or villages; this is the impression that emerges from several incidental references to prostitutes in the Languedocian municipal archives and from studies on prostitution in other regions.[2] We have seen that a majority of the women who farmed the brothel of Castelnaudary in the sixteenth century were from other towns.[3] The earliest complete list of prostitutes in an authorized house, that from Uzès dated 1357, although badly water-damaged, shows clearly that all five women listed were from outside Uzès.[4]

Three complete lists of the names of the women residing in the public house of Toulouse have survived from the years 1514, 1521, and 1528.[5] Geographical origins are not easy to determine, however, because the women are often listed only by first names or even nicknames. Of the women whose "foreign" origin is indicated in the list of 1514, seven seem to be from other municipalities in the southwest of France and six from farther away (including two from the Ile-de-France and two from Lombardy). The list of 1521 consists almost entirely of nicknames, several of which indicate physical abnormalities.[6] More place names are found in the list of 1528, although not all are easily identifiable. Out of thirty women, twelve seem to be from southwestern France and three from farther away (including one from Sardinia and one from the Piedmont). One might tend to assume that the women listed only by first names or nicknames were natives of Toulouse were it not for the presence, in the list of 1528, of a woman identified as "La Toulousane." This entry would seem to suggest, on the contrary, that most of the women were from outside Toulouse, even if they were known principally by their first names or nicknames.[7] It was apparently so rare for a prostitute to work in her native town that this fact was a sufficient means of distinguishing her from her colleagues.[8]

On the socioeconomic origins of the prostitutes, the Languedocian archives are mute. It is a standard observation of contemporary sociology that many women fall into prostitution because of material need.[9] J. Rossiaud, analyzing documents unusually rich in information concerning the social background of prostitutes in Dijon (1440–1540), has concluded that most were indeed of humble origin.[10] Documents testifying to a connection between poverty and prostitution are found in Germany and Italy. A Bolognese *catasto* from 1371 lists several prostitutes as living in a very humble quarter of town, among beggars and poor workers.[11] Notarial records from Perugia include contracts concluded in 1388 between prostitutes and the local brothel manager in which the women committed themselves to working in the brothel for from one to three years in exchange simply for food and clothing.[12] There were apparently even women who found their way into brothels as a result of personal or family debts, a practice that some municipalities, in Germany as well as in Italy, sought to modify or abolish.[13]

But there is surprisingly little in the Languedocian archives that suggests an association between prostitution and poverty before the late fifteenth century,[14] when the term *poor girl* came to be used to indicate a prostitute.[15] Several illicit prostitutes arrested in Toulouse in the early sixteenth century were excused from eventual punishment because of their poverty.[16] Charitable donations in the form of dowries for poor women grew in popularity in that period,[17] and some donations make explicit their intention to prevent possible prostitution.[18] The Franciscan preacher Olivier Maillard castigated contemporary mothers who forced their daughters into prostitution to earn a dowry.[19]

More numerous, on the other hand, are the Languedocian texts that serve to remind us that, while sometimes a palliative to poverty, prostitution could also be a lucrative profession for women. Throughout the period studied, one sees examples of women who managed to profit nicely from their profession. Guiraude of Béziers and Elys of Le Puy had money enough to plead their cause for a recognized place of business in Montpellier in 1285. Several prostitutes from Beaucaire at the end of the fifteenth century left wills disposing of money and property and indicating middle-class origins.[20] Katharine Friande, while referring to herself as *pauvre fille* in her appeal to the consuls for a reduction of the farm of the Toulousan brothel in 1507, had nonetheless managed to win that lucrative farm. In her petition she reminded the consuls that she had already paid the *quart de vin* (wine tax) and the *taille*, an indication that she was a propertied person indeed, and she complained that without financial relief she would be obliged to pawn her jewels, an argument unlikely to bring tears to the eyes of even the most charitable town council![21]

Examples of women profiting from prostitution are particularly numerous, however, from the end of the fourteenth and beginning of the fifteenth centuries. Small-town archives show several cases of women doing well in the business. The brothel of Foix was the property in 1387 of two women, one named Isabel, a resident of Foix, and the other Denauda dela Roqua, residing in Toulouse.[22] In Lodève it was also an Isabel, *abadessa*, who was the owner of the public house in 1401.[23] In 1399 Raynauda of Melius, *abesse* of Pézenas, paid 80 l. for the local brothel, which she then donated to the Great Charity of that town, wisely retaining the usufruct until her death.[24] There was no official brothel in Castelnaudary at that period, but a contemporary register of criminal cases brought before the consuls describes a prostitute, who had accused a number of youths of attempted rape and robbery, as follows: "Johanna, widow of Arnauld Denat, and daughter of Bernard Olive of St-Felix, aged 22 years, and possessing more than average goods, public woman."[25] This well-to-do young widow belies the stereotype of the prostitute born of misery.

The large towns, too, saw a couple of generations of propertied prostitutes. Two notarial acts from Arles dated 1360 and 1364 record that an enterprising *mulier publica* from Lyon named Margarita bought two houses in the local *postribulum*, the first for 26 florins and the second for 13 florins.[26] Cristina, the *abbatissa* of the Montpellier brothel in 1400, paid a tax on movable goods amounting to 9 écus.[27] One of the prostitutes of the brothel of Marseille, Françoise of Florence, drafted a will in 1361 in which she made legacies to various charities, including the considerable sum of 40 florins as dowry for a poor girl.[28] The goods of the public woman Thomasa of Barcelona, who died intestate in Perpignan in 1432, were apparently of such value that the clergy of her parish church and the local administrator of the royal patrimony disputed the right to succession.[29] Significant, too, are a royal privilege granted by the king of France to the Toulousan prostitutes in 1389 (presumably for a certain price)[30] and the royal safeguard accorded to the Toulousan brothel in 1425, providing protection of "the said women who . . . live in the said house, with their goods and all their possessions and household members staying in the same house." [31]

An anecdote that well illustrates the material self-sufficiency of certain prostitutes in this period is found in the court records of Florence.[32] The pious neighbors of a prostitute there proposed to provide her with a basket of bread each week if she abandoned her profession. But the woman was not the least tempted by the offer, countering that she earned much more than what they had proposed and that they must offer her at least two florins to make it worth her while to give up that line of work. Not all prostitutes pursued their trade freely out of desire for gain, but at the end of the fourteenth century such a situation seems at least not to have been exceptional.

The archives are somewhat more generous in information on the legal status of prostitutes, making it possible to advance a tentative hypothesis concerning the evolution of that status. It would seem that an attempt to limit the legal capacity of the prostitute, characteristic of the twelfth and thirteenth centuries, had dissipated in the fourteenth and fifteenth centuries. The evolution of the legal status of the prostitute seems to have been generally positive in these last years of the Middle Ages, in the direction of full legal capacity and even protection by rape laws.

Much of the justification for the limitation on the capacity of the professional prostitute declaimed in the twelfth and thirteenth centuries came from Roman law. As we have seen, the civilians of the twelfth century repeated all the restrictions on prostitutes in Roman law, placing them in the ranks of the infamous. Thus, the prostitute was theoretically barred from testimony.[33] A register of testimony in criminal justice from Cordes (Tarn) dating from the early fourteenth century shows a case in which a prostitute's testimony was actually called into question by persons against whom the testimony was aimed.[34] The prostitute, as an infamous person, had, moreover, no right to bring accusations, according to Roman law.[35] The inhabitants of Arles complained to Charles of Anjou in a petition dated 1257 that accusations by prostitutes and other infamous people had been heard, requesting that such accusations no longer be accepted.[36] Although no contemporary texts witness to an attempt to prevent prostitutes from making a will or from inheriting property, there is some indication of hostility toward the marriage of prostitutes.[37]

In addition to these limits on legal capacity stemming from Roman and canon law, prostitutes suffered also from deprivation of the right to normal judicial procedure when accused of small offenses. Many Occitanian customs acknowledged, for instance, that an honest person who had been insulted by a prostitute could strike her as punishment without fear of being called before the authorities.[38] H. Courteault cites three police ordinances of Bagnols-sur-Cèze that include articles authorizing honest people insulted by a prostitute to avenge themselves "with the fist or the palm of the hand, provided that there be no death, loss of a member or bone fracture."[39] Similar customs existed in Provence[40] and in several Italian cities.[41] A similar restriction on the right to judicial procedure has already been seen in the case of prostitutes found living in a neighborhood of honest people in the towns of Toulouse, Arles, and Bourg-Saint-Andéol. The prostitutes' neighbors in these towns were authorized to expel the women from the vicinity on their own authority.[42] Similarly, an honest woman of Arles who saw a prostitute wearing a veil (normally an article of clothing to be worn only by chaste women) was authorized to pluck it off.[43]

The last of these provisions for expeditive justice against prostitutes seem to have disappeared by the mid–fourteenth century. Punishment of offending prostitutes was by then firmly in the hands of the public authorities. One can trace, moreover, an evolution in the kind of punishment meted out to delinquent prostitutes by the authorities.[44] Infraction of a municipal statute regulating prostitution in the thirteenth and early fourteenth centuries was often to be punished (when punishment was specified, not left to the decision of the court) by confiscation of the prostitute's clothing.[45] Whipping (only in the case of residence outside the authorized district) was coupled with confiscation of clothing in some regulations.[46] Increasingly in the late fourteenth and fifteenth centuries, however, the principal punishment was simply a fine (usually of 5 or 10 s.), less infamous and less severe than corporal punishment or confiscation. Corporal punishment appears again in the sixteenth century (earlier in royal ordinances) in legislation aimed principally at procurers.[47]

By the end of the fourteenth century, limits on the rights of prostitutes and restrictions of their legal capacity would seem to have disappeared. The consular registers of criminal justice that have been preserved in Castelnaudary and Foix from this period show prostitutes testifying and accusing in criminal cases without any objection being made to the propriety of this procedure. Thus, a prostitute (*Johanna, mulier de luppanari Fuxi*) testified against two sergeants of the constable of Foix, stating that she saw them draw swords without provocation on Arnald Vital after they had left the town brothel.[48] It was perhaps the same woman (*Johanna, filia communis de burdello Fuxi*) who, two and a half months later, accused Stephen Petri of breaking his way into her room and beating her. He could not be convicted in the consular court, however, for he was a cleric.[49] Similarly in Castelnaudary, another

Johanna, *mulier publica*, accused a group of young men of robbery, assault and battery, and attempted rape. Several other town citizens testified in her favor.[50]

There were apparently no practical limits to the legal capacity of the prostitute in southern France in the fifteenth century. J. Rossiaud has found several marriage contracts of prostitutes from this period in which their profession is clearly stated.[51] Several wills of prostitutes have also been preserved, indicating that they were free to dispose of their possessions as they wished.[52] Last, as we have seen, there were apparently no limits on the capacity of the prostitute to conclude contracts; municipal brothels were farmed out to prostitutes as well as to men.[53] From the end of the fourteenth century to the sixteenth century, prostitutes would seem to have enjoyed the same legal capacity as honest women.

Whether the rape of the prostitute should be punished by the courts or not was a hotly debated issue in the Middle Ages. The Roman Codex extended no protection to the prostitute,[54] and the medieval canonists apparently were scarcely more generous.[55] Vigorous protection of the public woman, on the other hand, was provided by Emperor Frederick II, who, in the Constitutions of Melfi of 1231, decreed that rapists of prostitutes should be executed.[56] Frederick may have been inspired in this by the legislation of the Christian emperors, especially the Justinianic Novella 14, providing severe punishment for procurers.

The legislation of the German and Italian towns on this point was varied. Some explicitly refused to consider the rape of the prostitute to be an offense; others imposed a penalty on the rapist of the prostitute, although almost systematically this punishment was lighter than that inflicted on the rapist of an honest woman.[57] Vienna is an example of a town whose law evolved from exoneration of the rapist of the prostitute in the early thirteenth century to his punishment in the middle of that century.[58]

Regional and municipal law in France seems to have been favorable to the protection of the prostitute from rape.[59] There is to my knowledge no Occitanian text, moreover, that specifically exonerates the rapist of the prostitute from prosecution, as was so often the case in German and Italian towns. In general, the punishment was less severe than that which sanctioned the rape of honest women (very often the death penalty or castration in the case of the rape of a virgin).[60] A statute from the town of Bioule (Tarn-et-Garonne) dated 1273 states that the rapist of the prostitute should be corporally punished by the lord (*punit de corps a esgard del senhor*). Punishment was left to the discretion of the court in Lézat (Ariège) in a statute of 1299. The most common punishment established by the law codes, however, was a fine, the amount of which ranged from 1 to 100 s.[61]

That these statutes were actively enforced is clear from the early-fifteenth-century consular court records of the towns of Foix and Castelnaudary, which both show prostitutes bringing charges of attempted rape and battery.[62] Lists of fines imposed on the residents of Apt include numerous examples of fines for aggression against prostitutes in the fourteenth and fifteenth centuries.[63] Sanction of the rape of the prostitute was so widely accepted that foreign merchants, fearful of presumably trumped-up charges being brought against them, often solicited from the king the privilege of exemption from prosecution on such charges.[64] The early-fourteenth-century registers of the Inquisition of Jacques Fournier show that common morality deemed it necessary not only to pay a prostitute a reasonable price but also to obtain her consent.[65] Not until the sixteenth century did it become usual to assume that a prostitute's profession deprived her of legal recourse in case of rape.[66]

While the legal status of prostitutes seems to have improved markedly in the late Middle Ages, this progress may be more ambiguous than it would seem at first. One may wonder, for example, whether the impression of the widening of the prostitute's legal capacity may not be due in part to the fact that practical texts dealing with the enforcement of laws are more plentiful in the fifteenth than in the thirteenth century, and practice is often laxer than theory.[67] The prostitute's virtually unchallenged capacity to accuse and to testify in the fifteenth century, while it may be evidence of her rise in public esteem, may also be related to a general desire to repress criminality more effectively.[68] Well-enforced rape laws may indeed be testimony to the prostitute's integration into medieval society, but they may also have been intended to enforce a commercial rather than a personal protection, for the prostitute but also for the community boasting a municipally owned public house. Laws prescribing small fines as punishment for the rapist of the prostitutes may also have been intended to protect the citizens of the town against exorbitant punishment in the case of prosecution for the rape of a prostitute.[69] Was the improvement in the legal status of the prostitute real or was it only apparent? Marginality or integration—which best describes the place of the prostitute in late-medieval society?

Some writers, such as B. Geremek, have chosen to portray prostitutes as among the marginals of medieval society, along with criminals and beggars; others have claimed, on the contrary, that public women were so integrated into medieval society as to constitute a veritable professional guild.[70] Neither image is completely accurate, for, while prostitution was so unquestionably accepted and generally institutionalized as to preclude the marginalization of prostitutes, society did not grant them the dignity of a professional organization among others. In fact, the social group which prostitutes most resembled was that of the Jews. Like the Jews, prostitutes defied the teaching of the Church, yet were tolerated because of the importance of their services in an urban society. Jews were condemned not only for their disbelief in Christ but also because they practiced usury, forbidden by canon and secular law; yet urban life without that usury (which included most forms of lending at interest) was impossible.[71] Prostitutes' commerce was the antinomy of Christian mores, yet a town without prostitutes was as inconceivable as one without usurers. It is no accident that Saint Thomas Aquinas included his defense of the necessity of prostitution in a chapter dealing with the toleration of the Jews.[72] When Pope Pius V tried to ban both Jews and prostitutes from the city of Rome in 1566, the citizens, fearful of the effects such a measure might have on the economy and public order in that city, petitioned him to be more indulgent "in imitation of the Lord, who has tolerated in the world Jews, adulterers and prostitutes."[73]

Some contemporary Occitanian texts make explicit this association in the popular mind between Jews and prostitutes.[74] A regulation from the Avignonese customs of 1243 prohibits Jews and prostitutes alike from touching bread or fruit on the market, obliging them to buy all they did touch.[75] The thirteenth-century statutes of Marseille forbade bath keepers from allowing Jews and prostitutes to enter the public baths on other than specified days (Monday for prostitutes, Friday for Jews).[76] It may also be noted, even though no contemporary document draws the parallel, that prostitutes, like Jews, were required to wear distinctive signs and were prohibited from circulating through town during Holy Week.[77] Finally, it may be pointed out that, while both Jews and prostitutes were often the object of scorn or suspicion, both could find succor in society if they decided to convert or repent. This dual attitude—hostility toward practicing Jews and prostitutes but encouragement to those who converted—is seen in the words and actions of Saint Louis. A fierce enemy of usury and a stern critic of the Talmud, Louis IX nonetheless encouraged the conversion of Jews to Christianity and acted himself as godfather on occasion.[78] Similarly, while condemning prostitution, Louis is said to have been a generous benefactor to communities of repentant women, which included many former prostitutes.[79]

Similar as were the place of Jews and that of prostitutes in medieval society, the evolution of the social status of these two groups in the late Middle Ages seems to have been quite divergent. It is a commonplace of medieval history that the status of the Jews deteriorated at the end of the Middle Ages, when they were victims of popular hostility and official expulsion. The prostitute, on the other hand, seems to have gained in social stature in the same period, as we have already seen from diverse evidence: the relatively enviable economic position reached by certain prostitutes, the apparent amelioration of their legal status, and the adoption of a more neutral vocabulary of prostitution. These developments are connected to the increasing institutionalization of prostitution, which transformed the public woman from a free-lance worker to an agent of a positive public policy on prostitution and sexual morality, enjoying certain privileges as well as obligations.[80]

The role accorded to the prostitute in public life in the late Middle Ages is best conveyed by some Italian texts, as that in which a Venetian prostitute is rewarded with 25 ducats in 1498 for a patriotic act—having notified the authorities of the traitorous plans of the friend of a client.[81] Significant, too, is the Venetian court register that records, in the trial of a man who, accused of having had carnal relations with his goat, claimed as extenuating circumstances a physical infirmity preventing his having normal relations with a woman, that the judge called in two of the city's prostitutes to "do numerous experiments" in order to verify the accused's claim, much as today a psychiatrist is called in to verify a plea of insanity![82]

While the importance of the prostitute in public life must be recognized, it must not, on the other hand, be overemphasized. The role she played in public pageantry and festivities, for example, has probably been exaggerated. The oldest Languedocian reference to prostitutes' participation in festivities is an account-book entry dated 1399, which records that at Ascension the consuls of Nîmes gave 5 s. to the personnel of the city's public house.[83] This rather sober custom was elaborated only toward the end of the fifteenth century, when it became customary for the *abbesse* of the brothel to present a cake (*fogassia*) to the consuls (1479); only one text mentions a kiss (*osculum*) exchanged between the consul and the *abbesse*.[84] Detailed accounts of expenses for Ascension Day and other festivities in other Languedocian towns, however, make no mention of such a practice.[85] The few texts referring to prostitutes' participation in festivities are late and all from the lower Rhone River valley. There was, for instance, a race for prostitutes held on the feast day of Mary Magdalene (22 July) in Beaucaire in the fifteenth century[86] and one on Pentecost in Arles.[87] The earliest reference to such a race, to my knowledge, is in the ordinance for the fair of Saint Felix in the Italian town of Foligno in 1447.[88]

Although there is evidence from central Europe that prostitutes there participated in the entry of important persons, including the emperor, into towns,[89] such participation seems not to have figured in the entry of the kings of France.[90] A notary of Orange records that two young prostitutes (*deux jeunes garces*) were dressed up as a Turk and a Moor for the entry into the town of the local bishop.[91] But here, clearly, they were not an official delegation representing the town prostitutes but were merely hired to play a theatrical role in the pageantry. This kind of role, indeed, could hardly have been played by the honest women of the town, especially in cases calling for nudity or seminudity (allegorical representations of the virtues, for example).

One may also wonder to what extent the more favorable attitude toward prostitutes adopted by the public authorities in the late Middle Ages penetrated the rest of society. Contemporary documents would seem to indicate that, despite the official recognition of the prostitute as a person capable of making a positive contribution to the commonweal, scorn and distrust were perpetuated. Even in the period when the prostitute was for official purposes a "public woman," the word *whore* was still the greatest insult one could inflict on a female, and contemporary court records bristle with variations on that epithet. In 1469 a fine was imposed on an Arlesian woman who had dared to call a slave girl "whore"; [92] although she was at the very bottom of the medieval social pyramid, a slave might be "honest," which a prostitute, by (medieval) definition, could never be. In the personal journals of Italian merchants, as well as in the *fabliaux* of northern France, the prostitute is presented as a wily, greedy person not to be trusted.[93] Such a judgment is hardly surprising. In a society with an ambivalent attitude toward sexuality (both asceticism and libertinage found their advocates), an ambivalent attitude toward material gain (which was alternately condemned and praised), and an ambivalent attitude toward women (honored for Mary's sake, despised for Eve's), it would be unrealistic to expect a clear, let alone a clearly positive, attitude toward those women who commerced their sexuality.

Prostitutes, like Jews, were the object of proselytizing efforts in the late Middle Ages. Unlike Jews, however, prostitutes had a direct material interest in repenting, as had the community in helping her to do so. The prostitute knew well that her career would be short; there was little demand for elderly prostitutes, and by middle age, if she lived so long, the public woman was obliged to retire, if not to repent.[94] From the public authorities' point of view, both charity and wisdom dictated that they provide a suitable institution. A former prostitute of the municipal brothel was not only a deserving recipient of municipal charity but also a potential object of suspicion. It was feared that, if not aided by the community, the former prostitute might well resort to activities inimical to the commonweal: procuring for illicit prostitutes, arranging adulterous trysts and the deflowering of virgins, and concocting love potions and abortive mixtures, like Celestina in the famous fifteenth-century Spanish play of the same name.

The initiative in encouraging prostitutes to repent had first been taken, of course, by the Church, which had long preached "conversion" to public women[95] and which was experiencing in the twelfth century a revived interest in penitence in general. In a letter dated 1198, Innocent III urged Christians to aid the "conversion" of former prostitutes and offered remission of sins to those who married such women.[96] The movement took institutional form through the efforts of local preachers in the early thirteenth century. In Paris, Fulk of Neuilly, a student of Peter the Chanter, whose preaching of repentance was aimed principally at usurers and public women, founded, in cooperation with Peter of Roissac, a community for repentant prostitutes, which was erected into an abbey in 1206.[97] A similar community, based on the Augustinian rule and called the Filles-Dieu, was founded by the Parisian theologian William of Auvergne in 1226.[98] Saint Louis is said to have been a generous benefactor of this community.[99] In the same period in Germany, the conversion of prostitutes had become the principle concern of Rudolph, canon of Saint Maurice of Hildesheim, who had received a preaching mission from the legate Conrad of Zähringen in 1225[100] and whose efforts were lauded in a letter of Gregory IX dated 8 June 1227. Two days later the pope issued a bull giving a veritable juridical status to these communities, to whom the Augustinian rule and the institutions of Prouille were recommended.[101] Italy witnessed a similar enthusiasm for such institutions in the thirteenth century.[102]

In southern France most major towns seem to have had communities for repentant women by the late thirteenth or early fourteenth century. A will from Toulouse dated 1294 mentions a donation to such a community.[103] In Marseille it was a *bourgeois* named Bertrand who in 1272 founded a home for penitent prostitutes, which was later recognized by Pope Nicolas II.[104] Mentioned for the first time in a will dated 1293, the repentant sisters of Avignon later benefited from the generosity of the papal chamberlain Gasbert du Val, who financed the construction of a chapel and a house for the sisters in the second quarter of the fourteenth century.[105] This same Gasbert du Val, once he became archbishop of Narbonne, showed an interest in the equivalent institution there, which had been founded, apparently, by the archbishop Peter of Montbrun (1272–86).[106] A community of repentant sisters existed in Limoux by 1309.[107] Several *bourgeois* of Carcassonne founded a house for penitent prostitutes in 1321, during the episcopate of Peter of Rochefort.[108] Queen Esclarmonda, wife of James I of Majorca, is said to have founded the community of repentant sisters of Perpignan in the early fourteenth century.[109]

Little trace other than a foundation date has been left by most of these humble communities. Of all the Languedocian towns, it is Montpellier whose archives yield the most information about these institutions. A will dated 3 May 1204 indicates that a community of repentant sisters existed already in Montpellier,[110] by far the oldest testimony to such an institution in the region. Located near the Gate Saint Gilles, this community was granted a papal favor in 1247 and the authorization to build a stone staircase down to the town moat behind the convent in 1294.[111] Sometime in the next seven years, the community took the name Saint Gilles and ceased to be an institution for repentant women. A will of 7 May 1301 includes a legacy to the sisters of Saint Gilles and to the "new" repentant sisters.[112] By 1319, however, the municipality had two such communities, referred to in a will of April of that year as the repentant sisters of Saint Catherine and those of the Courreau (and in later wills as the sisters of Mary Magdalene).[113] These two communities existed side by side in Montpellier from 1319 to 1387, when they merged, probably as a result of the depopulation of urban monastic communities in the wake of the Black Death.[114]

Despite the similarity of these institutions—all were primarily intended for repentant women and welcomed former prostitutes—there seems to have been a wide range of norms and regulations set for individual communities. An idea of just how divergent the orientation of two such institutions could be is obtained by comparing the surviving statutes of two of these communities—the Occitanian statutes of the Sisters of Saint Catherine of Montpellier, dated 1339,[115] and the Latin statutes of the Repentant Sisters of Saint Mary Magdalene of the Miracles of Avignon, granted by Pope Gregory IX in 1375.[116]

We learn from the latter that the Avignonese community was open only to those female sinners who were under twenty-five years of age.[117] After a trial period of eight or ten days, a woman entering the community promised obedience and chastity in that convent for life. In this cloistered community, great attention was paid to the celebration of the divine office, and the sisters were required to confess once a week during Advent and Lent. Minor infringements of regulations were punished by a diet of bread and water, and all serious offenses were punished by imprisonment. The officers of the convent were directly responsible to the archbishop of the town.

The Repentant Sisters of Saint Catherine, on the other hand, were under the direction of the municipality of Montpellier, representatives of which approved the election of officers in the convent. The statutes, of which the first page is unfortunately missing, make no mention of an age limit; the community seems to have been open to all female sinners (*femena paccayris*). The only requirement was that the woman come equipped with a bed, clothes, and a sum of 100 s. A postulant was given a trial period of a year, during which, if she decided to leave the convent to marry, she was free to do so on condition that she not claim any of the dowry she had brought with her to the convent. At the end of the yearlong trial period, she was theoretically no longer free to leave the convent, but in fact, as the list of punishments shows, such departures were probably common enough, for the community reserved the right to expel a sister refusing to serve a term in prison to which she had been sentenced for fornication (!) or for rebellious and disobedient behavior. No elaborate ceremonies were required of the sisters at divine office; they were simply assigned a number of Ave Marias and Pater Nosters to say.[118] Members of the community were only required to confess once a month and were subject to very light punishment for infringement of regulations (for example, no wine at mealtimes for a few days), except in cases of sins of the flesh and major disobedience, which were punished respectively by imprisonment and expulsion from the community. This was not a cloistered order; the women were simply required not to eat or drink in town (*en la vila non auzon beure ni manjar*), a requirement strikingly similar to certain police regulations for prostitutes.[119]

The community of Montpellier served, it would seem, a social more than a religious purpose. As there was no age limit for prospective members, the house could serve both as a refuge for the truly repentant sinner, as a retirement house for old prostitutes, and, since the trial period lasted a year, as a kind of halfway house for the younger prostitute hoping to reenter honest society by marrying or by other means.[120] The community depended on the municipality, not on the bishop or other religious officer, and was, in fact, a municipal institution, like the numerous hospitals and charitable organizations patronized by the municipality—or like the red-light district, established by municipal initiative. The community of repentant sisters, originally an ecclesiastical institution, had become in many towns in the fourteenth century the logical charitable complement of the municipally authorized brothel. The control of secular authorities over these institutions seems to have increased throughout the fourteenth century.[121]

The documents are scarce for the fifteenth century but multiply toward the end of the fifteenth and beginning of the sixteenth centuries, a period that apparently saw a revival of interest in these communities.[122] The annals of the town of Toulouse narrate that in 1516 a Franciscan preacher, Mathieu Menou, succeeded in converting a number of prostitutes from the municipal brothel.[123] Known as the sisters of Saint Magdalene, they were given a house by the consuls, who made regular contributions to the convent and often paid for repairs of their house thereafter.[124] In Albi in 1526, the entire staff of the municipal house (probably five or six women) decided to retire from their worldly life to devote themselves to God, their retreat made possible by alms from the municipal council.[125]

The newly revived communities apparently offered a different sort of life and filled a different function in the sixteenth century from what they had earlier. Some of the repentant sisters of Toulouse worked in the town hospitals.[126] The convent also served as a prison for certain female criminals; an *arrêt* of the Parlement of Toulouse dated 3 September 1518 records that Condorine de Menville, whose crime is not mentioned, was sentenced to be "put in the convent of the repentant sisters of Toulouse to serve God and the said convent perpetually . . . with a prohibition never to leave . . . on pain of hanging and strangulation."[127] The communities of repentant sisters of the sixteenth century seem to have been a transitional institution between their medieval antecedents and the Maisons du Bon Pasteur of the seventeenth and eighteenth centuries, penitentiary houses of force for former prostitutes.[128]

Certain parallels can be drawn between the evolutions of institutionalized prostitution, of the status of prostitutes, and of the centers dedicated to their repentance or retirement. The period that witnessed the authorization and later municipalization of places of prostitution also saw the foundation of communities for repentant women, their progressive municipalization, and the growing emphasis on their function as a retirement center or halfway house for reintegrating former prostitutes into society. The doldrums of convents for repentant women in the early and mid–fifteenth century (and the apparent waning of interest in dowries for poor women) correspond to a period when the public woman held a relatively positive position in society, enjoying full legal capacity and even benefiting from seigneurial and royal privileges and safeguards. One may advance the hypothesis that, in an era when prostitution held certain material attractions and relatively few legal or social disadvantages and when reintegration or retirement by marriage seems not to have been rare, conversion from prostitution (or prevention through donations of dowries) seemed a less pressing problem. Only in the late fifteenth and early sixteenth centuries, with the growing hostility toward prostitutes and prostitution, did repentance again come to the fore and the revitalized convents become true centers of penitence for expiating sin, by a life of service to the poor and ill, or even for expiating crime, in the case of cloistered female criminals.

Chapter Five

Controlling the System: "Police" of Prostitution and "Government" of Houses

The details of the commerce of prostitution, which had formerly been a matter left to private initiative, became, in the late Middle Ages, a topic of growing concern to the public authorities and the object of increasingly detailed regulation and surveillance. In favoring an "interventionist" policy on prostitution, the Languedocian municipal authorities hoped to guarantee more effectively the maintenance of public order by making sure that the business of prostitution should be conducted discreetly, without inconvenience or scandal to the community.[1] The primary and most difficult task facing a municipality with such preoccupations was the choice and definition of limits of a site suitable for the municipal place of prostitution.

Authorized red-light districts, it may be observed, were often located outside the walls of the Languedocian towns.[2] In assigning prostitutes to these suburban districts in the thirteenth and fourteenth centuries, the municipal authorities may well have been consecrating already traditional centers of prostitution. The old custom of banning prostitutes from the center of town probably encouraged public women to congregate outside the city walls, far from the residence of the town's more affluent citizens. Residing and working outside the walls was an appropriate choice for practical as well as legal reasons: the modest real estate value of the outlying areas permitted lower overhead.

Common as the situation was, residence outside the city walls was not articulated as a general policy until the fifteenth century, when a French royal charter claimed that[3]

> from all time, it is customary in our country of Languedoc, and especially in the good towns, to be established a house and residence outside the said towns for the habitation and residence of the common girls.

In reality, as recently as the late fourteenth century, it had been common to house prostitutes within the city walls. The decimation of the urban population at that period had left land and houses vacant within the walls, and the climate of war and insecurity encouraged suburban residents to seek refuge there. The consuls of Castres, after much debate, decided to establish a house within the town walls for prostitutes who had formerly been relegated to the suburb Bela Cela.[4] The brothel of Uzès, which had been outside the town in 1326, was located in the very center by 1357,[5] and the town of Béziers, whose brothel had been *extra muros* in 1348, had a public house inside the town in the early fifteenth century.[6]

Examples of brothels located within the town walls can be found, moreover, both before and after the period of depopulation in the late fourteenth century. The *de facto* brothel of Toulouse mentioned in 1296 was in the very heart of town.[7] Although the red-light district of Montpellier was established in a suburb of the city, Villanova, a second place, which had been suggested by the committee convoked for finding a site, was located within the city walls.[8] The municipal brothel of Toulouse may well have been located within the city walls in the fifteenth century (as it was definitely in the sixteenth century),[9] as was the public house of Le Puy.[10] The red-light district of fifteenth-century Florence lay in the very center of town.[11]

The crucial problem in determining where a brothel should be located was not in deciding between *infra muros* and *extra muros* but in finding a place in which no one would be offended or protest, not an easy task in a medieval town. The difficulty of reaching an agreement is illustrated by the case of Montpellier in 1285:[12] there, no one seems to have opposed the existence of an authorized center of prostitution, but resistance to the establishment of such a center in particular neighborhoods had been so strong that an impartial committee representing all the quarters of town was needed to be able to settle the problem.

The most important principle respected when deciding where a brothel should be located was to place it far from neighborhoods of honest citizens. Another custom generally observed was that the house should be kept away from main streets and places where there was heavy traffic.[13] It was also a generally respected principle that prostitutes and brothels should be placed far from churches.[14] The archives reveal numerous examples of religious orders complaining about the proximity of houses of prostitution to their convents.[15]

A series of documents from Toulouse, dated 1526, gives a vivid illustration of the problems encountered when the authorities attempted to take all these principles into consideration in the choice of a site for a municipal brothel, following the destruction of the old brothel during reconstruction of the city walls.[16] The dispute over three possible sites for the new municipal brothel of Toulouse (all of which were located within the city walls) involved different priorities rather than conflicting principles. All the council members agreed in principle, for instance, that the brothel should be kept far from churches and religious orders, yet all three sites were near either one or the other: the garden of Saint Paul was near the convent of the Augustinians, the Petit Bernard was near the convent of Saint Orens, and the third site near the church Saint Sernin. Enthusiasts for the first two sites argued that the construction of a high wall between the brothel and the convent in question could solve the problem.

Another consideration, one that seems to have increasingly preoccupied public authorities in the fifteenth and sixteenth centuries, was the proximity of the public house to schools.[17] Two doctors from the University of Toulouse testified before the council that the proximity of the old brothel to their institution had created scandal and advised that the new structure be placed far from the university. In the ensuing debate the council seems to have split into two camps—those in favor of the site of Saint Paul and those against. The opponents claimed that this site was close to the new grammar schools of Dr. Paschalis, but supporters of the site scoffed at this argument, saying that the schools were in fact quite far from Saint Paul. They claimed that the real reason for the opposition was not the schools but the interest of "certain individuals who have their pleasure gardens [*jardrins de plaisance*] there." The leader of the opposition, Casaveteri, had in fact emphasized the inconvenience that the Saint Paul site would cause to persons having houses, gardens, and stables in the area. Casaveteri also protested that the site was too near the Square Saint George, where the wine market was held: the *roffiens* might take advantage of this proximity to siphon wine. The royal counselor de Vabres countered these arguments of the opposition by saying that "public good should be preferred to private good" (*le bien publicque doibt estre preferré au bien privé*). The supporters of the Saint Paul site also pointed out that this site, being near the town hall (*près de la maison commune, et si près de justice*), would discourage the commission of illegal acts. The conflict between the advocates of the Saint Paul site and its opponents seems to have split the town into two camps—the supporters of the public good, consisting primarily of "intellectuals," and the defenders of private interest, mainly merchants.[18] The Parlement of Toulouse was called in to settle the matter. The municipality finished by purchasing the garden of Saint Paul—a modest triumph for the intellectual defenders of the public good—despite continuing opposition. It was virtually impossible to place a brothel in a medieval town without offending someone.[19]

Once a site had been chosen for the local red-light district, the prostitute was obliged to limit her activity to that place. This was the principal, but not the only, directive issued to public women by the municipality in the so-called police regulations, municipal statutes that set rules of behavior for everyday life in the towns, in the interest of maintaining public order. Virtually all police regulations concerning prostitutes include a dress code, the earliest of which—dating from the period preceding the establishment of authorized centers of prostitution—prohibited prostitutes from wearing clothing usually associated with honest women. Thus, prostitutes in Arles were not to wear veils, and those in Avignon neither veils nor coats.[20] A similar provision is found in the undated police regulation of Nîmes.[21] In 1320 the constable and bailiff of Pézenas prohibited prostitutes from wearing "long dresses trailing on the ground."[22]

While dress codes for prostitutes continued to be important, the emphasis toward the middle of the fourteenth century was placed on forbidding rich and elegant clothing and decorations. In Nîmes (1350) and Bagnols (1358), prostitutes were forbidden to wear, among other luxurious apparel, silver and ermine. These measures were part of the sumptuary laws of this period, issued to restrict conspicuous consumption and to discourage the blurring of social and class lines by inappropriate dressing.[23] Restricting the elegance of prostitutes was especially important in the eyes of the municipal authorities, who believed that allowing public women to wear sumptuous clothing would have been tantamount to encouraging honest women to debauch themselves.[24]

Provisions obliging prostitutes to wear a sign indicating their profession appear in the statutes in the mid–fourteenth century; such insignia had been prescribed for Jews since the early thirteenth century.[25] In Languedoc the first reference to an obligatory sign for prostitutes is in the police regulations of Castelnaudary, dated 1333, requiring public women to wear a cord belt.[26] The royal court of Nîmes, which had issued a sumptuary law for prostitutes in 1350, decided on an obligatory sign in 1353: "Item, that such base women should be distinguishable from others by means of ornaments which they wear; that on their dress there shall be a sleeve of a different material and color."[27] Provisions for a distinctive sign became standard in most regulations on prostitution in the late fourteenth century. In Beaucaire (1373) prostitutes were required to carry a mark on their left arm (*aliquo signo in bracchio sinistro*), whereas in Castres (1375) the statutory sign was a man's hat (*capayro de home*) and a scarlet belt (*correg vermelh*).[28] It was against similar measures that the public women of Toulouse appealed to the king, whose privilege of 1389 allowed them to dress as they pleased provided they kept a discreet mark of the profession on their sleeves.[29]

Although the distinctive sign may be interpreted as a stigma for the women who wore it, it is clear that there were positive advantages to its institution, both for the community and for the prostitutes. As an instrument of public order, the sign helped avoid situations in which a customer might mistakenly proposition an "honest" woman. For the prostitute, too, helping potential clients to identify her was an advantage. The sign may have served, moreover, as Rossiaud has suggested for a slightly later period, as an emblem of the seigneurial or royal safeguard often enjoyed by prostitutes, thereby intimidating would-be aggressors.[30]

Police regulations were intended to control the activities of prostitutes as well as their dress. Most common were statutes restricting the residence of prostitutes and limiting their circulation in town.[31] The regulations issued in Nîmes in 1350 prohibited prostitutes from circulating in groups in town; in 1353 even these solitary promenades were forbidden.[32] The public women of Bela Cela were allowed into the center of Castres only on Saturdays or fair days, and even then they were not to enter the straight street of Saint John and were to go only one at a time to buy bread and fruit for the whole group. The town of Beaucaire was off limits to prostitutes only after the curfew was sounded.[33] There are numerous examples in early-sixteenth-century Toulouse of efforts to restrict the circulation of prostitutes.[34]

The authorities were particularly concerned with keeping prostitutes out of taverns. As early as 1251, prostitutes were barred from the taverns of Montpellier.[35] In Castelnaudary there was a fine not only for the public woman who frequented taverns (she was to eat and drink only in the *carreria publica*) but also for the tavern keeper who received her. The statutes of Saint-Félix forbade prostitutes to drink in taverns, and the consuls of Toulouse repeatedly exhorted their successors to keep the municipal prostitutes out of taverns.[36]

One of the major reasons for restricting the circulation of prostitutes was to avoid possible contact between them and honest women. A royal ordinance issued in Pézenas in 1461 stipulates that, when in church, prostitutes should stay "behind and segregated from 'good' women."[37] In Grasse in 1487 a prostitute was sentenced to pay a 50 s. fine for having disobeyed the vicar's regulation forbidding prostitutes to dance with honest women.[38] No medieval police regulations specifically forbade forced recruitment of honest women by prostitutes, but, when such a situation occurred, courts found the means to prosecute; in Castelnaudary in 1390 a public woman who had tried to force the barber's wife to the local brothel was booked on charges of blasphemy, as witnesses testified that she "denied God terribly" while tugging at the honest lady's arm.[39]

The municipal statutes of some towns regulated the way in which public women might solicit, as in Bagnols, where prostitutes apparently chanted their services.[40]

> Item, that no public woman be so bold as to sing or chant by night in the streets, nor to chant by day, unless in their street, except during the fair of Bagnols, at which time it is authorized for them to chant.

A similar provision is found in the regulations of Beaucaire (*nec audeat cantare per villam*).

By the fifteenth century prostitution in most Languedocian towns was limited to one brothel, and the problem of the "police" of prostitution had become, to a great extent, that of the "government" of such a house.[41] It was apparently common to issue a set of rules for the government of the municipal brothel in the late Middle Ages; the only extant copy of such rules for a Languedocian brothel are the undated "statutes and ordinances" for the public house of Pamiers, called Castel Joyos, written probably in the last years of the fifteenth century.[42] These statutes can be compared with similar regulations issued for brothels in towns outside France, many of which have been published.[43] Such ordinances were principally aimed at regulating problems concerning the women, the manager, the customers, and the maintenance of public order in the brothel.

A primary concern of brothel regulations was to define financial relations within the institution. In most brothels women paid room and board to the manager. The statutes of Castel Joyos outline two possible arrangements between the women and the manager (referred to systematically in this document as the "abbot"). Women wanting to eat at the abbot's table were to pay him four ardits for each meal, noon and evening; for this price the abbot was to supply good bread and wine and "other food according to the season" (*compainage rasonable segon lo temps*, §6). To women not wanting to eat at his table, the abbot was to sell bread, wine, and meat "according to the policy of the city" (*iuxta la policia de la ciutat*, §7). All women were obliged to pay the abbot two ardits a day for room, bed, fire, service, and light (§8). A similar arrangement concerning food existed in the brothel of Toulouse, where the women owed three doblas a day for board.[44] Rates per day or per meal, rather than for a longer period of time, as in some other regions,[45] may have been preferred because of the presence in the house of itinerant women as well as permanent residents.[46] The money for room, board, and other material seems to be the only payment made by the women to the abbot of Castel Joyos. The only mention in the ordinances of a payment from the customer to the abbot is in case the customer wished to stay overnight, when he was obliged to pay the manager a dobla for the bed (§9). It seems, therefore, that there was little relation between the turnover of customers and the income of the abbot, aside from any tips he might receive. This was not the case in Nürnberg, where the manager received a penny "as often as [the prostitute] did carnal work with a man";[47] there and in Ulm, it was the woman who was to pay the abbot if a man stayed overnight (*slaffgelt*).[48]

The intention of these regulations concerning abbot and women seems to have been, on the one hand, to guarantee an income to the farmer of the house and, on the other hand, to prevent the manager from exploiting the women arbitrarily or greedily. Intention to protect the prostitute is manifest in the statutes for the brothel of Sandwich, which forbade the bawds to beat or punish the women and allowed the women to bring all complaints of mistreatment to the mayor.[49] Italian municipalities, on the other hand, extended considerable power of jurisdiction over the women to the abbot. In Perugia and Foligno the farmer was authorized to hit the women when provoked, provided he did not kill or maim them;[50] the manager of the brothel of Genoa could put in the stocks prostitutes who had been involved in a brawl. In many Italian towns, moreover, debts could be freely contracted between the farmer and the prostitutes.[51] The Genoese farmer could imprison indebted prostitutes, but only for debts contracted within the *postribulo*. The purpose of the regulations of Strasbourg, by contrast, was exclusively the protection of the women. They forbade the custom of accepting women as pawns for debts; any woman pledged to the brothel was declared automatically free, and the manager was forbidden to use debts in order to oblige women to stay in the house.[52]

In many brothels the public women were virtually cloistered. Such was the case in Castel Joyos, where the women were obliged, according to the statutes of that house, to eat, drink, and sleep in the brothel unless excused (§12); the same rule was observed in the brothel of Toulouse. The lawyer who represented the prostitutes of Toulouse in their indictment of the brothel-farming system brought before the Parlement of Toulouse in 1462 implied that this system was an innovation, protesting "that the said girls are not free in the said house."[53] The prostitutes of Toulouse were allowed, however, to leave the house to go to mass,[54] a right that was guaranteed in the statutes for Nürnberg and Strasbourg as well. The prostitutes of Genoa and Venice were allowed out on Sundays, whereas those of Pavia could circulate freely on condition that they pay a sum for the privilege of sleeping elsewhere.

Several of the statutes of Castel Joyos deal with the brothel's customers. Admission to the brothel was selective, all customers having to be admitted personally by the abbot. Anyone who jumped the walls of the house or who otherwise entered "without permission of the abbot" (*ab voler e conget del abat*) was to be sentenced to prison and "running the town" (§10).[55] Once admitted to Castel Joyos, the customers were obliged to surrender their arms to the abbot; those who refused faced a prison term, a 60 s. fine, and confiscation of weapons (§4). In an era when violence was rampant, the office of brothel keeper must have been a dangerous one; it is no wonder that brothels were often fortified and that the statutes of many Italian towns (e.g., Perugia, Foligno, and Genoa) authorized the brothel keeper to carry arms.[56] The prime victims of this potential violence were the women themselves, hence the necessity of extending a royal or seigneurial safeguard to them, as in Pamiers, where anyone who caused the prostitutes injury—verbally, corporally, or materially—was punished for breaking the seigneurial safeguard (§2). The consuls of Castelnaudary apparently sought to discourage such violent attacks on the women by a system of public humiliation: in front of the public house was a pole on which were hoisted the arms of a person who had attacked one of the prostitutes.[57] In Genoa the customer who hit a prostitute was obliged to pay her medical expenses and to pay damages to the manager for work time lost because of injury. Theft within the brothel was also a problem; it was recommended that customers leave all jewelry and money with the abbot of Castel Joyos, who could not be held responsible for the theft of valuables not deposited with him (§5).

In Languedoc, the brothel keeper was not alone in patrolling the public house. External surveillance was provided by municipal and sometimes by royal officers. In Toulouse, for example, the brothel was protected by the subvicar during the day and the captain of the watch (*capitan del geyt*) at night; the house was also under royal safeguard.[58] In fact, the distinction between external surveillance of houses of prostitution and their internal government by a manager or abbot was not a clear one. In 1433, for example, Peter Darganhac, captain of the watch, shared the farm of the public house of Toulouse with Margarida Dargenta.[59] Similarly, in Tarascon (Bouches-du-Rhone) in 1441, the subvicar took the farm of the municipal brothel.[60] In Montpellier not only did the king guarantee a monopoly on prostitution to the private owners of the authorized brothels, but his royal officer established "ordinances concerning the government of that house."[61] In their proposed alternative to government by a brothel farmer presented to the Parlement in 1462, the public women of Toulouse suggested that their abbess be responsible to an overseer ("master of hours") to be appointed by the king.[62] Even in the case of royal officers, police of prostitution and government of houses were closely related.[63]

Some public-house statutes set norms for the admission of customers to the house, in the interest of social or moral order. It was frequent, for example, to refuse admittance to Jews, as in the mid-fifteenth-century police regulations of Avignon.[64] In the interest of public morality, the manager of the brothel of Ulm was obliged, by a statute of 1527, to refuse entrance to boys under fourteen years of age.[65] More frequent were prohibitions concerning priests and married men. The synod of Avignon of 1441 barred clerics and married men from postribular bathhouses there.[66] In many German towns married men who frequented brothels were fined;[67] the Nürnberg brothel ordinances forbade the manager ("host") to admit married men and priests and also prohibited him from keeping married women as prostitutes. Although no such restrictions are found in the statutes for Castel Joyos, the municipal law of Pamiers was hostile to any admixture of prostitution and matrimony, as is demonstrated in two cases brought before the consular court there. In 1501 a man and two meretrices were convicted of adultery and punished;[68] a married woman who was found in the brothel in 1497 was convicted by the consular court.[69] There seem to have been fewer scruples in Italy, where no such restrictions are found in municipal-brothel ordinances; in Moncalieri a law of 1457 specifically authorizes "all people, of whatever grade, sex or condition, clerics . . . and married men . . . to enter . . . for bathing, drinking, eating and sleeping, during the day or at night" the municipal *domus lupanaris*.[70] Only ducal officers were forbidden entry.

A crucial aspect of the maintenance of order in the brothel of Pamiers was the prohibition against procurers, which prescribed severe punishment for offenders. A prostitute convicted of having kept a procurer "as master or governor" (*per mestre ny per governador*) was to run the town, and the procurer in question was threatened with capital punishment (§1). Such a prohibition is also found in the farming contract between Maria Lanas and the municipality of Castelnaudary.[71] A prohibition against "beloved men" (*liebe menner*) is included in the regulations of Nürnberg. *Ruffiani* were excluded from some Italian brothels (Venice and Pavia) but were acknowledged in others (Genoa and Perugia).

Many brothel ordinances forbade gaming within public houses. A clause prohibiting gaming is found in the farming contract in Castelnaudary; the farmer found to be lax in enforcing this rule could be whipped. In Alès gaming was forbidden only during the time of the divine office; the negligent farmer was to be imprisoned for a month.[72] Gambling with prostitutes was forbidden in the Venetian brothel, and gaming was prohibited even in the lupanar of Moncalieri, otherwise so lax in matters of morality. No such prohibition is found in the statutes of Castel Joyos, but municipal laws there against both gaming and blasphemy were actively enforced.[73] Blasphemy was specifically prohibited in Castel Joyos; offenders were sentenced to three days in irons on bread and water (§14). A similar prohibition, again, is found in the farming contract of Maria Lanas.

A last provision guaranteeing order on the public house of Pamiers, which is apparently without parallel in the legislation on such houses in other towns, is that prohibiting sick customers from entering the brothel (§11). Access to the prostitutes was forbidden to victims of venereal disease (*mal e ronha de Naples*), to lepers (*ladre*), and to people carrying any other contagious disease (*autre tocat de deguna malautia contagiosa*).

An important aspect of the government of certain public houses in late-medieval Languedoc, although not outlined in the regulations for Castel Joyos, was the custom of stopping business during Holy Week. Traditional periods of abstinence from sexual intercourse, even within marriage, were common in western Christendom in the late Middle Ages.[74] The first indications of such restrictions applied to prostitutes in Languedoc are found in the early-fourteenth-century police regulations; the undated regulations of Nîmes forbade prostitutes to enter the city during Holy Week,[75] and a municipal deliberation of 1326 obliged the prostitutes of Uzès to leave the town for the period of a month.[76] A similar regulation was issued in Nîmes in 1353 for Holy Week, but it allowed prostitutes the possibility to circulate for the purpose of prayer or confession.[77]

With the establishment of authorized public houses, however, the problem could not be restricted to a simple barring of prostitutes from town. The consuls of Uzès made the following provisions in 1357: the five women of the authorized house were solemnly led by municipal officers and sergeants to the hospital for the poor, where they were to remain for the duration of Holy Week, food and drink being provided by the consuls.[78] Similar measures aimed at stopping the business of prostitution during Holy Week were taken in other regions. The public house of Ulm (1430) was to be closed for holy days, and a Venetian law of 1438 forbade prostitutes to work on Christmas and on the feast of the Virgin Mary, as well as during Holy Week.[79] In his statutes of 1430, Amadeus VIII of Savoy ordered prostitutes to be confined to one place during Holy Week, where a preacher was to exhort them to repent.[80]

Similar customs were practiced in Albi and Toulouse in the late fifteenth and early sixteenth centuries, but from the Uzès text of 1357 to those late-medieval western Languedocian documents there is no archival evidence of observation of Holy Week in Languedocian brothels. Quite the contrary, an incidental text from Foix shows that there, at least, such a custom was not regularly observed. In a criminal case brought before the consuls of Foix in 1402, Johana, "*mulier de luppanari Fuxi*," was a witness of events that took place Easter evening (*in vespera Pasche Domini*); as she was leaving the brothel (*exiens foras luppanar de Fuxo*), she saw a fight between a dyer and two officers of the constable of Foix, who were also leaving the brothel (*exeuntes de dicto luppanari*). Not only was Johana residing in the brothel and circulating freely, but the brothel was apparently serving clients at the same time, a state of affairs that seems to have been taken for granted.[81] Yet in neighboring Roussillon, a document from 1442 declares that the prostitutes of Perpignan had traditionally been confined during Holy Week to the town leprosery—vivid testimony not only to the public authorities' pious intentions but also to their blithe ignorance of the most fundamental notions of contagion and hygiene![82]

Information on Holy Week observances in the brothels of Albi and Toulouse at the end of the fifteenth and beginning of the sixteenth centuries is found in the consular account books. In Albi the custom is first mentioned in the account book of 1506, which records that 7 s. 6 d. were paid "to the poor sinners of the Good House of Albi . . . so that they stop sinning for Holy Week."[83] It is recorded that the women spent Holy Week of 1513 in the town hospital (as had been decided in Uzès in 1357). In 1515 the sum of 30 s. went to the consul Radanier, who had supplied food to the women during Holy Week. In 1547, 5 s. were given to each of the six women. The last entry concerning these observances is from 1554.[84]

The first document attesting to such a custom in Toulouse is from 1496, when the brothel farmer was granted 5 l. "so that [the prostitutes] should not do evil [*mal*] during Holy Week and Easter Week."[85] As is specified in an account-book entry from 1501, business was interrupted for the week before and the week following Easter, during which time the women, moved to another house, were to refrain from sin and go to the sermon and to church,[86] "acting," as the town scribe noted in 1507, "like good Christian women" (*fesson coma bonas Chrestianas*).

The brothel farmer John Amery, to justify the subsidy of 20 l. that he had requested from the consuls for this Paschal retreat in 1514, submitted a detailed list of sums expended for this purpose.[87] On the eve of Palm Sunday, the thirty-four residents of the public brothel had been led to another house, where they were to stay until the Tuesday after Easter (at the expense of 50 s. for rent and beds). The manager spent 30 s. daily on their food, which consisted of the traditional Lenten fare—various kinds of fish. None of the prostitutes wanted to fast on Wednesday and Thursday, but about a third of them decided to do so on Good Friday. The majority of the women received communion on Holy Saturday, and on Easter Sunday they all feasted on beef, mutton, and kid. Expenses also included a total of two barrels of wine consumed during their stay, plus heat and the wages for one male and one female servant.

In a separate order, the consuls reimbursed the sergeant whose task it was to lead the public women to the sermon every day.[88] This daily religious activity seems to have lasted all or most of Lent, not just during the ten days of professional inactivity.[89] The prostitutes heard sermons in various churches.[90] In 1511 and 1514 this sermon was preached in the morning, but by the 1520s the women went twice daily for sermons.[91] Attendance seems to have been obligatory for all the women, but the degree to which they actually participated in the services may be reflected by the number of rosaries purchased for them by the sergeant. In 1517, for example, the sergeant bought twenty-two rosaries for the women, whereas the manager for the same year listed thirty prostitutes as being in the public house. The obvious goal of these arrangements was to give the women ample opportunity to do penance and to encourage them to repent. Although only one financial document from Toulouse mentions a Holy Week convert, in 1523,[92] one learns from the town chronicle that the year 1516 (from which no financial documents remain) witnessed the mass repentance of prostitutes, who were given a house in which to retire to the religious life.[93] In March 1526 all the women of the brothel of Albi decided to withdraw from their former worldly life to dedicate themselves to God.[94]

In 1509 the Toulousan brothel farmer stated that observing such a Holy Week retreat "is customary . . . in all the good towns of France." No other Languedocian town has left archival records of such a custom, but we know that sermons for prostitutes were sponsored during Holy Week in Rome in the sixteenth century. The Roman courtesan Beatrice of Ferrara wrote to Laurence of Medicis, nephew of Pope Leo X, in 1516, that she and the other prostitutes of Rome went to the sermons of a Dominican preacher and confessed to him; two colleagues converted to the religious life, and she herself gave alms of two ducats—which she later regretted![95]

Renewed concern with the spiritual fate of prostitutes was only one aspect of an increasingly strict police of prostitution practiced by the Languedocian municipal authorities toward the end of the fifteenth and the beginning of the sixteenth centuries, manifested in the legislation aimed at the definition of relations between the prostitutes and the brothel manager, the admittance of customers, and the maintenance of public morality and order in the municipal brothels. Contemporary documents occasionally refer to the municipal brothels as "abbeys," and the comparison is understandable: governed by an abbot, cloistered within the brothel walls, led to bidaily sermons during Lent, the municipal prostitutes of the late fifteenth and sixteenth centuries seem indeed to have been living in a peculiar kind of nunnery.

Chapter Six

Eliminating Competition: The Prosecution of Procurers, Illicit Prostitutes, and Keepers of Illegal Houses

The institutionalization of prostitution in Languedoc in the late Middle Ages did not imply an unlimited toleration of prostitution, but, rather, it resulted in a dichotomy between authorized and unauthorized prostitution. Existence of official public houses implied the illegality of other brothels, protection of the *filia communa* was paralleled by the condemnation of the illicit prostitute, and the legal activities of the town brothel keeper implied that all other procuring was to be outlawed. The counterpart of regulating authorized prostitution was repressing illegal competition.

Legislation on procuring (*lenocinium*) and the procurer (*leno*) appear in Languedoc in the thirteenth century, well before the establishment of authorized centers of prostitution.[1] Certain texts give the impression that *lenocinium* was considered a very serious offense in this period. *Lenocinium* was included, along with homicide and adultery, among the cases of high justice reserved to the archbishop of Narbonne in 1253.[2] The case of a man hanged for this crime in Narbonne in 1331 indicates, however, that more than mere procuring was involved; he was accused of being a mercenary accomplice to the rape of his young virgin ward, not a common procurer.[3] As this example shows, *lenocinium* was an ambiguous term in the thirteenth century. Only in the case of the corruption of an honest woman was it considered to be a matter of high justice.

The ambiguity of the term *lenocinium* is well illustrated by two charters from Cordes. In the first, granted in 1222, Raymond VII of Toulouse retained the right to judge and confiscate the goods of any person accused of "homicide or *lenoscinium* . . . or other similar crimes."[4] In a charter of 1282, Philip III confirmed the privileges of 1222 and added a paragraph concerning

89

adultery and *lenocinium*: "If anyone commits *lenocinium* in his own house, the house shall be ceded to us in feudal commission; if indeed it be a rented house, the perpetrator shall be obliged to pay us 20 l."[5] *Lenocinium* was thus transformed from a capital offense in the former text to a morals charge in the latter, severely punished but assimilated to common procuring rather than corruption of honest women.

Interpreted as common procuring or brothel keeping (the two were often assimilated), *lenocinium* inspired diverse legislation in the thirteenth century. Capetian legislation, as is seen above, provided punishment for those people renting houses to prostitutes.[6] According to the "moderate" ordinance of 1256, echoed in the statutes of Marseille, only people renting in the center of town or other honest streets were guilty, but the "repressive" ordinances of 1254 and 1272 (and the charter of Cordes) forbade renting anywhere to prostitutes. These provisions may well have been inspired by canon law, which had kept the strictures against procuring published in the Council of Elvira (c. 300),[7] and Roman law, especially the Justinianic Novella 14 punishing procurers.[8] A thorough discussion of the different types of *lenones* and provision for punishment of common procurers (banishment from town) as well as corrupters of honest women is elaborated in the famous Castilian law code of the late thirteenth century, the *Siete Partidas*, also profoundly influenced by Roman and canon law.[9] The *Livre de jostice et de plet*, written in Orléans and influenced by the same sources, called for the banishment of procurer (*maquerel*) and brothel keeper.[10] In the thirteenth and early fourteenth centuries, northern French town authorities banished men and women convicted of procuring (*bordellerie, makelerie*),[11] and the Parlement of Paris confirmed such convictions.[12]

The Languedocian municipal authorities of the thirteenth and early fourteenth centuries seem not to have been influenced by these ideas. The early-thirteenth-century documents from Carcassonne and Toulouse are, as we have seen, mute on this point.[13] The statutes of Avignon and Arles, on the other hand, refer to the *leno* but do not consider his activity to merit punishment; the procurer was simply subject to the same restrictions as the prostitute—prohibited from living in the streets of honest citizens.[14] Regulations placing the same restraints on the *leno* as on the *meretrix* are found also in Narbonne (a town in which *lenocinium*, taken in a different sense, was considered a capital offense); in 1299 *lenones* as well as *meretrices* were prohibited from residing in Narbonne,[15] and, once the Hot Street was established there, prostitutes and procurers were to leave all honest neighborhoods, the implication being that both were welcome to set up residence in the *postribulum*.[16] In the Castelnaudary police regulations of 1333, the paragraphs dealing with prostitutes also mention procurers.[17] The statute prohibiting prostitutes from staying in Lunel more than once a week, unless in the *postribulum*, applied to procurers as well.[18] This text, dated 1367, is the last explicit Languedocian acknowledgment of the procurer, whose status changed dramatically in the fifteenth century. Either ignored or put in the same category as the prostitutes in the thirteenth and fourteenth centuries, the procurer became the target of the hostility of the Languedocian authorities in the fifteenth century.

Royal initiative was important in this condemnation of procuring. In the letter of 1425 placing the municipal brothel of Toulouse under the royal safeguard, the criminals and vandals who had been damaging the house and abusing the women, necessitating royal intervention, are described as "procurers and malevolent people, believing neither in God nor in justice." [19] A number of royal ordinances concerning Languedoc denounced procuring and prescribed punishments for individuals found engaged in such activity, as in an ordinance on morals published by order of the seneschal of Carcassonne in 1438, which chastises men who earn their livelihood by "procuring . . . keeping women in public or secret brothels." [20] Any such men discovered in the seneschalsy eight days after the proclamation of the ordinance were to be punished by "running the town," beating, and pillory. [21] A royal order of 1445 to the three seneschals of Languedoc commanded them to be more rigorous in their enforcement of ordinances against *ruffiens* and other criminals who "take women by force, putting them to evil and to following their life of damnation." [22] In an ordinance on police of fires, published by the Parlement in 1475, *ruffians* and *ruffianes* were prohibited from living in Toulouse; punishment for offenders included running the town and beating, banishment from the town, and confiscation of all goods. [23]

Municipalities also took measures against common procurers, often in cooperation with royal officers. As early as June 1429, the town council of Arles banned procurers from its limits under pain of beating, repeating the same prohibition in August and again in 1435, when they condemned the profession of procurer as "abominable in the eyes of God and the king." [24] In 1465 the council of Toulouse established ordinances against hotelkeepers who received *rufiens* and against procurers who stayed in town longer than three days; the punishment in both cases was running the town and beating. [25] Avignon added a prohibition of procuring to its police regulations of 1458 and set the fine for infringement at 200 l. [26] The consuls of Castelnaudary threatened the town brothel keeper with the whip if she were to tolerate procurers, and the regulations of the public house of Pamiers prescribed the death penalty for procurers found within the house. [27]

The correlation between the establishment of municipal brothels and the condemnation of procuring is unmistakable. The municipal authorities and the Crown, responsible for the authorization of municipal brothels and their protection by safeguard, took the legal initiative against procuring. Procurers were regarded as fomentors of disorders and trouble and also as illicit competitors to the system of institutionalized prostitution. The condemnation of the procurer was the obverse of the legitimization of the official municipal brothel keeper. The connection between the authorization of a center of prostitution and the condemnation of procuring is explicit in Pavia, where strong measures against *lenones* accompanied the earliest documents concerning the *postribulo*.[28] A statute from Cremona dated 1387 punished procuring with a 25 l. fine and a year's banishment.[29] The punishments prescribed for procurers caught in Venice increased in severity throughout the fifteenth century.[30] Condemnation of procuring in Italy was not so unanimous, however, as it was in France in this period.[31] The ordinances for the *postribulo* of Genoa, for example, issued in 1459, acknowledge the presence of procurers (*amicus vel rofianus*), forbidding them only to take their *protégées* out of the brothel.[32] Procurers were recognized in Perugia, where their petition against the high rate being charged in the *postribulo* instigated a law on maximal rates in 1452. Only toward the end of the fifteenth century did the law become stricter, requiring that all *ruffiani* register with the Podestà in 1486.[33] In Florence there was a confraternity of procurers (Società dei lenoni), to which one of the members left a legacy in a will of 1439.[34] Yet the same city enforced draconian penalties against procurers found guilty of inducing honest women to prostitute themselves.[35] Only in the late fifteenth and early sixteenth centuries was there a concerted movement against common procuring in Naples and Sicily.[36]

It may be partially due to Occitania's constant contact with Italy, where laws on procuring were often lax, that made enforcement difficult.[37] Procurers often had protectors in important positions, impeding effective prosecution.[38] A particularly colorful example of successful evasion from punishment for procuring is the case of Guillot del Cung, "enfant de la ville de Toulouse."[39] This young man, accused of procuring for the first time in 1448, was released by Parlement into the hands of the seneschal. In 1452 Parlement ordered the vicar to imprison del Cung despite the opposition of the seneschal, while officers of the court interrogated two young women for whom he had procured; the result of these investigations was a conviction and sentence of banishment from the kingdom and confiscation of all goods. Yet del Cung turned up again in Toulouse in September of 1455 in the company of other *mauvais garçons* and was carried off with them to prison, where he was put in chains and fed on bread and water. He was then released from prison on a solemn promise to stay in the parish of Saint-Etienne working as a shoemaker, but he took advantage of the plague to jump probation. He was again brought before the court in May and July of 1460, where the royal prosecutor accused him of twenty-four offenses.[40] His return to Toulouse after his banishment had been authorized, one learns, by a letter of remission from the king in 1454. After his escape from prison and from probation, he installed himself in the public house as *abbé des fillettes*. Later he abducted one of the women, Jehanete, and sold her charms throughout Languedoc—Carcassonne, Narbonne, Béziers, Montpellier, Avignon, and Marseille—clearing a profit of 50 or 60 écus. After this adventure he returned to Toulouse once again to exploit the public house, this time taking a partner as a front man. To top off his exploits, del Cung arranged through a procuress a liaison with a married woman for 6 écus; afterward, with the help of a notary and some sergeants, he managed to extort 10 écus from the woman in question. The royal prosecutor concluded, "It's a shame that the said Guillot has not been hanged," calling on the court to refuse to accept a second royal letter of remission obtained by del Cung on 26 May 1459. The lawyer for the defense cited the royal letters of remission, maintained that the charges against del Cung were "errors of youth [*cas de jeunesse*], including no murder or robbery," and, later, cited the accused's good family and his excellence as a shoemaker. He recited a different version of his client's travels in Languedoc and pointed out that del Cung had worked in the service of the subvicar of Avignon and of the duke of Calabres in Marseille. His client denied the more serious charges against him and "intends to act well in the future." The final outcome of the case is unknown. What is known is significant enough: an incorrigible *mauvais garçon* was able to engage in procuring and other illicit activities for twelve years with relative impunity, enjoying the confidence of well-placed men and managing to acquire two royal letters of remission.

But one must not allow del Cung's impressive record of evading punishment to obscure the Parlement's remarkable perseverance in prosecuting him. Despite the fact that there were clearly still many people for whom common procuring was a mere *cas de jeunesse*, it is significant that the Parlement pursued its prosecution. The very fact that such cases came before the Parlement at all indicates that the crime was considered serious enough to warrant the attention of such a high court. The punishments were severe and the cases of conviction apparently more common toward the end of the fifteenth century. In April of 1474, Peter Fontanes and his wife, Katherine, appealing a decision of the seneschal to the Parlement, were sentenced to beating and banishment; their goods were confiscated for the benefit of their victim, Catherine, their ten-year-old chambermaid.[41] Three years later a bathhouse keeper, Jacques Roy, convicted of "procuring and dishonest life . . . in the stews of Toulouse," was sentenced to run the town naked and be beaten and to be banished from the vicarage for a year.[42] The Parlement overruled the lenient judgment of the court of the seneschal and refused to accept the royal letters of remission in the case of Mengard Servante, convicted of "procuring and dissolute life, blasphemy and other excesses," sentencing him to running the town, beating, and banishment from the seneschalsy.[43] Often persons convicted by the higher courts for procuring had, like Mengard Servante, been accused of other crimes, too. Thus, the hanging of a *leno publicus* in the seneschalsy of Beaucaire in 1480 and the amputation of the hand and banishment of one of his accomplices do not reflect the typical punishment for procuring, since the men were also accused of carrying arms, attacks, and other crimes.[44] To find typical punishments, one must look in the records of the lower courts, which, unfortunately, are rare. The early-fifteenth-century criminal-court records from the towns of Foix and Castelnaudary contain no cases of prosecution of procurers. Only in two towns can one find archival documents attesting to lower-court prosecution of procurers—Aiguesmortes and Toulouse.

The royal court of Aiguesmortes punished procurers by imposing fines on them, according to the budget of the vicarage of that town for the year 1460–61, which lists four cases of fines imposed on procurers; for example, "From Stephen Vaudimont, *leno*, because he lived from the evil commerce [*de turpi questu . . . vivebat*] of Johanne Badouine, paid 20 s." [45] There is no evidence of any additional punishment (e.g., payment to the town executioner for whipping). The policy of the vicar seems to have been to punish procurers actively—four cases in one year for a small town like Aiguesmortes is a respectable number—but to punish them more leniently than was recommended in royal ordinances.

Evidence of the enforcement of laws against procuring in Toulouse is found in the consular account books, which include several lists of prisoners and payments made to the town executioner for punishments inflicted on criminals. In a list of miscellaneous expenses for the year 1494–95, an entry reads, "Paid to M. Bernard, executioner of justice, because he whipped a woman named Johaneta, procuress [*macarela*] of her daughter, 5 s." [46] In 1501 the executioner was paid 10 s. to whip "two women, the twelve-year-old girl . . . and the other, who was a procuress [*macarella*]".[47] A list of prisoners from 1503–4 makes it possible to see how many out of all the accused were punished. Of three women listed as *macarella*, only one (Bartholina de Longages) was actually punished—sentenced to run the town.[48] In 1510 Berthomen Teulet and his wife received the whip as a result of their procuring activities.[49] In a list of prisoners from the year 1520–21, out of four prisoners specifically accused of procuring (although there were people accused of other morals charges that may have included procuring), one seems to have spent a long time in prison (the cost of his stay came to 3 livres), and one, Michelle Jaque, was punished by whipping.[50]

The number of actual convictions for procuring in Toulouse was small, but the evidence of corporal punishment contrast with the simple fines charged by the vicar of Aiguesmortes half a century before. The evidence from these documents, although laconic and sporadic, is sufficient to prove that the municipal and royal ordinances on procuring were enforced as well as proclaimed, by lower and higher courts alike, at the end of the fifteenth century.

Once prostitution was institutionalized, a distinction developed between the *filia comuna*, the agent of municipal prostitution, and the illicit prostitute flaunting the police regulations by working outside the authorized center. The days of free-lance prostitution were over; any prostitute caught plying her trade outside the official center was considered as illicit and was punished.[51]

Punishment in most late-fourteenth- and early-fifteenth-century police regulations was limited to a fine.[52]

The distinction between the public woman and the illicit prostitute became sharper as the latter was increasingly associated with procurers. The royal and municipal ordinances of the fifteenth century aiming principally at procurers prescribed corporal punishment for their protégées as well. The ordinance of the seneschal of Carcassonne published in Narbonne in 1438 banning procurers from town on pain of beating also prescribed the same rigor of justice for "women . . . publicly leading a damned life . . . living in good streets."[53] The series of expulsions of procurers promulgated by the council of Arles included some references to "fallen women" (*mulieres falhite*) living in honest neighborhoods who were also to be expelled.[54] The royal ordinances on fires promulgated by Parlement in 1474, which prescribed punishments for procurers, dealt with illicit prostitutes as well: "that these dissolute public women not live nor be so bold as to live in public streets, but should stay in the public house or in nonpublic streets." First offenses were punished by fines and a third offense by a fine of 10 l., running the town, beating, and banishment from the town.[55] This toleration of prostitutes living outside the authorized center but in private streets is seen also in Avignon, where a police regulation of 1458 refers to "*meretrix publica vel privata.*"[56] But the policy of most towns concerning these "secret" prostitutes was to oblige them to move to the brothel. Such was the case in Montpellier.[57] In Perpignan and in Genoa, the official municipal brothel keeper himself was given authorization to round up illicit prostitutes and bring them to the public house.[58] J. Rossiaud reports that it was the women of the brothel of Dijon themselves who rounded up the *filles secrètes* of that town.[59]

The laws against illicit prostitution seem to have been enforced with less rigor, however, than those against procuring. The Parlement of Toulouse convicted several women on morals charges in the fifteenth century, but it was in cases of concubinage rather than prostitution.[60] The vicar of Aiguesmortes apparently inflicted no punishment on the prostitutes discovered with procurers during the year 1460.[61] The financial documents from Toulouse indicate, however, that illicit prostitutes were, in fact, arrested and sometimes punished by the municipal authorities there in the early sixteenth century. As we have seen above, the consuls paid the executioner 10 s. in 1501 to whip a procuress and her twelve-year-old *protégée*.[62] Later lists of prisoners include women probably arrested for illicit prostitution. In 1510, for example, a certain Laysetta, called a *cantoniera*, was imprisoned but released without punishment, and, in the same year, payment was made to the executioner for ropes and bars purchased on the occasion of the running of the town by three thieves and three lecheresses (*palhardas*).[63] In 1514 a *filla publica* was arrested several times.[64] The list of prisoners from 1520–21 includes the names of eighteen different women arrested for *palhardise*, only two of whom were whipped, these two, mother and daughter, having been caught with a monk.[65] Although not un-known, punishment seems nonetheless to have been less frequent for illicit prostitutes than for procurers. There is also some indication that the consuls took into account the socioeconomic situation of the woman arrested. Thus, Johana de Sancta Fe, arrested in 1503 as a "whore . . . living in a house where a brothel is kept," was released "because she was a poor unmarried girl."[66] In 1520, Catharina D., "poor debauched girl," was sentenced to the whip but was excused because she was illegitimate, and, in the same year, Leysette Goultiere, arrested for *pailhardize*, was released "because she was poor."[67]

By the early sixteenth century, moreover, even the women of public houses were not immune from arrest and corporal punishment in case of infringement of police regulations or house statutes. A woman resident of Castel Joyos in Pamiers could be sentenced to run the town if caught sheltering a procurer or could be put in the stocks for three days if she blasphemed.[68] The brothel-farming contract of Castelnaudary provided that the farmer, herself a prostitute, was to be whipped if she admitted procurers.[69] The lists of prisoners from the Toulousan archives include specific mention of women from the public house who had been imprisoned. Perrona Beseda and Isabel Martina, listed as "*filles del bon hostal*," were both imprisoned for two days in 1514,[70] and the 1520 list includes three women from the public house.[71] Apparently none of these women were punished, although those who could were required to pay for their prison costs.

By the 1530s there was no longer a clear distinction made between the licit *fille publique* and the illicit prostitute, and even the former could be severely punished for infringements of municipal police regulations that had merited no more than a small fine a few decades before. The severity of the enforcement of police regulations in this period is demonstrated in two cases that came before the royal court of Toulouse in 1535.[72] In the first, five prostitutes (three from Pamiers and two from the Château Vert of Toulouse) were charged with circulating about the town (*vagabonder parmi la ville*). They were found in front of a painter's shop, "where they were having flowers gold-leafed and the names and nicknames of their pimps written in gold letters in the leaves, a capital offense."[73] The women from Pamiers, "because they wanted to go to the public place, but were not aware of the proclamations," were sentenced to be banished from the town and vicarage, whereas those from Château Vert were sentenced to run the town, to be whipped, and to be banished, "given that they were well informed of the said proclamations." In fact, all five were released without punishment (they claimed they had only been shopping for food), those from Pamiers pledging not to return to Toulouse, and the prostitutes from the Château Vert not to wander about town. Far from making her immune from punishment, being a resident of the public house made a prostitute that much more responsible not to transgress the regulations and that much more guilty when caught doing so.

The second case concerns another woman from the Château Vert, a *putain publique* who was found wandering (*vagant*) in town. She was sentenced to running and perpetual banishment from the town. Just as in the case cited above, her defense was that she "only went to town to buy victuals." The sentence was only slightly modified this time. It was decided "that she will be delivered to the executioner of high justice, who will make her run, beating her until the blood flows, and then sent back to the public [house], forbidden to wander about town on pain of hanging." [74] In comparison with the late fourteenth and early fifteenth centuries, when even plying the trade outside the authorized center of prostitution was punishable by no more than a small fine, the sentence pronounced against Antonia Fragut for illicit circulation seems harsh indeed, especially considering the threat of capital punishment in the event of a second offense. Authorized as well as unauthorized prostitutes were being punished severely for even minor offenses, well before the official abolition of public houses in 1561.

In the thirteenth century, procuring, brothel keeping, and tolerating fornication in one's house were often assimilated. By the late fourteenth century, however, with the precise spatial definition of places of prostitution, legislation became more discriminating. The police regulations of many towns, in addition to forbidding women to work outside the official *postribulum*, prohibited town citizens from receiving prostitutes in their homes. A citizen of Lunel caught receiving a prostitute "with any man" in his house was to pay a fine of 60 s. plus the bed. [75] The inhabitants of Castres were prohibited from receiving prostitutes in their homes even for a drink. [76] The fifteenth-century regulations of small municipalities having no public house and observing the custom of "once a week" often punished the man who received the prostitute, whereas similar statutes from the early fourteenth century had punished the woman. [77]

If receiving a prostitute was a punishable offense, running an actual brothel was even more serious, as it posed a permanent threat to the monopoly on prostitution enjoyed by the municipality or its notable citizens. Complaints about illicit brothels were often brought before royal officers. When Paul Dandrea opened an unauthorized house of prostitution in Montpellier in 1458, offended monopoly holders and indignant neighbors of Dandrea brought their complaint before the seneschal of the Limousin and the Estates of Languedoc; it was the king himself who confirmed the guarantee of the monopoly in 1462. [78] The Parlement of Toulouse was particularly vigorous in prosecuting illicit brothels. It confirmed the sentence of the consuls of Toulouse against Peter de Donasse in 1454, prohibiting him from receiving "in his house girls, procurers, or other people of bad life, on pain of running the town." [79] Its officers seem sometimes to have been more zealous than the consuls in their prosecution of illicit brothel owners, as is seen in a request brought by the royal prosecutor before the Parlement in 1498, urging the court to oblige the consuls to enforce the ordinances on illicit brothels by punishing the people involved in an illegal house rented by a notary in the Place Mage. [80]

It has been suggested that, although only one official house of prostitution existed in each town in the fifteenth century, in fact, prostitution was tolerated in the numerous urban bathhouses. [81] Although abuses were surely not rare, the texts from southern France indicate that considerable efforts were made by the authorities to maintain the "honesty" of public bathhouses. [82] A solution found in Avignon was to distinguish between honest and dishonest stews, the latter being located in the authorized red-light district of the city. Thus, in 1441 a council recognized that the stews of Pont Trocat were "prostitutional"; instead of closing them, they simply forbade clerics and married men from bathing there. A few years later in the same city, Genin del Geline advertised his honest bathhouse as "beautiful and honest stews for honorable and honest women to bathe." The stew keepers of the Cervelière were given permission in 1448 by the temporal court to operate a bathhouse that was both honest and dishonest, as long as there was strict separation between the two, including separate entries. [83] In Nîmes the honest bathhouse and the brothel *cum* stews belonged to the same owner, who farmed them out to the same woman, stipulating that prostitution be strictly limited to the brothel. [84]

In Montpellier the owners of the official house of prostitution incurred the expense of constructing a bathhouse attached to the brothel so that the house's prostitutes should not disturb the honesty of the municipal stews. [85] When two dishonest bathhouses opened in the suburb of the Saunerie at the end of the fifteenth century, the consuls, who were also the prostitutional monopoly holders, dissatisfied with the insufficient measures taken against these stews, brought the case before the Parlement of Toulouse. [86] The consuls argued that there existed in Montpellier an "appropriate place" (*lieu proporcionné*) for the residence of the public women, "as is permitted by law" (*ainsi qu'est permis de droit*), and also "stews . . . for the service and health of the human body in all honesty" (*estuves . . . au service et sancté de corps humain par toute honnesté*). In the two new dishonest stews, frequented by "procurers and other people of bad life" (*ruffians et autres gens de mauvaise vie*), the rules of public order and decency were flouted. The divine service in the neighboring Convent of the Observance was frequently disturbed; the women apparently sometimes climbed onto the wall near the convent, exposing themselves to their pious neighbors! Young boys from the neighboring university were debauched there, and the baths had been the scene of gambling, thefts, and even murders. The consuls asked that these offenses be punished and the prostitutes led to the "public place." The kings' prosecutor called for the closing and destruction of these dishonest stews. Both were, in fact, closed, and one was converted to the use of poor plague victims.[87]

There were undoubtedly many abuses in the system of honest bathhouses in the fifteenth century.[88] But the principle of the separation between honest and dishonest houses was well established and, as the case of Montpellier proved, could be enforced. Hostility to all competitors of authorized prostitution siphoning off the gains of the monopoly holders and municipalities was a strong motivation. But the exigencies of public morality and security were important, too.[89] It is perhaps for this reason that royal officers were sometimes more rigorous than the consuls themselves in the enforcement of the legislation against illicit houses. This concern with public morality should not be neglected, for similar arguments were later used in the polemic against authorized houses of prostitution. The mid-sixteenth-century critics of authorized brothels, brothel keepers, and prostitutes found models for their protest against institutionalization in the fifteenth-century attacks on illegal houses, illicit prostitutes, and procurers. The morality of the Reformation found its roots in the fifteenth century.

℘ *Epilogue to Part Two*

Institutionalized Prostitution: Demography, Public Utility, and Sexual Morality

A study of the evolution and dynamics of prostitution in the Middle Ages, no matter how carefully traced or how vividly depicted, is bound to leave the reader with a sense of dissatisfaction if it restricts itself to the what and how of the matter without at least attempting to answer that most tantalizing and elusive of all historical questions—Why? Why was prostitution tolerated in the twelfth and thirteenth centuries, institutionalized in the fourteenth and fifteenth, condemned in the sixteenth century? What reasoning impelled the public authorities to develop a positive policy on prostitution in the late Middle Ages? The answers to these questions, of course, can only be hypothetical and speculative, but it is nonetheless essential to formulate them.

The demographic features of late-medieval society have been invoked as a major reason for the development of institutionalized prostitution in this period by J. Rossiaud and R. Trexler. Rossiaud argues that the large percentage of the population that was celibate and the late age at which people, and especially men, married—a peculiar aspect of western European population structure, distinguishing it from that of other societies—resulted in a positive policy on prostitution.[1] There is an undeniable relation between these peculiar demographic structures and the dimension of prostitution in the late Middle Ages; without engaging in the debate on medieval population figures, one can note simply that there was *at least* one prostitute for every thousand inhabitants of a medieval town (probably even more, when one considers the secret and occasional prostitutes who escaped head counts).[2] What is less evident than the connection between massive prostitution and the peculiar demographic features of late-medieval society is the relation between these structures and the *policy* of institutionalizing prostitution. It is not obvious that a large demand for prostitutes necessitates institutionalization. In a situation of passive tolerance, the simple law of the market is usually sufficient to assure a supply of prostitutes.

There is, moreover, little correlation between the demographic trends of the era and the tendency toward authorization. Demographic movements in the last centuries of the Middle Ages were sudden and dramatic, fluctuating from the extreme of overpopulation to the opposite extreme of depopulation, whereas the tendency in the policy of public authorities was a relatively steady, continuous progression toward increased and elaborated institutionalization. The trends were, moreover, sometimes contradictory. If one period can be singled out as witnessing a relative "quantum leap" in the institutionalization of prostitution, it is the decades of recurrent plagues following the Black Death, which saw the creation of the municipally owned brothels and the extension of royal safeguards to the same. Yet, at the very same time, a period of depopulation in the wake of the plague, marrying age would seem to have dropped, thereby, according to Rossiaud's own reasoning, diminishing the demand for prostitutes.[3]

R. Trexler draws a closer parallel between population movements and the contemporary policy on prostitution, focusing on these difficult decades of plague and population decline in the late fourteenth and early fifteenth centuries. Trexler believes that the primary motivation in this elaborated positive policy was to fight against the declining birthrate of this period, a trend that perpetuated the depopulation wrought by the plague. By converting men from homosexuality to heterosexuality, Trexler argues, prostitutes made an indirect contribution to boosting the sagging birthrate. This argument, while seductive, is not without weaknesses, for the popularity of prostitution may dissuade men from marriage and family as effectively as the charms of homosexuality. In the absence of explicit proofs,[4] it is not obvious that the municipal authorities believed that the most direct path from the sodomic bower to the connubial bed passed through the municipal brothel.

Another hypothesis might be advanced to explain the intense phase of institutionalization in the late fourteenth and early fifteenth centuries. The studies of D. Herlihy and C. Klapisch-Zuber have shown that there were more men than nubile women in medieval Tuscan society[5]—another factor, along with late marrying age, conducive to prostitution on a large scale. But, while the high marrying age apparently dropped in the wake of the Black Death, the male-female disproportion, on the other hand, would seem to have been aggravated. Some contemporary texts and modern research would tend to indicate that women, especially poor women, suffered a disproportionately higher mortality rate than men.[6] Contemporary chroniclers observed that the decline in population made it easier for people to marry.[7] If the male-female disproportion was indeed further aggravated, women in particular must have found it much easier to marry than in the period before the plague. The motivation to become a prostitute in a society in which women could marry easily, one can imagine, must have been considerably reduced. Society may well have been suffering, quite simply, from a very real, if temporary, shortage of prostitutes.

While the above hypothesis is tentative indeed, it has the advantage of tying in with contemporary documentation. It may explain the numerous cases of relatively well-to-do prostitutes that are found in the texts of this period;[8] insufficient supply relative to demand should have resulted, in fact, in a greater remuneration for prostitutes. A real shortage of prostitutes may also explain the extraordinary efforts on the part of the municipalities actually to recruit prostitutes in this period.[9] This tentative demographic explanation fits well, too, into the social context of the period. The municipal deliberations of Albi make explicit the connection in the public mind between municipal security and strong control by the municipal authorities of the business of prostitution.[10] Fear of insecurity came not only from the threat of military invasion but also from the menace of social unrest. The second half of the fourteenth century was a period, in Languedoc as in the rest of Europe, of social turmoil and upheaval. The testimony surviving from Bagnols concerning the most spectacular uprising of this period—the Tuchin movement—describes the Tuchins unanimously as frequenters of brothels.[11] The authorities may well have feared, not only the danger of inadequately controlled red-light districts, but also the risk that hostility arising from insufficient sexual outlets for the lower classes due to the dearth of prostitutes might be the spark capable of transforming the kindling of discontent into the flame of open revolt.

Uprisings of the lower classes, while one of the more spectacular aspects of the social history of the period, are not the only significant one. The late Middle Ages witnessed the rise of a new bureaucratic class, the result of the growth of "public administration."[12] One may wonder whether they, at least in their celibate youth at the university or elsewhere, may not have constituted an expanding source of clients. Surely the soaring price of slaves in this period placed beyond the reach of most of them the alternative of concubinage,[13] which had been the premarital and sometimes the extramarital mainstay of the great Mediterranean merchants in the thirteenth and early fourteenth centuries.[14]

Another factor in the development of institutionalized prostitution that one cannot ignore is the financial attractiveness of the business of prostitution. A municipally owned brothel, for example, was an interesting affair for the large towns, both in a period when financial straits encouraged authorities to seek money where they could find it (late fourteenth–early fifteenth century)[15] and at a time when expanding commerce made investment in a house of prostitution a form of speculation (late fifteenth century).[16] But this precise motivation cannot explain the trend over the whole period or the institution of prostitution in small municipalities where it was a subsidized service rather than a source of profits.

Clearly, demography and even social and financial factors are not sufficient explanations for the evolution of prostitution in the late Middle Ages. The demographic trends in particular, abrupt and dramatic, while they may explain some aspects of institutionalized prostitution (especially its developments in the second half of the fourteenth century), cannot account for the relative continuity in the development of this institution, the gradual evolution of an increasingly structured institutional framework of sexual life of the period. It is also important, finally, to support speculation and hypothesis with direct evidence of motivation—the justifications given by Languedocian municipal authorities themselves, even if they are so general and vague as to be open to diverse interpretations.

A classic formula cited in Languedocian documents justifying an authorized center of prostitution is that such a place was needed in order "to avoid greater evil." [17] The debate is open as to just what, if anything precise, constitutes this greater evil. Trexler believes that, for the municipal authorities in Italy, the greater evil was homosexuality and the promotion of prostitution a means of defending heterosexuality. The late Middle Ages was indeed a period of increasing repression of homosexuality.[18] Thomas Aquinas makes explicit the role of prostitution as a defense against a potential wave of homosexuality.[19] Rossiaud, on the other hand, has suggested that the authorities hoped, by authorizing and structuring prostitution, to protect their wives and daughters from rape at the hands of the violent groups of young men who roamed the towns in this period.[20] This is, of course, the classic argument for prostitution in any civilization in which the dominant classes prize the chastity of their womenfolk, made more pressing in a society in which male celibacy was widespread.

While such reasons may well account for part of the motivation, conscious or subconscious, of the late-medieval municipal authorities, a closer analysis of the documents would seem to show that the phenomenon was broader and deeper than the above arguments might imply. The medieval texts, besides citing the avoidance of greater evils, often invoke the interest of the common good. This is manifest in the creation of the red-light district of Montpellier in 1285, where concerted agreement was necessary in order to choose a site that would be "the most appropriate and with the least scandal and detriment to this town." [21] In Albi the theme was not only the security (*securitas*) of the town but also "public utility" (*utilitas publica*).[22] The words that appear often in the fifteenth century are *res publica, la chose publique* (commonweal).[23] A situation in which prostitutes could be found in any street, in any house, was manifestly "harmful to the commonweal of the town." [24] Prostitution was inevitable but should be limited, in the interest of public morality, to the confines of one place. The nascent sense of public order, public utility, public good demanded a policy of confinement of prostitution, and confinement could not be satisfactorily effectuated without a certain institutionalization. [25]

What exactly was feared in a situation where prostitutes wandered freely through the town? The documents concord, the danger that threatened was a bad example to the community (*exemplum pessimum plurimarum personarum*, in the Villefranche text). The lasciviousness of prostitutes was considered to be a bad example for all; toward the end of the Middle Ages, its effect on children was particularly feared. [26] But the theme that pervades the documents is the effect that contact with prostitutes might have on honest women. In 1358 a royal officer in Montpellier closed off an alleyway that had been a notorious center of illicit prostitution, where "many good and honest women were made whores." [27] The illicit stews that operated in the same town in the 1490s were closed by order of Parlement because the women there debauched young children and "gave a bad example to the girls and married women and widows who have their gardens near the said stews, and many have been debauched." [28] The roundups of secret prostitutes to the public house there were necessary because of the "bad example which is taken by good women of the city from such lecheresses." [29] Languedocian police regulations insist on the strict segregation of dishonest from honest women for this reason. [30] The dominant medieval concept of female nature was that women were the more carnal sex, ruled by passion rather than reason. [31] The municipal authorities feared that honest women, once having witnessed the material as well as the pleasurable rewards of sin, would abandon the connubial bed for the street. "One diseased ewe," warned the authorities of Lacaune in 1337, "infects the whole flock." [32] In case of contagion, the best remedy was quarantine. Authorized red-light districts were the guarantee of female virtue, not only against those who threatened, but also against that which tempted.

The danger, as a psychoanalyst would be gratified to know, came not from a precise external or marginal enemy that threatened good society but from within the heart and bowels of society itself. Sexual desire was natural, prostitution was inevitable, but the need to limit prostitution by defining its perimeters, sealing it off from the mainstream of society, reflected a need to protect society from itself, as it were, by relegating incitement to a limited place. Prostitutes in Languedoc were not so much the heroines of heterosexuality or the guardians of honest women's besieged virtue as they were the sometimes mistrusted pawns in the effort to hedge off sexual and social disorder. The ambiguous role of the prostitute in the maintenance of social and sexual order explains also the ambivalent attitude of the authorities and of society to municipal prostitutes, [33] an attitude that would seem irrational in any strictly "functional" theory of prostitution. These contradictions, this ambiguity, cannot be understood without a comprehension of the place of prostitutes in the evolution of sexual morality in this period.

The late-medieval period has often been presented, in historical and fictional literature alike, as a morally decadent era.[34] One of the examples of licentiousness cited most frequently to illustrate this moral decadence is the legitimization of prostitution. A brothel named Castel Joyos, prostitutes called *filles de joie*, public houses often municipally owned and royally protected—these are so alien to contemporary mores that it is difficult to know how to weigh their moral value for the people of the fifteenth century, and it is tempting to attribute them to a low or declining moral sensitivity on the part of late-medieval society. In fact, there is evidence that could lead one to believe that, far from being a symptom of moral decline, institutionalized prostitution was a sign of increasing concern with problems of sexual morality, a veritable instrument of increasing moral rigorism.[35]

In order to understand the moral significance of prostitution in the fifteenth century, it is necessary to place it in the context of that society's sexual morality, determined to a large extent by the great moral arbiter, the Church, but influenced, too, by secular factors, such as the Germanic tradition and the influence of Roman law. A thorough analysis of the changing sexual morality of the late Middle Ages being beyond the scope of this study, the following discussion will focus on the changing attitudes toward three problems of sexual morality: adultery, concubinage, and so-called simple fornication (sexual relations between unmarried people).[36] The Church's position on these issues will be presented, followed by the point of view of the Languedocian laity in three different periods: the thirteenth, the fifteenth, and the sixteenth centuries.

By the twelfth century, with the compilation of canon law and development of the scholastic method of analysis in theology, a coherent schema of sexual morality was emerging in the Church, at first for the clergy and later for the laity. The great movement for clerical celibacy, one of the hallmarks of the Gregorian reform, was followed by major developments in the theory of marriage, especially its sacramental aspect.[37] The indissolubility of marriage followed logically from its sacramental nature. The consequence of these changes in the theory of marriage was a growing campaign against those practices that posed a threat to the sacred status of marriage, principally divorce, adultery, and concubinage. Repudiation of the adulterous wife had been permitted in the Frankish church, but all divorce was rejected by the canonists and theologians of the twelfth century, who insisted on the indissoluble nature of marriage.[38] The denunciation of lay concubinage by the Fourth Lateran Council was echoed in many provincial councils.[39] Male adultery was also denounced by these councils; the statutes of Paris, for instance, imposed a seven-year penance on a married man having had intercourse with an unmarried woman.[40] Most of the legislation on sexual morality of Languedocian councils was aimed at sins that offended the marriage bond. Adultery was declared a cause for excommunication by the council of Béziers in 1342. Lay concubinage incurred the greatest indignation, however, and was universally declared a cause for excommunication.[41] Simple fornication, while it did not entail excommunication and was not a *casus episcopalis* (a case in which judgment was referred to the bishop), was nonetheless considered a mortal sin.[42]

Lay opinion did not accept docilely the strict sexual morality of the Church, based as it was on a certain equality of the norms of sexual behavior for men and women. Both German and Roman tradition encouraged a double standard of sexual morality, strict for women and lax for men, especially unmarried men. There seems to have been a virtual consensus in Languedoc, for instance, that simple fornication, far from constituting a mortal sin as the Church insisted, was a mere peccadillo. A confrontation of these two ideas appears in the registers of the inquisition of Jacques Fournier, an early-fourteenth-century document. Inquisitors often interrogated suspected heretics about their views on sexual morality, since the Cathars believed that intercourse between a married couple was no different from illicit intercourse. While most heretics seeking to hide their beliefs were able to answer correctly that adulterous and incestuous intercourse were mortal sins, a favorite trap laid for them by the inquisitors was to ask if intercourse with a prostitute was a sin. One suspect who fell into the trap answered innocently that "he did not believe it to be a sin, on condition that one pay what one had promised to the said prostitute, and that she agree [to the act]."[43]

The double standard that prevailed in lay society is seen clearly in the Languedocian interpretation of adultery in the thirteenth century. The majority of the urban Languedocian law codes considered adultery to be an offense committed only by a married woman and her lover. It was usually in towns having an ecclesiastic as lord that the adultery of the husband figured as a punishable offense in the customs.[44] The tendency to exonerate married men from possible adultery charges found its origin in Germanic law and was reinforced by the revival of Roman law.[45] A desire to maintain the strict definition of adultery as a primarily female offense in the face of enforcement of a broader definition of adultery by Church and king alike was one of the principal motivations, as we have seen, for the creation of red-light districts in the early fourteenth century;[46] the town residents were eager to define a zone reserved for professional prostitutes, within which men could not be arrested for adultery.

There are few texts concerning lay concubinage from this period. The statutes of Arles, exceptionally, included a paragraph calling for the expulsion from the city of a husband keeping a public concubine, as well as expulsion of a married woman cohabiting with a man other than her husband.[47] But no other customs included such provisions. The author of the first commentary on the customs of Toulouse, moreover, seems to have been as tolerant of concubinage as he was of male adultery. In a lecture on a different topic, he casually threw in a reference to a certain woman as "my former concubine" (*concubina nostra quondam*). There was apparently nothing shocking about making such a remark in this context.[48] Concubinage was, after all, a tolerated institution in many regions surrounding Languedoc.[49] One may note, moreover, that Louis IX, for all his reforming fervor against gaming, blasphemy, and prostitution, took no initiatives against concubinaries.[50]

But lay opinion in Languedoc, despite its vigorous resistance to ecclesiastically defined norms of sexual morality in the High Middle Ages, had undergone significant modifications by the fifteenth century, the most striking of which was precisely a growing lay opposition to concubinage, seen clearly in certain archival documents. In 1387 the consuls of Béziers submitted to the royal court of that town a list of kept women and their companions, exhorting the court to take stronger action against these individuals, especially the women.[51] The consuls complained that most of those on the list, which included several royal sergeants, remained unpunished by the court, contrary to royal ordinances and written law (*instructiones regias et ius scriptum*). A similar document is preserved in the municipal cartulary of Mirepoix,[52] where the consuls complained to their lord that certain women were being kept publicly by various citizens of the town. They requested that the unmarried concubines be required to wear the mark of public women and that the married ones be sent back to their husbands. General prohibitions of concubinage are found, not only in such exceptional documents, but also in a number of mid-fifteenth-century police regulations. Concubinaries faced a 2 l. fine in Saint-Michel-d'Euzet (1466),[53] a 9 l. fine or running in Alès (1454),[54] and a 50 l. fine in Avignon (1458).[55] The presence of these articles in a number of fifteenth-century police regulations becomes significant when one realizes that *none* of the fourteenth-century police regulations preserved for Languedoc include such a disposition. The change seems to indicate a real transformation of public opinion.

The Parlement of Toulouse also was active in prosecuting concubinaries, especially royal officers. Jacques Artisel, a court attorney, was threatened with removal from office and was eventually put in prison, then released on 200 l. bail, for keeping a concubine.[56] A royal order to the judge of Castelnaudary urged punishment of married men keeping concubines and of concubines; men were threatened with prison and a 25 l. fine, women with the whip and banishment.[57] There are numerous examples of fines imposed on concubinaries in Apt and other Provençal towns from the mid–fourteenth to the mid–fifteenth century.[58] Royal and municipal authorities alike undertook a serious effort to enforce an aspect of sexual morality that had been proclaimed for centuries by the Church.[59] One even finds instances of private individuals' having made notarial declarations of concubinage in order to "make up for evil acts" (*male geste reparare*).[60]

There seems to have been, as well as a general condemnation of concubinage, less tolerance for male adultery in the fifteenth century than in the
thirteenth. One no longer finds references in this period to the privilege protecting men found within the official red-light district from arrests for adultery; indeed, the official fiction was that brothels existed for the use of unmarried men. The synod of Avignon banned entrance of married men (and
priests) to prostitutional bathhouses,[61] and the royal letter granting permission
to the consuls of Castelnaudary to establish a house of prostitution in that
town stated clearly that the existence of such a house was justified by the presence of so many young unmarried men in the town (*jeunes hommes et serviteurs non mariez*).[62] The lawyer for the archbishop of Lyon, whose illicit
bathhouse there had drawn protest from neighbors, argued that the establishment was not scandalous because it admitted no married men.[63] In the lists of
prisoners preserved in the financial documents of Toulouse, one finds many
references to men arrested as *paillards*, who may have been adulterers.[64] The
police regulations of Aubignan and Loriol (Comté Venaissin) of 1487 forbade
prostitutes to "commit adultery with any man, nor any man with her."[65] In
Pamiers a man caught with two unmarried prostitutes was charged with adultery in 1501.[66]

The last bastion of lay society's double standard was simple fornication.
There is no indication of a campaign against simple fornication, either by the
Church or by municipal or royal officials. Yet the perception of fornication
seems to have changed in some subtle ways. More than just accepted behavior, youthful fornication became a kind of behavioral norm, justified by appeals to nature as a guide for human behavior.[67] At the same time, one senses
in some texts a certain disapproval of such fornication, especially venal fornication, relegating it to the lower classes of society. There was something
suspect about a person who frequented brothels habitually.[68] A number of the
humanists of fifteenth-century Florence voiced their disapproval of excessive
lust or passion, which they considered to be inimical to the civic and patriotic
spirit of young people, as well as harmful to the health and spirit of the individual.[69] The limitation of sexual life to the marital bed had found secular as
well as ecclesiastic apologists by the fifteenth century.[70]

This gradual change of lay sexual morality in the late Middle Ages laid the
foundations for the dramatic transformation in morals which took place at the
end of the fifteenth and throughout the sixteenth centuries and which were
presented in a coherent manner in the theological works of the Reformation
leaders and in the corpus of the canons of the Council of Trent. In general,
their effect was to tighten sexual moral discipline by constructing a more coherent model of Christian marriage. Despite the important differences between the Catholic and Protestant models—Protestant marriage being neither
a sacrament nor indissoluble—both resulted in the total condemnation of concubinage and the much stricter enforcement of laws against male adultery.[71]

Sexual morality was also fundamentally transformed by the Protestant rejection of asceticism and introduction of marriage for the clergy, a transformation whose roots are found, like so many other Protestant reforms, in the fifteenth century.[72]

At the heart of this transformation of sexual morality in the sixteenth century was the condemnation of simple fornication. Regarded as acceptable and natural by most of the laity in the fifteenth century, the sexual activity of unmarried men drew increasingly harsh criticism in the sixteenth century. The records of the Protestant consistories are full of accusations of lechery (*paillardise*) made against young unmarried women and men.[73] The Protestant movement to close the brothels in the sixteenth century was part, then, of a general reaction against toleration of sexual activity on the part of young unmarried men. The Counter-Reformation, too, took a firm stand against youthful fornication. Brothels were regarded no longer as a necessary escape valve for male sexual appetites, but as centers of corruption in which young men were initiated in the ways of lust.[74]

Which is not to say, of course, that the early modern period was an era of sexual puritanism, of "Victorianism" before the Victorians. We have all been struck by the offhanded bawdiness of Rabelais, Shakespeare, and their lesser-known contemporary chroniclers, diary writers, and storytellers. But this should not blind us to the moralistic element important in this period. The point is not to compare the sixteenth century with the nineteenth century but with the High Middle Ages, when concubinage (a heritage of the Franks) was common, male adultery not even officially an offense, according to most Languedocian city laws, and simple fornication so accepted that laymen sometimes mistakenly believed it to be tolerated by the Church. By contrast, the sixteenth century—and even the fifteenth century—was a period in which municipalities took the initiative in punishing concubinage and when secular thinkers advised, to those who would listen, in the interest of *raison d'état*, a sober life of moderate sexual activity within the bonds of marriage.

These changes in morality were far broader than those evoked in this book. The late Middle Ages witnessed an intensified prosecution of sexual practices considered to be unnatural—homosexuality, as we have seen, and also bestiality. The increasingly intense enforcement of laws on morals went beyond sexual offenses, moreover, and included such infractions of public order as gaming and blasphemy.[75] Procedural changes in the courts made prosecution easier (the change from accusatory to inquisitorial procedure was complete by this period), and municipalities created organs of justice specialized in prosecuting what modern sociology has dubbed "victimless crimes."[76]

If the fifteenth century has been seen as an era of moral decadence, it is surely because the growing sensitivity in that period to the exigencies of sexual morality led to the prosecution of people on morals charges that had not even been considered offenses a century before and to the condemnation by contemporary social critics of an "immorality" that would have passed unnoticed in an earlier period. We must focus not on the immorality presented but on the tightening moral standards that defined such activity as immorality. Likewise, the municipalization and protection of brothels is evidence not of the decadence of the late Middle Ages but of the attempt of secular authorities, both municipal and royal, to impose a uniform standard of sexual conduct on lay society.[77] Sexual morals had become an affair of state by the fifteenth century, and institutionalized prostitution, approved and protected by the public authorities, was not a sign of the decadence of a society in moral chaos but rather the earliest manifestation of the imposition on society by the secular authorities of an increasingly coherent, albeit changing, notion of public sexual morality.[78]

Institutionalization was not primarily conceived—excluding the exceptional period of dearth of prostitutes in the late fourteenth and early fifteenth centuries—in terms of demographic exigencies, and it was not intended, generally, to encourage the frequenting of prostitutes. It was an instrument of public order, relegating prostitution to one spatially defined part of town, limiting the spread of the "infection." Municipal prostitutes were the (albeit sometimes mistrusted) defenders of public order only so long as simple fornication was considered inevitable because it was "natural"; once the possibility of a profoundly reformed society became a conceivable alternative in the public mind, the role played by the brothel in the maintenance of public order was called into question, and the public authorities, with a relative ease made possible by decades of prosecution of illegal prostitution, moved from a policy of institutionalization to one of repression of prostitution.

Conclusions and Perspectives

The High Middle Ages witnessed a renewed interest in the problem of prostitution, expressed in the works of the jurists and the customs of the Languedocian towns. Prostitution was considered to be inevitable, despite the efforts of Saint Louis to impose a repressive policy on a manifestly unresponsive society. The policy followed in Languedoc was primitive and negative in tone, defining places where prostitutes should *not* work; customary centers of prostitution probably developed, but they had no legal status. There was little concern with brothels or procuring in the Languedocian towns; prostitution was a free-lance affair, provided the persons involved stayed out of the more respectable neighborhoods of town. The prostitute's position in society was low and her legal capacity limited, although provisions were made for her conversion by the foundation of communities of repentant sisters.

The late thirteenth and early fourteenth centuries marked a period of transition from this negative policy to a more positive one, the essential element of which was the recognition by the municipal authorities of official centers of prostitution, where prostitutes had the obligation and the right to reside. Contemporary police regulations enforced a behavior and dress code for prostitutes, as well as obligatory residence in the authorized *postribulum*. Primarily a consequence of the concern for public order, a means of protecting honest women and honest neighborhoods, this positive policy of authorizing red-light districts also played a role in the limitation of adultery arrests of the male residents of certain towns.

In the late fourteenth century, as a result of depopulation and the concern to supervise brothels more strictly, most places of prostitution were reduced to one house, in western Languedoc often the property of the municipality. Municipalization continued throughout the fifteenth century; where houses remained private, they were often in the hands of the great *bourgeois* or nobles. Direct exploitation of brothels gave way, in the big towns, to brothel farming; the masculinization of brothel management in Toulouse underscores the increasing importance of the farmer and the interest in the profits of prostitution. Places and personnel of authorized prostitution enjoyed the protection of municipal and royal authorities, who assured the security of the brothel (sometimes the haunt of suspect people) and defined the rules for the house, concerning finances, customers, and conduct. Only the king could grant a private or municipal monopoly on prostitution, and his officers, as well as municipal agents, prosecuted unauthorized competitors. Municipal prostitutes enjoyed full legal capacity and protection by rape laws, and their eventual reinsertion into society was assured by the municipally supervised centers for repentant women.

A certain malaise pervades the documents of the late fifteenth and early sixteenth centuries. In western Languedocian towns, the closing of brothels during Easter Week was institutionalized, and considerable effort was made to convince the public women to repent. Morals offenses were enforced with increasing severity; concubinage and male adultery were taken seriously, not only by the Church, but by laymen themselves—Parlement and consuls—who took the initiative in enforcing a stricter self-discipline. The prosecution of procuring and other morals offenses had put in place a machinery of repression that was to be used to attack all manifestations of prostitution once the Reformation/Counter-Reformation condemnation of simple fornication eliminated the public house's social justification.

This is what we know about late-medieval prostitution—or what we seem to know. Many of these conclusions are, in fact, hypotheses that sometimes hang by slender threads of evidence. Much research remains to be done before more definitive conclusions can be drawn. One would like to see more monographs, especially those that might elucidate the very different policies on prostitution followed in northern European countries and in the Mediterranean regions, or concentrate on the less well-documented yet crucial period of the High Middle Ages. Research in other fields could facilitate interpretation of data one has already. A study of the legal capacities of marginals and the lower classes and a synthesis of the history of women in the Middle Ages (if such is feasible) would permit a more accurate evaluation of the prostitute's place in society. The domain that needs the most exploration, however, is that of the social and cultural history of prostitution's clientele. Little is known of the sexual morality of the new emerging bureaucratic classes of the fourteenth and fifteenth centuries, who seem to have been both the clients and the critics of prostitution. Could they, raised to social heights by their knowledge of and reverence for law rather than by military exploit or commercial adventure, be a source of the increasing moral rigorism of the laity in this period?

It is this rigorism that sets the sexual morality of early modern Europe apart from that of other preindustrial societies, and that has intrigued social historians in recent years. Serious investigation of its etiology is but in the early stages. The goal of this essay has been achieved if it can serve as an orientation for further studies of the roots and development of this peculiar sexual morality, thus adding a small and tentative piece to the vastly complex puzzle of the cultural, institutional, and social transformation of western Europe in the late medieval period.

℘ *Appendix A*

Published Documents

No. 1. AM Albi, FF 43, no. 2. 3 May 1366. Letter of the king's lieutenant in Languedoc ordering the expulsion of prostitutes from the street assigned them by the bishop of Albi. (Discussed in chap. 2.)

Ludovicus regis quondam Francorum filius, domini nostri regis germanus eiusque locumtenens in partibus Occitanis, dux Andegavensis et comes Cenomanensis, . . . senescallo Carcassone, vicarioque et iudici regiis Albie et Albigesii et eorum cuilibet vel loca tenentibus eorundem salutem. Dilecti et fideles nostri consules ville Albiensis nobis graviter conquerendo monstrare curarunt quod curiales temporales episcopi dicte ville Albie meretrices et publicas mulieres de loco seu carreria in quibus morabantur et morari consueverant in aliis loco et carreria prope ecclesiam seu monasterium gloriosissimi confessoris Sancti Antonii dicti loci mutaverunt seu mutari fecerunt, et prope ac recte portale dicte ville vocatum de Vicano pro quo gentes magis continue intrant et exeunt dictam villam quam pro nullis de aliis portis eiusdem ville et intrare et exire consueverunt per eundem cum sit in loco magis comuni et utili ad intrandum et exiendum, in quibus locis et carreria a paucis diebus citra plura mala et orribilia ac innumerabilia peccata propter mantionem ipsarum mulierum devenerunt, et de die et de nocte multa pericula atque dampna irreparabilia possent evenire non solum dicte ville sed toti lingue Occitane propter custodiam ipsius ville que una clavis est trium senescalliarum Tholose, Carcassone et Bellicadri et tocius lingue Occitane, quare nobis humiliter supplicarunt ut tantis periculis irreparabilibus providere dignaremur, nosque eorum supplicationi annuere volentes et tantis periculis providere cupientes, vobis et vestrum cuilibet si opus fuerit commitendo mandamus quatenus si vobis legitime constiterit de predictis visis presentibus et absque morosa dilatione dictas meretrices seu publicas mulieres de dicto loco et carreria expellatis et in alio loco magis condecenti ad securitatem dicte ville et honorem dicti gloriossimi confessoris Sancti Antonii, vocatis consulibus dicte ville et aliis qui fuerint evocandi, mutetis et mutari faciatis, appellationibus, recusationibus, cavillationibus frivolis et subterfugiis, hiisque in contrarium subrepticie impetratis seu impetrandis non obstantibus quibuscumque. Datum Bitteris die tercio Madii, anno domini M° CCC° LX° sexto. Per dominum ducem ad relectionem consilii P de Vergin.

No. 2. AM Castelnaudary, FF 22 (parchment). 19 November 1445. Letter of Charles VI ordering his judge in the Lauragais to assign a place suitable for a brothel in Castelnaudary. (Discussed in chap. 2.)

Charles, par la grace de dieu roy de France, au juge du Lauragois ou à son lieutenant, salut. Les consulz de la ville de Castelneuf d'Arry nous ont exposé que ladicte ville est assez grande et peuplée et y affluent ou demeurent plusieurs jeunes hommes et serviteurs non mariez et aussi despourveuz de femmes ou filletes publiques, aumoins icelles femes pubiques qui y sont n'ont point d'ostel et maison expresse en laquelle elles doyent estre trouvées et y demourer toutes séparées de gens honnestes, ainsi que es autres villes de bonne police est acoustumé de faire, dont sordent aucunesfoiz noises et inconveniens oudit lieu. Et pour ce ont lesdiz exposans délibéré entre eulx de faire construire et édifier à leurs despens un hostel hors de la ville et séparé de gens honnestes, qui sera appellé le bordel, ouquel demeureront et seront trouvées icelles filletes. Mais qu'il nous plaise donner auxdiz exposans de ce faire congié ou permission et licence, ainsi qu'ilz dient requerans humblement icelle. Pourquoy nous, les choses dessusdictes considerées, et pour éviter lesdiz noises et inconveniens, vous mandons et pour ce que vous estes nostre plus prouchain juge illec, commectons se mestier est que appellé nostre procureur ou son substitut en vostre iudicature et autres qui feront à appeller, vous élisez et consignez place ou lieu convenable et illec permectez et donnez licence de par nous auxdiz exposans de faire faire et edifier à leurs coustz et despens hors de ladicte ville en place convenable ledit hostel appellé bourdel pour la cause dessusdicte, et y faites retraire et demourer icelles filletes ou femmes publiques, et vuider ou bouter hors de ladicte ville quant ou regard de continuelle résidence. Car ainsi nous plaist il estre fait, et auxdiz exposans l'avons octroyé et octroyons de grace especial par ces presentes, non obstant quellesconques lettres sur ce impétrées ou à impeter à ce contraires. Donné à Tholouse le XIX jour de novembre l'an mil CCCC quarante et cinq, et de nostre regne le XXIIII. Par le conseil.

No. 3. AN, JJ 181, 16v–17r. January 1452. Letter of remission granted by Charles VII in favor of Poncelet Paulin, who mortally wounded John Sudre in the brothel of Toulouse in August 1448. (Discussed in chap. 3.)

Charles, par la grace de dieu roy de France, savoir faisons à tous presents et à venir. Nous avons receue humble supplication de Poncelet Paulin, aagé de vint-et-cinq ans ou environ . . . que ou mois d'aost mil CCCC quarante et huit, ledict suppliant, estant demourant en nostre ville de Tholouse, fut prié et requis par ung gentil homme d'aler avecques icellui gentil homme et le acompanger avecques autres à aler querir une jeune femme au bourdeau de ladicte ville de Tholouse que l'abbesse ou maistresse lors dudict bourdeau avoit promis de bailler à icellui gentil home; auquel ledict suppliant, voulant lui faire plaisir, accorda d'aler avecques lui au lieu dessusdict. Et après ce à ung certain jour ensuivant dont ledict suppliant n'est bonnement retors, ledict gentil home et avecques lui ledict suppliant et autres alerent audict bourdeau en esperance d'y avoir ladicte femme. Et eulx venuz là, trouverent ladicte abbeesse ou maistresse, à laquelle ledict gentil homme demanda ladicte femme, que promise lui avoit. Et elle luy respondy que elle n'y estoit point et qu'il ne la povoit avoir, et sailly hors de l'ostel et dist audict suppliant et autres qui en la compaignie estoient qu'ilz s'en retournassent, ce qu'ilz firent tous, excepté ledict suppliant qui après les autres demoura audict lieu. Et lors vint à lui ung nommé Jehan Sudre et lui dist telles ou semblabes parolles en substance, que demande ce seigneur, demande il une femme, il fauldroit qu'il chantast premierement une chançon. A quoy ledit suppliant respondit qu'il ne sauroit chanter à la guise du païs. Et lors lui dist ledict Sudre qu'il n'auroit donc point de femme. Et ce voiant ledict suppliant et que ledict Sudre se mouquoit de lui, ala prandre une des jeunes femmes qui là estoient par la main, et lui dist qu'il convenoit qu'elle s'en alast avecques lui, et eurent grans parolles ensemble. Et quant ledict Sudre vit que ledict suppliant la vouloit emmener, icellui Sudre, plain de mauvaiz courage, tira sa dague et lui en donna deux ou trois cops. Et ce voiant ledict suppliant, doubtant que ledict Sudre lui fast encores piz et le mist en exoine[1] de corps et de membres, tira aussi sa dague . . .
[Subsequent testimony deals exclusively with the fight between the two men and Sudre's eventual death.]

No. 4. AM Toulouse, FF 117. 1462 (date noted on back of document). Excerpts from a case brought before the Parlement of Toulouse by the *fillettes communes* of Toulouse, concerning the brothel farm. (Discussed in Chap. 3.)

En la cause pendant par devant nous Pierre de la Talle et Nicole Barthelot, conseillers du Roy notre seigneur en sa court de parlement à Thoulouse, et commissaires par icelle depputez en ceste partie. Entre les pouvres filletes communes de l'ostel public de ceste ville de Thoulouse, suplians et demanderesses d'une part, et les capitolz de Thoulouse, deffendeurs d'aultre part. Groselier pour lesdictes suplians et demanderesses, replicando, dit que par ce qu'il dit et propose en sa demande, son intention est très bien fundée. Et oultre *cum protestatione, de qua supra est facta mencio* en ladicte demande, dit *pro fundamento istius materie*, qu'il est escript en droit, *quod inter opera caritatis, non est minimum errantem ab erroris sui semita revocare,*[2] par quoy est clairement remonstré *quod circa incrementa virtutum debemus omnis avelare, et multiplicacionem viciorum possethemus vitare.* . . . Et par ainsi soubz corexion l'en doit extirper et mectre auneant toutes choses provocans à luxure, et non pas les norrir, et porter soubz umbre et couleur de arrendement de grosses sommes de deniers à appliquer. . . . Et ne se trouveroit en ville de cest royaulme ne ailleurs ung semblant abus, et le roy, la court et vous mesdictz seigneurs les commissaires y devez avoir grant regard *ad fine vitandi iram dei omnipotentis cui multiplicatio ardoris libidinis multum displicet.* Et doncques en continuant tousiours la matiere audict hostel commun par les prepos desdictz deffendeurs prins en leur prejudice, il y a acoustumé d'avoir ung arrendeur, lequel comme plus offrant et derrenier encherisseur *ad extinctum candelle, consuevit recipere regimen et gubernamen* desdictes filletes de jour et de nuyt etc. Et cellui arrendeur vrayment les roigne et taille tout ainsi que bon lui semble. Et proprement parler il semble que iceulx deffendeurs ont honte de nommer ledict prethendu arrendeur par son nom propre et notoire audict Thoulouse, nommé par derision en leurs registres l'abbé du bordel. *Et proprie nommen abbatis non est honoris, sed solitudinis,* ainsi le dient noz maistres. Et pour ce fault dire que les deffendeurs baillent le gouvernement dudict hostel a ung roffien, qui *gaudet pluralitate dictarum muliercularum et non parcitate.* . . . Et seroit honneur ausdictz deffendeurs que laissassent laquerele, pour ce que aucune foiz prouffit n'est pas honneur. . . . Et par ainsi fault dire que lesdictz deffendeurs ayment mieulx concubitger, que les enfans, ce que n'est pas honnorable, *officio de curionatus.* Et à ce que lesdictz deffendeurs maintiennent en leurs pretenduz deffenses que en ceste ville a ung hostel public ouquel les filletes publiques doivent et ont acoustumé demourer, et ne leur est permis selon les ordonnances de ladicte ville observées, de tant et si long temps en ça qui n'est memoire du contraire, demourer, converser, boire, dormir et manger ailleurs par la ville que audict hostel, lequel est grand et espacieulx et y plusieurs estages, chambres et aultres maisons, et est tout clos en celle maniere que de nuyt, nul n'y puet entrer ny offandre lesdictes filletes sans licence et congié d'icellui ou d'iceulx qui ont le gouvernement dudict hostel, etc. Respondent lesdictz suplians que par le propos desdictz deffendeurs, prins toutesfoiz en leur prejudice, il appert que ledict hostel leur appartient, et illecques publiquement doivent faire leur residence et non ailleurs, et ainsi le confessent elles, et n'ont point besoing de gouvernement de jour ne de nuyt. Car par ledict propos prins comme dessus, il appert que l'ostel est bien clos, en telle maniere que nully ne puet offandre lesdictes demanderesses. Car de jour est l'office du soubz viguier de Thoulouse, de les garder ou faire garder de toute offance, et de nuyt c'est le gouvernement du capitaine du guet. . . . Et n'y vault riens coustume ne observance, au contraire, cestassavoir que lesdictes filletes ne soient audict hostel à leur liberté, mesmement dedans ledict hostel public, car puis que ainsi est qu'il est public, destiné à la residence publique des filletes, ledict hostel ou dict cas est de chacune et illecques puet demourer tant que bon lui semble *Nam talia loca publica* ne regardent pas la faveur d'iceulx deffendeurs, mais la faveur de la chose publique, et *ne maius malum subsequatur*. Et queque soit, les deffendeurs veulent enbourser l'argent que lesdictes filletes guangnent en leur usaige vile et deshoneste, et ne leur en chault dont il viengue. . . . Car puet chacun sçavoir, que si au temps passé, la matiere fust venue en jugement comme maintenant, *non fuisset tolleratum, sicuti non tollerabitur quid quid fulsiatur exadverso*. Et sembleront que lesdictz deffendeurs vueillent maintenir que lesdictes filletes doivent demourer *invite et contredicentes* audict hostel public, ce que ne se pourroit soubtenir *Dum tamen ad semitam honestatis vellent avelare*, ce que jamaiz ne permectroit ledict ruffien appellé l'abbé ne ses complices, *quia non sunt castitatis amatores ut predictum est*. Et seroit grand honneur maintenant ausdictz deffendeurs, si ladicte pernicieuse et fole costume, si coustume se doit nommer, estoit decirée, et mise hors et auneant, en leur temps comme sera si dieu plaist. Car parlant soubz correction, ne y a raison qui la puisse soubstenir. Or dient ilz plus les deffendeurs que ce n'est pas sans cause, ainsi autrement avoir esté trouvé, pour raison de plusieurs inconveniens qui s'en porroient ensuyr, comme batures, mors, mutilacions et aultres, etc. Dient lesdictz deffendeurs que à cecy en effect a esté dessus respondu, car le soubz viguier de jour, le capitaine de guet de nuyt, en ont le gouvernement et *non lenones qui exterminant*. Car ung ruffien, entre telles pouvres et miserables femmes, est comme ung reynart entre les gelines, *tanquam fera pessima*. . . . Et dient plus lesdictz deffendeurs que lesdictes filletes communement sont femmes de grand disolucion et de plus grand despense en leur boire et manger que aultres gens, car il leur a acoustumé donner chacun jour quatre foiz à manger c'estassavoir de matin à desiuner fricheures[3] ou pastez, à disner boully et roty, et à respriller [?] aussi quelque chose de friant, à souper aultres bonnes viandes et tousiours bons vins blanc, rouges & clarez tellement que leur despense, est plus grand coustange que aultres gens, etc. Par les propos d'iceulx deffendeurs prins tousiours en leur prejudice, appert clerement que ledict ruffien nommé abbé est in causa de nourir lesdictes femmes en plus grand disolution par le moyen des bons vins et aultres viandes *et datus est ad multiplicanda vicia, et inconveniencia*. Ce que est repprouvé *tamquam adsurdum et detestabile quia vicium et mulieres apostatare faciunt, etiam sapientes*. Et est vray *quot parcitas cibi potusque therit et renprimit luxuriam*, ainsi le remonstrent noz maistres en plusieurs lieux. Et aroient les deffendeurs quelque raison, si *aliquid petebatur* pour le loage *aut pro repparacione dicte domus*. Maiz pour leurdict propos prins comme dessus *ipsi pocius tendunt ad inflamacionem luxurie et libidinis, quam admitigacionem*, ce que n'est pas bien fait, que l'en vueille dire ou maintenir, etc. . . . .

Et est ainsi que sans bruit et noise de jour et de nuyt elles pourroient aler là où bon leur semble, et ainsi est acoustumé de faire à Paris, et partout le royaulme de France et ailleurs. . . . Et afin que ladicte court, et vous messieurs les commissaires puisses clerement appercevoir que lesdictes suplians et demanderresses ne entendent poursuyr cause en ceste partie, si non que soit raisonable, elles et chascune d'elles offrent à ladicte court qu'elles sont contentes de payer cinq solz turnois pour chascune d'elles *qualibet septimans*, lesquelx soient employés à la reparacion dudict hostel, de chambres, de lictz et aultres choses necessaires par les mains du maistre des heures, depputé par le roy à Thoulouse ou par aultre que la court saura mieulx adviser. Et seront ses cinq solz enregistrés à ung livre, avec les noms des filletes, qui y sont et survendrent au temp advenir par aucun marchant de Thoulouse, lequel lacourt advisera, et lequel en randra chacun au compte et reliqua au viguier de Thoulouse ou à son lieutenant satisfacto audict receveur de son salaire raisonnablement pour sa poine. Et elles mesmes se feront la despense de bouche si voulent manger ne boyre. Et que la plus ancienne d'elles, laquelle l'en a acoustumée à Thoulouse nommer l'abesse du bourdel, soubz correction de laquelle les aultres ont acoustumé de faire, *circa familiaria dicte domus*, avecques ledict maistre des heures, qui est au present, ou sera pour le temps advenir, deviseront et pourveront chacun moys en visitant ledict hostel, des choses neccessaires à la relasion duquel maistre des heures et de ladicte abaisse ensemble ledict receveur sera tenu de fournir, et ce qu'il fornira en prenant cedule dudict maistre des heures contenent en effect la raison pour quoy, et en quoy a esté emploié, lui sera rebatu de ses comptes. Et par cest moyen sera obvié, que fera pessima, que sont ruffiens ne sera trouvée entre les berbis, et quant l'en y trouvera, l'en sçet bien comment ils doivent estre punis. Offrent comme dessus.

No. 5a. AM Montpellier, Louvet 147.[4] 13 September 1498. Letter of Louis XII ordering his officers in Montpellier to prosecute all offenses committed in two illicit bathhouses. (Discussed in chap. 5.)

Ludovicus dei gratia Francorum rex, nostris gubernatori baiulo que et judicibus ordinario et partis antique Montispessulani aut eorum locatenentibus salutem. Visa per nostram parlamenti, curiam Tholose sedentem, supplicatione seu requesta eidem pro parte consulum ville Montispessulani porrecta hunc qui sequitur tenorem continenti.

A nos seigneurs de parlement supplient humblement les consuls de Montpellier que, comme en ladicte ville y ait lieu proporcionné auquel les filles publicques doivent demourer et soy tenir pour eviter esclandres, ainsi qu'est permis de droit, et aussi y a estuves tant dedans ladicte ville que dehors, lesquelles sont trouvées au service et sancté de corps humain par toute honnesté et non autrement, ce neantmoins, hors les murs de ladicte ville y a deux estuves, les unes près de l'estude et université, et les autres sont quasi vis à vis de l'eglise de l'Observance. Et en icelles estuves se font de grans desordres et continuelement se trouvent cinq ou six putains, lesquelles sont entretenues par leurs ruffians et autres gens de mauvaise vie. Et illec les escolliers sont desbauchez et se desbauchent tous les jours, ensemble autres enffans de la ville occieux tant en paillardie, gormandie, jeux de detz et de cartes, que en autres dissolucions, et despendent ce qu'ilz n'ont pas acquis. Et le service divin est maintesfois interrompu en l'eglise de l'Observance qui est prouchaine desdictes estuves. Et aussi donnent mauvaiz exemples aux filles et femmes marriées et vefves qui ont jardrins près desdictes estuves, et maintes en sont desbauchées. Et à l'ombre desdictes estuves se commectent beaucop de murtres, larrecins de nuit et pilleries, sans ce que jamais en ait esté fait aucune justice, ains les sergens en prennent de l'argent et composicion. Et soubs umbre de ce que les officiers ordinaires dudict Montpellier se dient estre inhibez par lectres de nelitependente de la court de ceans en laquelle l'on dit y avoir esté introduict certaine cause d'appel entre Nicolas Mazi et Jehan Maupel appellans du juge de la part antique de Montpellier ou de son lieutenant d'une part, et de Guillaume de la Croix, maistre Guillaume Pavez et Jaques Bucelli apellez d'autre, pour raison et à cause si lesdictes estuves y devoient estre ou non, lesdicts officiers ne veulent ou osent faire aucune punicion desdicts exces qui sont excecrables et se commectent tous les jours à la grand foule, dommaige et destruction totalle de la chose publicque dudict Montpellier, et discontinuacion et diminucion du divin service et office dudict couvent de l'Observance, et qui est exemple pernicieux des habitans de ladicte ville. Et plus seroit si par la court de ceans n'y estoit donnée prompte provision de justice. Ce considéré, il vous plaise de vostre grace faire declaration que la court n'a entendu ne entend que *propter usus modi inhibiciones et illis non obstantibus* il soit permis tenir ne demourer icelles femmes dissolues et de mauvaise vie dedans lesdictes estuves et qu'elles soient mises dehors de ladicte maison, et au surplus que les magistratz de ladicte ville facent les informacions et procedent contre les coulpables et delinquans tant desdicts exces qui ont esté faiz et commis, et des autres qui se feront doresenavant, et en faire la punicion selon l'exigence du cas, et que verront estre à faire par raison, et vous ferez bien et justice.

Vobis et vestrorum cuilibet ex ipsius nostre curie deliberatione tenore presencium commictendo mandamus quatinus appellatione necnon inhibitionibus factis in vim licterarum de nelitependente de quibus in requesta eadem cavetur absque tamen dicte appellationis in futurum in prejudicio non obstantibus de et super requesta in eadem contentis facinoribus provideatis celeriter prout iuris fuerit, et insuper de et super in ea mentionatis excessibus et maleficiis vos diligenter et secrete informetis, et contra quos de eisdem inveneritis culpabiles, iuxta casuum exigenciam procedatis sub omnibus autem iusticiaris officiariis et subditis nostris vobis et vestrorum cuilibet in hac parte pareri volumnus et jubemus. Datum Tholose in parlemento nostro XIII^a die septembris anno domini millesimo CCCC^{mo} nonagesimo octano, regni vero nostri primo. Per comunam De Borrassol.

No. 5b. AD Haute Garonne, B 2010, 239v–24or.^{5} 29 April 1499. Excerpts from pleading before the Parlement of Toulouse in the case of the illicit bathhouses of Montpellier.

Entre Nicolas Mazi, habitant de Montpellier, appellant du juge ordinaire de ladicte ville de Montpellier ou de son lieutenant commissaire royal deputé en icelle partie d'une part, et les consulz de la ville de Montpellier appellez. . . .

De Selna, por lesdictz consulz, dit qu'il y a proces ceans entre ledict Mazi et ung nommé Malpel appelans d'une part, et lesdictz consulz appelez d'autre . . . à cause de deux estuves. . . . C'est assavoir celles de Malpel sont assises près les escolles de l'université de Montpellier, et les autres qui appartienent audict Mazi sont assises près le couvent des Freres Mineurs . . . car en icelles estuves on mectoit femmes dissolues et ruffiens, s'ensuyvoient beaucop de maulx *quoniam escolares ab eorum distrahebantur studio*, et les femmes honnestes de ladicte ville en allant en leurs jardins d'icelles femmes dissolues veoient leurs insolences et mauvaise vie et deshonneste conversation, et se trouva qu'elles montoient sur les paretz assises près du couvent de l'Observance *et illec eorum discoperiebant et utroque demonstrabant pudibunda*. Et aucunes foiz ausdictes estuves lesdictes femmes et rufiens faisoient si grant bruyt qu'ils destourboient audict couvent le divin service, par quoy lesdictz consuls qui pour lois estoient se tirerent devers les officiers de ladicte ville pour pourveoir donner ordre et mectre fin ausdictes insolences et qu'ils voldrent faire, mais parties adverses avecques certaines lectres de ne lite pendente obtenues de ladicte court de ceans firent inhiber. . . . Or dit il que s'il semble à la court que les estuves doivent demourer, *quod maneant*, pourveu que les femmes dissolues, rufiens, ne autres de mauvaise vie ne habitent en icelles, mais que aillent faire leur demeure au lieu publique, et que soit fait inhibition et defense ausdictz Mazi et Malpel qu'ilz ne parmectent que lesdictz hommes et femmes dissoluz entrent ne habitent ausdictes estuves. . . .

Or dit il [de Prato, pour le procureur general du roy] que lesdictes estuves ont donné et donnent dommage à la chose publique, car au moyen d'icelles, les femmes dissolues habitans et conversans en icelles ont destourné et destournent les escoliers qui estudient *in universitate ville Montispessulani, et sic in hoc res leditur publica*. Aussi le divin service à la foiz est empesché audit couvent des Freres Mineurs par les grans caz et folliez que lesdictes femmes dissolues et rufiens font ausdictes estuves assises près dudict couvent appartenans audict Mazi, car les autres estuves appartienent audict Malpel. Se conclud à ce que par arrest de ladicte court lesdictes estuves soient ostées et abbatues, et les maisons appliquées en autres usaiges par maniere de provision pendant le proces et jusques à ce que par la court autrement en soit ordonné. . . .

No. 6a. AM Toulouse, CC 2364, no. 71. Granted 13 December 1514. Request by the Toulousan brothel farmer for reduction from the farm of expenses incurred during observation of Holy Week and Easter Week. (Discussed in chap. 5.)

A vous nobles seigneurs messieurs les capitols de Tholouse. Supplie humblement Jehan Aymery, arrantier de la Bonne Mayson de Tholouse, disent que comme mieulx se avise et aussi est de bonne coustume et par vos predecesseurs observée, les filhes estant en icelle Bonne Mayson se doivent abstenir de faire aulcun péché de leurs corps en pailhardise ny autriament saltim despuis la vigile de Pasques Flories jusques au mercredi après Pasques prochain. Et par ce qu'est de coustume de pourveoir ausdites filhes d'autre logis que de ladite Bonne Mayson et néantmoins durant ledit temps de aliments, par vous autres mesdiz seigneurs a esté donné charge audit suppliant d'y pourveoir surtout aux despens de la présente cité de Tholouse et aussi a esté commandé audit suppliant de fornir ausdites filhes en déduction de son arrentement, lequel suppliant, voulant fer comme ung bon serviteur, a loué mayson, achepté boys, charbon, pain, vin, posson, [cher] et autre companaige pour lesdites filhes estant en [?] que appert par le papier cy actaché au quel est le nombre et mise de tout. . . . Ce considéré, vous plaise de voz benignes graces avoir consideration aux chouses susdites et visiter sa myse cy actachée, et considere le nombre des filhes, services, poynes en tel cas et serviteurs, et tout considéré, desduyre la somme spécifiée en sa déclaration de son arrentement. Si ferez bien, et ledit pouvre suppliant priera dieu pour vous.

Habeat viginti libras turonensis decembris XII anno domini M V^c [XIV].

No. 6b. AM Toulouse, CC 2364, no. 72. 1514. List of expenses incurred by the brothel farmer during Holy Week and Easter Week. (Discussed on p. 87.)

S'ensuit le nombre des filhes de la Bonne Mayson de Tholouse de l'an mil cinq cens et quatorze, et du temps de la Sempmayne Saincte dernierement passée, et mesmement de celles que ont vescu au despens de l'oste deladite Bonne Mayson durant ladite Sempmaine Saincte et jusques au mercredi après Pasques, et aussi la despence par ledit hoste pour lesdites filhes durant ledit temps sancts.

[For the list of women, see appendix B.]

Ce qu'a esté despendu pour lesdites filhes:

Et premierement la vigile de Rams pour donner à disner ausdites filhes, a fourny le susdit hoste tant en pain, huyle, merlins, arans, escaramdes estimars tant cuitz que rotiz et poisson froiz   17 s.   6 d.

Item le lendemain jour de Pasques Flories dit le jour de Rams, a forny ledit hoste pour lesdites filhes pour companage que dessus 30 s.

Item le lundi ensuyvent, a forny pour lesdites filhes et provision d'icelles 30 s.

Le mardi ensuyvent, a forny pour la provision desdites filhes comme dit est 30 s.

Item le mercredi ensuyvent, pour ce que lesdites filhes ne vouloient point jeuner, a forny 30 s.

Item le jeudi sainct, a forny ledit hoste pour lesdites filhes et leur provision 30 s.

Item le vendredi sainct, pour icelles filhes a forny ledit hoste, pour ce que aulcunes jeunoient et les autres non 20 s.

Item la vigile de Pasques, pour ce que lesdites filhes, ou aulmoins la plus part d'icelles, avoient receu nostre seigneur et ne jeunoyent point, a forny ledit hoste 30 s.

Item le jour de Pasques, a forny pour lesdites filhes ledit hoste en cher tant chevreaux, moton que beuf et pain 30 s.

Item le lundi ensuyvent, a forny tant pour le disner que souper 30 s.

Item le mardi, a forny tant pour le disner que souper des filhes 30 s.

Item a forny en vin deux pipes lesquelles luy coustoient huit excutz petitz et par ainsi monte par pipe quatre escuz petitz 27 s. 6 d.

Item en boys pour brusler et abilher le manger ausdites filhes, a forny 15 s.

Item en charbon une charige, a forny 16 d.

Item una carrada de fagotz pour lesdites filhes, ledit hoste a forny 15 s.

Item pour le loyer de la mayson là out lesdites filhes ferent leur Pasques et les litz out dormoient durant ledit temps, a forny ledit hoste 50 s.

Item pour ung serviteur et une servante que hont servy lesdites filhes durant le temps, a payé 20 s.

No. 6c. AM Toulouse, CC 2364, no. 61. Granted 24 April 1514. Request by a sergeant for reimbursement for expenses and labor expended leading women of the brothel to sermons during Lent.

Supplie humblement Anthonius Nanvielas, sergent iuré de vostre court et pourtant vostre livrée, disent que de vostre commandement icelluy suppliant a vacqué toute ceste présente Caresme dernier passée à conduyre les pouvres filhes de la Bonne Mayson de Tholouse au sermon, là out tous les jours demeuroit depuis le matin jusques à neuf heures et non sans grand peyne et trevailh, occasion de quoy ledit suppliant a layssé à faire ses besonhes. Et pour sa peyne et son interetz ledit suppliant n'a en rien esté remuneré, combien selon droit l'ait bien de merite, qu'est chouse grandement preiudiciable audit suppliant, ainsi que verrez selon conscience de sa peyne et travailh, et neantmoins le rambourser de trante et deux arditz qu'a fournitz pour avoir des pater nostres ausdites filhes. Et feriez bien.

Habeat duas libras turensis XXIIII aprilis anno domini M V^c decimo quarto.

No. 7. AM Castelnaudary, BB 1, 12r. 19 September 1515. Brothel-farming contract. (Discussed in chaps. 3 and 5.)

Anno domini millesimo quingentesimo decimo quinto et die decima nona mensis septembris, domino Francisco etc. Noverint etc. quod apud Castronovo de Ario etc. existens etc. videlicet providus vir Turandus Le Bolier, receptor dominorum consulum Castrinovi de Ario, grate de mandato expresso huius Johannis magistri, Johannis Cosselenti, Johannis La Rocha et Bertrandus Turret, consulum anno presento Castrinovi de Ario, arrendavit et per modum arrendamenti tradidit Marie Lanas dicti loci Castrinovi de Ario et abbadesse domus lupanaris dicti loci, videlicet dictam domum lupanaris eiusdem loci. Et hoc per unum annum continuum et completum incipiendo in festo beati Luce proxime venturi et finiendo in simili festo, precio triginta libras turenses monete curente, de quo precio ipsa Maria realiter in mei etc. exsoluit eidem receptori duodecim libras turenses, restum vero soluere promisit terminis sequentibus, primo in nundinis Epiffanie domini proxime venturi quinque libras turenses, et in nundinis Pasche alias quinque libras turenses, in aliis nundinis beate Marie Magdalene alias quinque libras turenses, et tres libras restantes in tunc sequenti festo beati Luce anno revoluto. Precize etc. bona sua obliganda etc. Fuit tamen pactum quod idem receptor tenebitur reparare domum predictam in sibi necessariis sumptibus ville et facere gaudem de dicto arrendamento. Item quod ipsa Maria non tenebit lenones, neque permitet lusores neque blasfematores in eadem domo, sub pena fustigationis. Compromissa ipse partes tenere promiserunt etc. Bona eorum obligando videlicet ipse receptor bona villa obligando et ipsa Maria bona sua propria renuntiandi etc. voluendi compelli per omnes rigores etc. jurandi de quibus etc. Testes Johannis Marescal laborator, Guillelmus Malhabuo et ego Hugoni notarius.

No. 8. AM Albi, FF 43. 23 March 1526. Request by women of the brothel for alms. (Discussed in chap. 4.)

A mestres honnorés seigneurs messieurs les consolz d'Albi. Sy vous supplient très humblement en pitié, charité et aulmone les pouvres filles de la maison commune, quatre qu'il en y a, lesquelles pouvres filles ont vouloir de leurs retirer et fer comme femmes de bien, aidant dieu et la vierge Marie, et aussi que d'isi en avant leurs fault penser de servir dieu e de leurs mectre en bon estat; et davantaige il en y a qui sont loing de leur pays et n'ont de quoy vivre en ce monde, synon que part vous autres leurs soit faict aucune aulmone pour l'honneur de dieu. Ce considéré, mestres honnorés seigneurs vous plaira de vos benignes graces de leurs fer aucun bien pour l'honneur de dieu et de la vierge Marie, car l'aulmone y est bien faicte, et en ce faisant, lesdites pouvres suppliantes se mectront en bon estat et priront dieu de bon cueur qui vous doint à tous ensemble à la fin de vos jours le royaume de paradis. Amen.

Fuit quod requestantes personaliter compareant ad hunc actum Albie die XXIII mensis martii anno domini millesimo Vᶜ XXV.

No. 9. AM Toulouse, BB 9, 100r–101r. 20 May 1528. Deliberation in which the city council decides to attribute the money from the brothel farm to the city's hospitals. (Discussed in chap. 3.)

Le tiers poinct pour estre mis en deliberation, que au commencement de cette presente année entre aultres arrentements que feust de faict est le Chasteau Vert, dict la public, que se arrenta deux cens livres ou environ. A pour ce que comun fama l'on dict parmy la ville que les capitoulz chescune année font fer leurs reubes des deniers provenans dudict arrentement, combien le contre soit la verité, toutesfoys est le comun dire du peuple, qui est une chouse qui redund à la dishonneur de la cité. Et davantage car ce sont deniers qui procedent de male acquisition, à ceste cause et par plusieurs aultres considerations, avoit advisé lesdictz capitoulz, si ainsi semble au conseil, que feust fait statut et ordonnance ceans que a cetero ledict esmolument que proviendra du public soit applicqué aux alimens des pouvres de tous les hospitaulx de Tholouse, car aussi fault il que la maison de la ville fournisse aux pouvres *tempore necessitatis*, a quant le domayne desdictz hospitaulx n'y peult inspecter, sauf et reservé que là et quant sembleroit audict conseil, ledict arrentement soit faict en la maison de ceans et par les capitoulz, tout ainsi que se font les aultres arrentements, et aussi qu'ilz puissent applicquer le revenu dudict public à la reparation de ladicte maison et aultres chouses plus necessaires, quant bon leur semblera.

Jehan Bertrandi, docteur, et touchant le public, il ne faut poinct de doubte que ne doibt estre donné aux hospitaulx, toutesfoyz par aultre consideration est d'advis que acetero ne soit arrenté aucunement.

De Olsonio, docteur, que a cetero n'en soit faict nul estat *in favorem civitatis*, mais soit arrenté *per manos civitatis* et applicqué aux alimens des pouvres ou aultres usaiges pyes.

Pierre de Garguas, doucteur, que pour cette année soit applicqué aux pouvres, mais *in futuro* soit arrenté comme a esté acoustumé *in favorem civitatis*. [Of the next five persons, three agree with Bertrandi, one with Olsonio, and one with Garguas.]

Pons Imbert, bourgeois, *cum* de Olsonio, *hoc addendo* que ce que en proviendra soit applicqué à la reparation de la maison du public. [Of the next eleven persons, seven agree with Imbert, three with Olsonio, and one with Bertrandi.]

Jehan Allemand, bourgeois, *maneat in statu in quo est de presenti.*
Azemar Mandmolli, notaire, *cum* Imbert, et que ne soit mesté avec l'autre domayne de la ville.
[The next four persons agree with Imbert.]
Jehan Ferrier, cirurgien, la moytié aulx hospitaulx et l'autre à la ville.
[Of the last nineteen persons, thirteen agree with Imbert, five with Bertrandi, and one with Allemand.]
Et tant que touche l'arrentement de Chasteau Vert, dict le public, est ordonné, conclud et arresté que acetero l'esmolument que proviendra du arrentement qui se faira de ladicte maison du publicq sera appliqué aux alimens des pouvres de tous les hospitaulx de Tholouse. Sauf et reservé que l'arrentement d'icelluy sera faict en la maison de ceans et par les capitoulz, tout ainsi que se font les aultres arrentements. Toutesfoyz n'en sera faicte prinse et mise ne mester entre les aultres deniers comuns et esmolumens de ladicte ville, ains sera tenu les hospitaulx susdictz le thesaurus prendre le double du registre du conterollent de ceans et faire prinse et mise dudict esmolument duquel sera tenu rendre compte comme estant de la recept. Sauf et requerir que iceulx capitoulz porront applicquer le revenu dudict esmolument à la reparation de ladicte maison et aultres chouses plus necessaires quant bon leur semblera.

No. 10. AM Pamiers, BB 11, 123r–v. Undated [late fifteenth or early sixteenth century]. Statutes of the brothel of Pamiers, called Castel Joyos. (Discussed in chap. 5.)
Statutz et ordenances feytes sus la forma que per assi avant sera tenguda en la mayson comuna de la ciutat de Pamias, appellada Castel Joyos, tant sus lo vivere de las donas que aqui voldran demorar et que pagaran per cascuna taula, et aussi per aquelas qui la noeyt y voldran lotgiar et autrament, aixi que sen sieg:
Et prumierament foc statut e ordenat que deguna filha estant dedins la maison de Castel Joyos no sia si ardida de amparar ny entretenir degun roffia per mestre ny per governador, ny li fe part del gasanh que fara. Et aussi fa hom inhibition e defenssa a tota persona de quinh estat o condicion que sia que no aia a enparar ny entretenir deguna filha deldit Castel Joyos ny per mestre ny governador se gerir, ny li occubar ny pendre res del sue ny del gasanh que fara, sus pena de estre pendutz et estranglatz, et alas donas de corre la vila.
(2) Item fa lom assaber et notiffica que las donas que habitaran aldit Castel Joyos seran mesas et meten los cosenhors dela presenta ciutat en lor protection et salvagarda. Et fen inhibicion lesditz cosenhors et defenssa que degun de quinh estat o condicion que sia no lor aia a fer iniuria ny los mal tractar de feyt ny de paraula en corps ny en bes. Et asso sus pena de carce et de estre punitz coma infrictors de salvagarda.
(3) Item foc statut e ordenat que tot home que volera lotgiar dedins ladita

mayson de Castel Joyos o dormir de noeyt en aquela sera tengut de balhar et delivrar al abat deladita mayson son armes, et autremens sas bagas et argent per conte, e lodit abbat sera tengut restituir lo tot lo mati ab conte aixi que ly aura balhat. Et asso sus la pena de LX s. aplicadora alsdits cosenhors et de pagar aquo que aura pres en garda delquel tal.

(4) Item et si era lo caas que aquel tal qui voldra intrar dedins la mayson de Castel Joyos no volas leychar l'arnes si ly es mandat per l'abat, encorrera la pena de carce et de LX s. et perdicion del arnes, et deladita carce no partira entre per tant que aura pagada ladita pe[n]a de LX s., laquala sera applicada alsdits cosenhors.

(5) Item foc statut e ordenat que si aqual tal que voldra dormir dedins ladita mayson no volia balhar son argent et bagas en las mas deldit abat, et ac perdra dedins ladita mayson, que ental cas ledit abat no sera tengut en aqual tal de res mes sera son perdut.

(6) Item foc statut e ordenat que cascuna dona que volera habitar dedins ladita mayson de Castel Joyos, si vol estar et vivere ala taula de l'abat, pagara per cascuna taula so es a disnar et a sopar quatre arditz. Et lodit abat lor sera tengut tenir bon pa, vi et compainage rasonable segon lo temps.

(7) Item foc statut et ordenat que aqualas talas donas que no voldran vivre a la taula de l'abat, mes voldran vivre a lors pessas, lodit abbat sera tengut de lor vendre vivrez, pa, vi e carn iuxta la policia de la ciutat ab lor argent.

(8) Item foc statut e ordenat que otra so dessus, lasditas donas seran tengudes donar e pagar aldit abat tant per la habitacion, lieyt, foc, servicy e lum cascun jorn per elas tant solament, dos arditz.

(9) Item foc statut e ordenat que si alcun stranger o dela ciutat dormira de noeyt en ladita mayson ab dona, pagara aldit abat per lo lieyt una dobla.

(10) Item foc statut e ordenat que degun de noeyt ny de jorn no sia si ausart de intrar dedins ladita mayson de Castel Joyos ny salher per las muralhas suir per las portes et ab voler e conget del abat. Et asso sus la pena de estre metut en carce e de corre la vila.

(11) Item foc statut e ordenat que degun malaud ronhos del mal e ronha de Naples ny ladre ny autre tocat de deguna malautia contagiosa no sia si ausart de grad ny per forssa de compellier degunas donas dela mayson de Castel Joyos a se abandonar atal malaud e ronhes, ladre o autre malaud contagios, per los scandols que totz los jorns se vesen e poden endevenir. Et asso sus la pena de estre metut en carce et de corre la vila sensse remission delguna et de estre forabanditz de ladita ciutat, et als ladres de estre brulatz et cremmetz sense misericordia.

(12) Item foc statut et ordenat que las donas deladita mayson deldit Castel Joyos seran tengudas manjar e beure dedins ladita mayson, et no permit per vila, et dormir en ladita mayson la noeyt sino que agossan legitima desencusa.

(13) Item foc statut e ordenat que degun hoste dela presenta ciutat no sia ausart de reculhir de noeyt deguna delas donas deldit Castel Joyos, sino que

fos venguda de novel en ladita ciutat et ignores ladita mayson de Castel Joyos. Et asso sus la pena de LX s. aplicadora alsdits cosenhors dela medixa ciutat et de estre metutz en carce et d'aqui no pertir entro ajan pagada ladita pena.

(14) Item foc statut et ordenat que d'assi en avant no sia si ardit degun de blaphemar Dieu ny los sanctz dedins ladita mayson de Castel Joyos. Et asso sus la pena als homes de carce et de LX s. et d'aqui no partiran entre per tant auran pagada ladita pena. Et alas donas de estre botadas al seps per l'espase de tres jorns al pa et ayga. Et apres demanda perdo a Dui al loc de la on sera ordenat per la iusticia et aquals tals qui ac ausiran sian homes o fenmas et no ac revelaran seran botatz als seps al pa et ayga per losdits tres jorns.

Item sean reservat losdits cosenhors la facultat, auctoritat e potesta de interpretar los presentz statutz, de y ajustar, diminuir, corregir et amendar. Et si lor es avist en tot o en partida totalment los abolir et anichilar aixi que bon lor semblara.

Notes

1. *Exoine*, danger. F. Godefroy, *Dictionnaire de l'ancienne langue française* (Paris, 1884; reprint Liechtenstein and New York, 1961).

2. X 4. 1. 20. Letter of Innocent III dated 29 April 1198. See p. 72.

3. *Frixures, frissures = fritures*. Godefroy, *Dictionnaire de l'ancien français*.

4. Partially quoted by A. Germain in his "Etudes archéologiques sur Montpellier," *MSAMtp* 5 (1860): 305.

5. The reference is found in Viala, *Parlement de Toulouse*, 1: 554.

🎗️ *Appendix B*

Lists of Prostitutes

1. AM Uzès, BB 1, 29v–30r. 4 April 1357.

Valentina de Romano	Romans (Drôme)
Johanetta de Privite	Privas
Johanetta de Valencia	Valence (Drôme)[1]
Janseranda de Livrono	Livron (Drôme)
Pieret de [illegible]	

2. AM Toulouse, AA 5, no. 371. 13 February 1425. (incomplete)

Johaneta de Corneri	[2]
Marieta de Navarra	Navarre
Johaneta Maleta	[3]
Bernarda de Sancto Petro	Saint Pierre (Haute-Garonne)[4]

3. AM Toulouse, CC 2364, no. 72. 13 December 1514.

la Bordelesa	Bordelaise
la Johana	
la Tonyna	diminutive of Antonia (Tonia)?
la Serena	"gentle" or "siren"
la Lyonnesa	Lyonnaise
la Ramonda	
la Francesa	
la Maurilhaca	Mauriac (Cantal)[5]
la Vinhala	"vine-keeper"

la Garacha	"ploughing field" (or *garcha* = "ewe")
la Ysabel	
la Borgueta	"little town"
la Petit Hoeyl	*oelha* = "ewe"
la Blanca	
la Granda Lombarda	Lombard
la Johanna de la Terrada	[6]
la Petita Lombarda	Lombard
la Anthonye de Lymos	Limoux (Aude)
la Catharina de Bourdeaulx	Bordeaux
la Johanna de France	Ile-de-France
la Soillarda	"dirty woman"?
la Maria de Paris	Paris
la Margot	
la Jacquelyna	
la Clareta	
la Bedossa	"stutterer"
la Gasconna	Gasconne
la Johanna dela Crotz	probably Lacroix-Falgarde (Haute-Garonne)
la Johanna de Castras	Castres (Tarn)
La Tuffayna	"hairy"?
la Catharina de Tors	Tours
la Marieta	
la Granda Maria	
la Porreta	"little leek" or "little mulberry bush"

4. AM Toulouse, CC 2371, no. 510. 2 April 1521.

la Berena	*bera* = "old ewe"
la Rossa	"redhead"
la Mª de Guera	
la Domenga	
la Petita Fransesa	
la Torta	"gimpy"
la Tomasa	
la Laurensa	
la Johana de Rebelh	Revel (Haute-Garonne)
la Feloy	
la Joana	
la Bastoyna	"pack animal"?
la Bordalesa	Bordelaise

la Marieta
la Olyna
la Clareta
la Fransesa de Beumont   Beaumont-sur-Lèze (Haute-Garonne,
                                arr. Muret)[7]

la Jaquelyna
la Quataryna
la Guirauda
la Jammeta
la Quatalina del Mas
la Marta
la Morelesa   "negress," "Moor"
la Pastra
la Margarida
la Petit Delh
la Mandeta   "vixen" (or *mandreta* = "prostitute")
la Fransesa de Nogarolis   Nogaro (Gers, arr. Condom)
la Bornieta   "one-eyed"
la Puta Nonela
la Esclopiera   "gimpy"

5. AM Toulouse, BB 72, 596–97. 6 April 1528.

Bertrande de Camsas   Campsas (Tarn-et-Garonne)
Margarette Sarlade   Sarlate-la-Caneda (Dordogne)?
Mondette de Montalba   Montauban
Anne Lansaquanette   Lansac (Girone, arr. Blaye)?
Marette de Montat   La Montat (Lot)
Angelline la Pymontoise   Piemont
Marguaritte du Puy   Le Puy (Gironde, arr. Langon)[8]
? Compaignere   Compains (Puy-de Dôme, arr.
                                Issoire)?

Peyrrine Bernade
Ysabel de Feurillet   ?
Loise de Saulmuves   ?
Ysabel Bastarde
Jehanne dela Couste   La Coste (Hérault, arr. Lodève)?
Jehanne Vendomes   Vendomes (Loir-et-Cher)?
Lisette de Montalba   Montauban
Jehanne Serere   Sere (Gers, arr. Mirande)?
Jehanne de Sartaigne   Sardinia
Peyrinne de Valenssa[9]
Magdalaine Seguine

la Tholosane	Toulousaine
Domenge de Castilhon[10]	
Lisette Gaulbert	
Lisette Cassaigne[11]	
Astrugue Peche	Pech (Ariège)
Jehanne Morlhone	Morlhon-le-Haut (Aveyron, arr. Villefranche-de-Rouergue)
Jehanne de Moyssac	Moissac (Tarn-et-Garonne)
Catharine dAlby	Albi
la Compaignere	Compains?
la Jehanne Blancque	
la Repentye	

Notes

1. There is also a Castelnau-Valence in the Gard near Uzès.

2. Possible suggestions: Corn (Lot), Corneillan (Gers, Hérault), Cornier (Haute-Savoie).

3. Possibly Malause (Tarn-et-Garonne).

4. There also exists a Saint-Pierre de Lages (Haute-Garonne) and a Saint-Pierre de Mons (Gironde).

5. Or possibly Mauriac (Gironde, arr. Langon).

6. Possibly Terre-basse (Haute Garonne, arr. St-Gaudens), or possibly a nickname ("sown field").

7. There are many other towns of this name in southwestern France (e.g., in the Gers).

8. Or possibly Le Puy (Haute-Loire).

9. Besides the better-known towns of this name, the following exist in southwestern France: Valence (Gers, arr. Condom), Valence (Tarn-et-Garonne, arr. Castelsarassin), and Valence d'Albi (Tarn).

10. There are numerous towns of this name in southwestern France, including two in the Haute-Garonne, two in the Gironde, one in the Gers, and one in the Ariège.

11. There is a Cassaigne (arr. Limoux) and a La Cassaigne (arr. Carcassonne) in the Aude, and a Cassaigne in the Gers (arr. Condom).

🎜 *Appendix C*

Brothel Farms and Farmers

Source	Date	Years	Price	Farmer	Remarks
Beaucaire (private)					
IIE18–31, 56v	16 July 1490		27 fl.	Stephan Vincedy de Beaucaire	
"	14 July 1492		"		
Nîmes (private)					
IIE¹ 199, 178v	15 Oct. 1482 (18 Oct)	3	26 fl. (19 9s)	Pierre Massot de Nîmes	—owner responsible for repairs, farmer for roof upkeep
IIE¹ 206, 123v	4 July 1498	5	22½ fl.	Deyderia Colina *relicta* de Anthôny Mosche	
IIE¹ 207	1506		—	Beton Petit	
Lodève					
IIE39/155	12 Aug. 1471	1	17s 7d	Johan Assalhit de Lodève	
Pézenas					
BB4	5 Feb. 1455	5	33	Johan de Laya alias Anesconi	
BB5, 3v	17 May 1481 (Pentecost)	1	27	Jehan Capelle	
Cart. B, 58r	7 Dec. 1514 (Quasimodo)	5	+	Bertrand Gast, natif de Toulouse	+32 sestiers *de blé* due before Ascension

Source	Date	Years	Price	Farmer	Remarks
Castelnaudary					
CC80, 4r	1505–6	4	+22 10s	Maria Lanas	+90 for 4 years
BB1, 12r	19 Sept. 1515 (18 Oct.)	1	30	"	—5 payments —town pays repairs —no procurers, gamers, or blasphemers
", 32v	13 Nov. 1526	1	25	"	—no procurers —can close if plague
BB2, 53v	13 Nov. 1526	1	34 10s	Margareta Boleta filie Vitalis de Montpellier	—3 payments —*cum pactis consuetis*
", 157v	12 Oct. 1527	1	20 10s	Bernarda de Cos	—4 payments —pay *rata pro rata* if closed for plague
", 172v	+21 Sept. 1528	1	30	Maria de Rebieyra	—*cum pactis consuetis* + canceled 24 Jan. 1530
BB2, 224v	31 Dec. 1533	1	12	Marieta del Pen de Toulouse	
BB3, 14	1534	1	12	Anne Martine de Pechandier	—3 payments
", 101r	23 Oct. 1536	1	10	"	
", 169v	15 Nov. 1538		9	Johana Roleote de Tratino	
", 210r	3 Oct. 1539	1	15	Astrugne de la Crox de Montaudran-lèz-Toulouse	
BB3, 235v	3 Jan. 1541	1	25	Jehanne Merine d'Aragon	
", 238v	23 June 1541		8	Guilhemete Jugnole de Blois sur Loyre	
", 277r	6 Oct. 1541	1	12	Magdalena d'Or-léans en France	
", 296r	5 Dec. 1542		9	"	
", 341v	12 Sept. 1543	1	10	Magdalena de Beauregard	
", 375r	18 Sept. 1544	1	10	"	
BB4, 303v	15 Oct. 1545		11	Jeane Gautier	
", 320r	3 Feb. 1547		6 15s	Johana Aurela et Antoniete de Pavites	—3 payments
", 335v	25 May 1550		20	Guilhemete Jugnole	
", 351r	14 Dec. 1552		18	Magdalena de Beauregard	

Appendix C

Source	Date	Years	Price	Farmer	Remarks
", 293v	19 Sept. 1553	1	12	Richarde Chevalier de Chambiry en Savoye	

Alès

Source	Date	Years	Price	Farmer	Remarks
1D8, 36r	27 Jan. 1510	6	—	Glaudius Pelhos textor. hab. Alès	—must make repairs
1D8, 71r	6 Dec. 1511	6	—	Guillelmus Elzere de Privas	—must make repairs
", 154r	12 Sept. 1513	3	—	Anthony Naze, barberius, or. Avignon	"
", 205v	7 Feb. 1515	6	—	Glaudius Pelhos textor	—repairs so brothel can be farmed for 6 l.
1D9, 99r	23 Apr. 1518	6	—	+Germanus Andree serviens regis	+left 29 Aug. 1519 because he married
", 146r	29 Aug. 1519	5	—	Stephanus Deylice de dioc. de Nîmes	—repairs
", 355r	10 Dec. 1524	—	—	Aubertus Perret dit Tartas cardator	—repairs —must keep *filias publicas* —no *excessum*
1D11, 135r	4 Mar. 1533	5	—	Johanus Albi lapicid., or. St. Andre Vallesbornie	—no games during divine office
", 268r	8 Aug. 1535	3	—	Maistre Anthony des Plans Chardr. de Dioc. de Valence	—repairs
1D12, 7r	13 Jan. 1537	—	—	Georges Richard chapellie	—repairs —*tenir belles et plaisantes filhes putains pour entretenir le bordel*

Montpellier

Source	Date	Years	Price	Farmer	Remarks
Inv. IX, 109	1521	—	+58 5s 8d	Pierre Lepontyer	+22s 5d paid weekly
IX, 112	1524	—	78	Janot de Bougac (Mogiat)	
IX, 117	1536	—	80	Annet Charenton	
IX, 123	1537	—	56	Antoine Coste	
IX, 132	1539	—	35	Antoine Gerbaut	
IX, 249	1541	3	40	"	
IX, 249	1542	3	50	Mia Vincens, veuve d'Antoine Gerbaut	

Source	Date	Years	Price	Farmer	Remarks
IX, 134	1547	¾	30	Guilhaumeta Sales	
IX, 250	1548	3	15	Mye, relicte d'Antoine Pascal	
IX, 251 Toulouse	1552	5	25	Anthony Cost	
CC2284	1372–73		60	—	
CC1855	1404–5		173¾ écus	Galhardina del Pont Guilhona de Labatut, abadessa	
BB3, 57	1417		230	woman	
"	1418		—	man	—3 or 4 women rent another house
CC1856	1420–21		150	Geletat de Serranois, filha deld. bordel	
BB6, 7r	1428–29		125	—	
CC1859, 53v	1431		70	Johaneta Delascura Johan Sudre e sos companhos	
CC1859, 55v	1432		140	Margarida Dargenta, femma publica +Robin Clerc	+name crossed out
CC1859, 57r	1433		42	Margarida Dargenta Peyre Darganhac, capitan del geyt	
CC1863	1450–51		151	Guiraut Vinhas	
CC1836	1454–55		210	Guilhem Prebost	
CC1866	1464–65		303	Peire Pris	
CC1868	1469–70		200	Johanna Belenquiera, abadessa e arrendeyra	
CC1870	1470–71		+100	Peyre dela Fourie La Lanchunanda	—*s'en era anat*; house refarmed; *s'en anet et leysset tout* + collected only 36 1.
CC2833	1487–88		200	Johan de Londres Pellet, Marti	
CC1871	1488–89		200	arrendier	
CC1872	1493–94		307	—	
+	1494–95		266	—	+Chalande, "Maison Publique"
CC1874	1497–98		150	Ehuefric Frurla alias lo prince	
CC2348, no. 93	1499–1500		—	Nandet del Pech	
CC2350, 58, 130	1500–1501		—	Johan Melet alias Rabanas Anthony Chevalie	
CC2350, no. 129	1501–2		—	"	

Appendix C

Source	Date	Price	Farmer	Remarks
CC2351, no. 87	1502–3	170	—	
CC1875	1503–4	211	Johan Melet alias Rabanas Anthony Chaler alias Gulhola	
CC2356, no. 89	1506–7	—	Katharina Frianda	
CC2358, 59r	1507–8	—	Katharina Frianda	
CC1877	1509–10	376	+Johan Chaveric	+Johan Stieve alias Eymeric, according to CC2359
CC1875	1511–12	370	Johan Estebe dit Eymeric	
CC2363	1512–13	—	"	
CC1880	1513–14	281	+Eymeric	+CC2364, no. 70
CC2365, no. 6	1514–15	—	Johan Eymeric	
CC2367, no. 87	1516–17	+160	Johana Dangiera, molher de Johan Eymeric	+CC2367, no. 76
CC1576	1517–18	261	"	
CC1882	1518–19	210	"	
CC2352	1519–20	200	—	
CC1883	1520–21	200		
CC1884	1521–22	+170	Johanna Dangiere	+ only the first quarterly payment (42 10s) collected *pour ce que elle a eu le fouet et a esté forabadie*
CC1885	1523–24	103	Peyre Fabre	
CC2374, no. 1	1524–25	+145	Armasse Venie	+131 l. deducted because the brothel had been razed (CC1669, 12 Dec. 1525)
CC1670	1527–28	+162	Pierre du Val	+116 l. deducted because of plague (Dec. 1528)
CC1671	1528–29	—	+Pierre du Val	+died Aug. 1529; his widow required to find man to replace him
CC1673	1529–30	+151	Domenge de la Font	+*au proffit et utillité du scindic des hospitaulx* from this year onward
CC1674	1531–32	165	"	
CC1675	1532–33	226	Mondete Ticarde, dite La Blanca	

Source	Date	Price	Farmer	Remarks
CC1676	1533–34	251	Jacques du Tilh	
CC1677, DD10	1535–36	330	Jehan Virbailh	
CC1678	1538–39	458	Antoine Andrieu	
CC1879	1539–40	513	Bernard de Lors de Toulouse	
CC1680	1540–41	587	"	
CC1681	1541–42	439	Jaumes Calviete, sartre	
CC1682	1542–43	531	Anthoine Andrieu	
CC1683	1543–44	680	Jehan de Mans Benoist Jauran	
CC1684	1545–46	815	Jehan Andrieu, bolanger	
CC1685	1546–47	801	Pierre Regis, peinctre, demeurant à la porte de St. Estienne	
CC1686	1547–48	950	Jehan de la Mazere, cardaire, rue de Villeneufve	
CC1687	1548–49	1020	Pierre Casaulx Trenagade de Toulouse, Maison des Ballantes	
"	"	+627	Jehan la Font	+*remise à la chandelle* 15 Jan. 1549
CC1688	1549–50	807	Arnauld de Hot Jehan de Vit, habitant de Lors	
CC1689	1550–51	927	Nando Durand, pescador, demeurant à Villeneufve	
CC1690	1551–52	1175	Pierre la Garda dit Pierre de menant, à Villeneufve	
CC1691	1552–53	950	Jehan Andrieu dit Sardune	
CC1692	1553–54	800	Arnauld de Lot de Toulouse	
CC1693	1554–55	715	Jehan de la Maziere de Toulouse	
CC1695	1556–57	522	" dit le Nebour	
CC1697	1557–58	—	—	*L'esmolument de Ch^{au} Vert n'a poinct esté arrenté, occasion qu'il estoit infaict.*
CC1703	1559–60	—	—	*La maison où souloit estre le Chasteu Vert*

Graphs of Brothel Farm Prices

I.
PRICES (IN LIVRES) OF BROTHEL FARM
CASTELNAUDARY
* = only partially paid

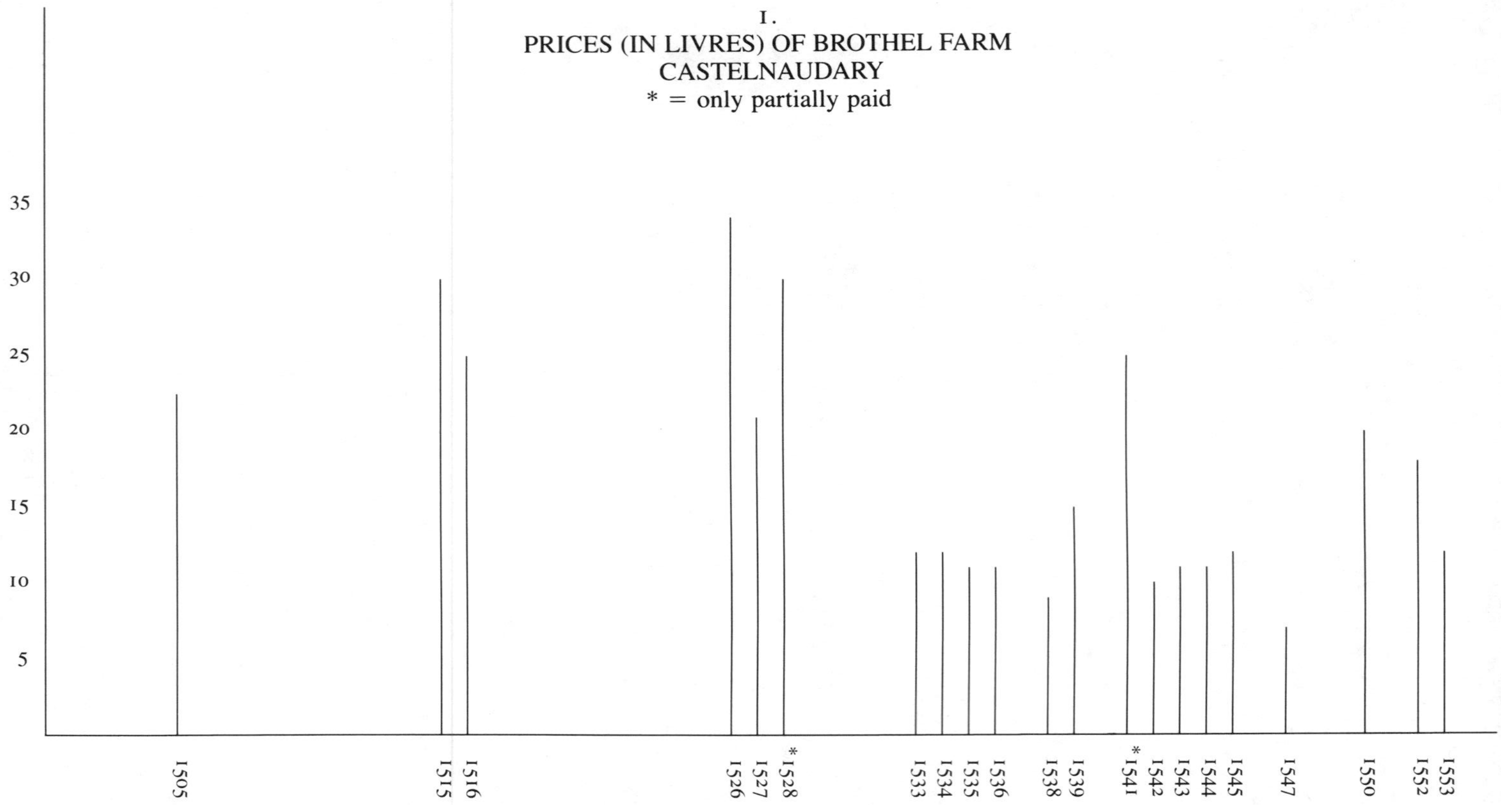

1553
1552

1550

1547

1545
1544
1543
1542
*1541

1539
1538

1536
1535
1534
1533

*1528
1527
1526

1516
1515

1505

35 30 25 20 15 10 5

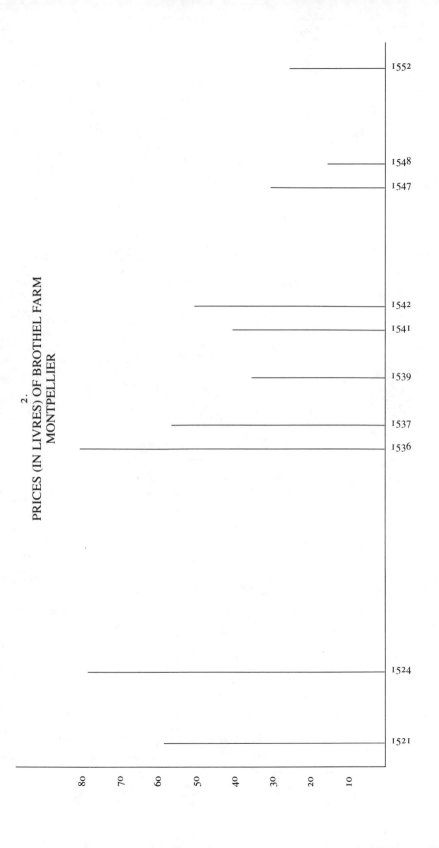

2.

PRICES (IN LIVRES) OF BROTHEL FARM
MONTPELLIER

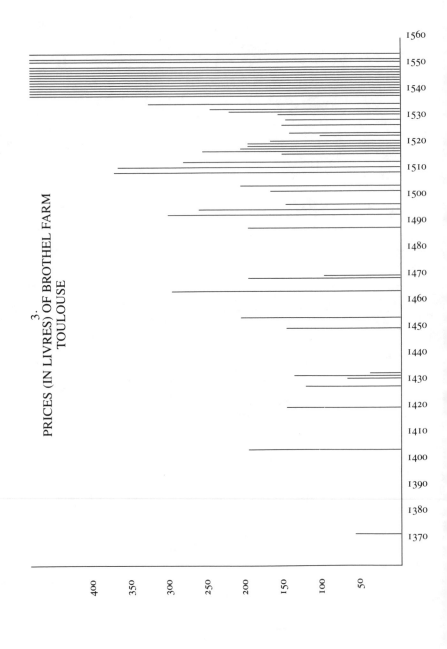

3.
PRICES (IN LIVRES) OF BROTHEL FARM
TOULOUSE

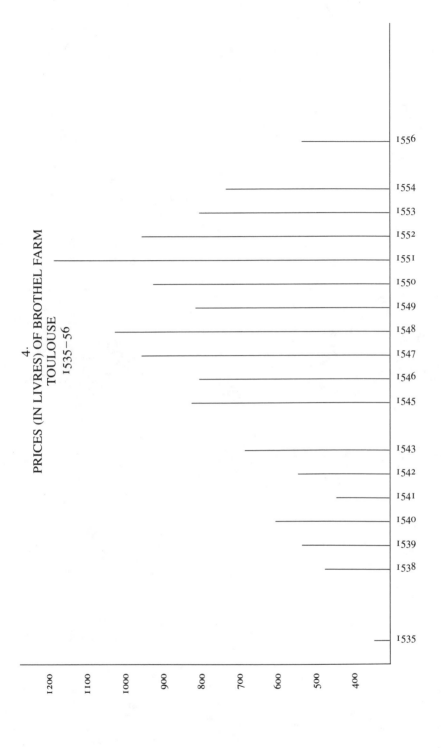

4.

PRICES (IN LIVRES) OF BROTHEL FARM

TOULOUSE

1535–56

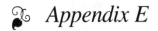 *Appendix E*

Easter Week Expenses, AM Toulouse

Source	Date	Sum	No. of Women	Remarks	
CC2344	1496	5			
CC2348	1500	10			
CC2350	1501	10			
CC1875	1504	8			
CC2356	1507	8			
CC2359	1510	26			
CC2360	1511	1		for the sergeant	
CC2345	1512	24	26	5 ardits per woman per day	
CC2363	1513	27			
CC2364	1514	20	34	P.D. no. 7	
CC2365	1515	28	32		
"	"	1 10s		sergeant	
CC2367	1517	27	30		
"	"	3		sergeant	
CC1576 CC2369	1518	27	28		
CC2371	1521	40	34		
"	"	1 10s		sergeant	
CC2372	1524	2 15s		sergeant	repentie
CC1669	1525	3		sergeant	
CC2378	1527	2		sergeant	

CC1670, BB72	1528	36	30	
CC1671, CC2380	1529	40 1	40	5 lezards per day sergeant
CC1674	1532		54	18 d. per day
CC2402	1541	1		sergeant

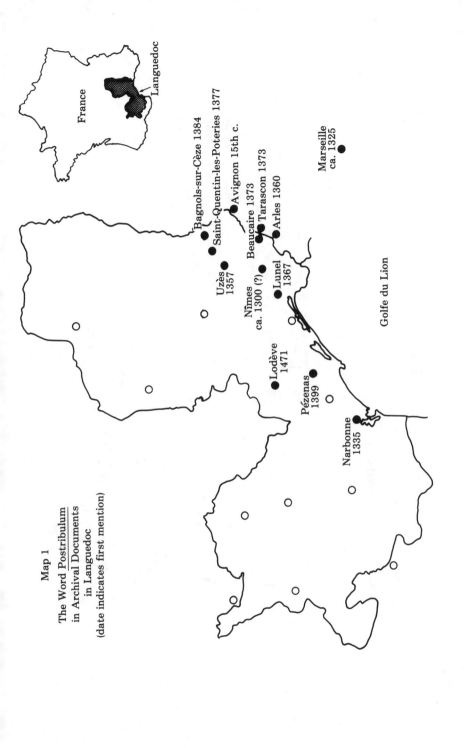

Map 1

The Word Postribulum
in Archival Documents
in Languedoc
(date indicates first mention)

France

Languedoc

Bagnols-sur-Cèze 1384

Saint-Quentin-les-Poteries 1377

Avignon 15th c.

Beaucaire 1373

Tarascon 1373

Arles 1360

Marseille
ca. 1325

Uzès
1357

Nîmes
ca. 1300 (?)

Lunel
1367

Lodève
1471

Pézenas
1399

Narbonne
1335

Golfe du Lion

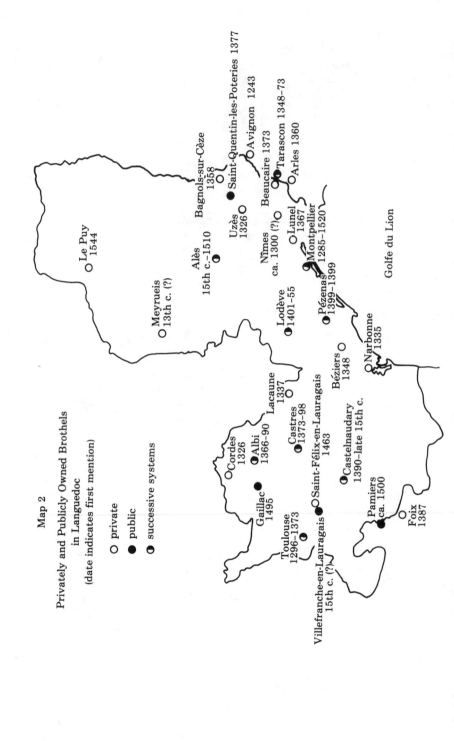

Map 2

Privately and Publicly Owned Brothels
in Languedoc
(date indicates first mention)

○ private

● public

◐ successive systems

Le Puy
1544 ○

Meyrueis
13th c. (?) ○

Alès
15th c.–1510 ○

Bagnols-sur-Cèze
1358 ○

Saint-Quentin-les-Poteries 1377

Uzès
1326 ○

Avignon 1243

Beaucaire 1373 ●

Tarascon 1348–73

Arles 1360 ○

Nîmes
ca. 1300 (?) ○

Lunel
1367 ○

Montpellier
1285–1520 ◐

Lodève
1401–55 ●

Pézenas
1399–1399 ●

Béziers
1348 ○

Narbonne
1335 ○

Golfe du Lion

Lacaune
1337 ○

Cordes
1326 ○

Albi
1366–90 ●

Castres
1373–98 ●

Saint-Félix-en-Lauragais
1463 ○

Castelnaudary
1390–late 15th c. ●

Gaillac
1495 ●

Toulouse
1296–1373 ●

Villefranche-en-Lauragais
15th c. (?) ●

Pamiers
ca. 1500 ●

Foix
1387 ○

Marginal drawing of prostitute and client, late fifteenth century. AM Perpignan, BB 7, 373v°.
Photograph courtesy of the Services des Archives des Pyrénées-Orientales (France).

✑ *Notes*

Introduction

1. The reader is asked to consult the Essay on Bibliography and Sources.

2. See the prologue to part 1.

3. For the geographical limits of Languedoc, see Introduction. The period covered is roughly from the twelfth to the sixteenth century. The documents for the twelfth century being quite scarce, prostitution in that period cannot be studied in great depth, whereas the proliferation of archival material in the sixteenth century makes it impossible to study the topic systematically beyond 1515 (the beginning of the reign of Francis I). The texts for the period from 1515 to 1561 (the date of the prohibition of brothels by the ordinance of Orléans, an otherwise logical terminus for this study) constitute a sufficient basis for a separate book. Many documents from this later period have nonetheless been consulted.

4. See the Essay on Bibliography and Sources.

5. Only recently has the topic of prostitution been changed in the *International Bibliography of Sociology* from a subcategory of "Deviance" to a subcategory of "Sexual Relations." Some social scientists have sought their models, quite the contrary, in the historical literature on the problem. See, for example, the questioning of the marginality of the prostitute in U. Erler, "Prostitution—ein Randgruppenproblem?" *Vorgänge* 13 (1974); 98–107. A helpful book is H. Schelsky's *Sociologie der Sexualität* (Hamburg, 1955), of which I consulted the French translation (Paris, 1966). Despite its outdated analysis of homosexuality, the section on prostitution (65–80) is interesting for its structural analysis and historical perspective.

6. Some recent studies of traditional societies in contact with urbanization have provided interesting analyses of prostitution. See in particular J. M.

Bujra, "Production, Property and Prostitution: 'Sexual Politics' in Atu," *Cahiers d'etudes africaines* 17 (1977): 13–40.

7. See the Essay on Bibliography and Sources.

8. For the Latin text, see n. 1, chap. 1. Although Ulpian says literally that the prostitute accepts customers "without choosing," I have preferred to emphasize the turnover of customers, as some higher-class prostitutes (courtesans or call girls) *are* selective about customers. The choice, however, is usually based on certain objective qualities of the client (wealth, social standing) rather than on personal factors.

9. In this study, which is social and institutional in orientation, it seems preferable to define prostitution in this strict professional sense, distinguishing it from occasional prostitution (women offering sexual services from time to time to supplement another, principal income). Defining prostitution strictly in terms of a professional group, rather than extending it to mean all sexual activity in exchange for some material benefit, has the advantage of setting clear limits and therefore avoiding such theoretical quandaries as whether to characterize marriage as a form of prostitution or to qualify the behavior of lower primates that offer sexual favors in exchange for food as prostitution. Most important, this strict definition has the virtue of corresponding approximately to the medieval definition of the prostitute as a professional public woman (see chap. 1). I refer to "women" rather than "people" because only female prostitutes constituted a recognized professional group. Homosexual prostitution existed, of course (see A. Méray, *La vie au temps des libres prêcheurs* [Paris, 1878], 2: 194), but, given the contemporary condemnation of homosexuality, was not authorized. J. Boswell has found a reference to male "brothels" in northern France in a polemical, antihomosexual poem (in *Christianity, Social Tolerance and Homosexuality: Gay People in Western Europe from the Beginning of the Christian Era to the Fourteenth Century* [Chicago, 1980], 261–62); one wonders how much credence should be given to such a reference. M.-T. Lorcin notes the appearance of gigolos in *fabliaux* (*Façons de penser et de sentir: les fabliaux français* [Paris, 1979]), but they, too, do not form a professional group.

10. For confirmation of this assumption, see Bujra, "Prostitution in Atu"; C. C. Zimmerman and P. C. Vaidhyakara, "A Demographic Study of Eight Oriental Villages Yet Largely Untouched by Western Culture," *Metron* 2 (1934): 179–98; R. van Gulik, *Le vie sexuelle dans la Chine ancienne* (Paris, 1971), 95 (translated from *Sexual Life in Ancient China* [Leiden, 1961]).

11. Hence, urban and commercial structures can engender prostitution even on a relatively small scale, such as the tiny hill towns of medieval Languedoc, often no larger than a good-sized village but exhibiting all the administrative and commercial trappings of a city.

12. Cash plays an essential role in prostitution because of its very impersonality and interchangeability. Although other remuneration is possible, it becomes difficult, in that case, to distinguish between a payment and a gift. The importance of the exchange of gifts in sentimental sexual relations is a phenomenon well known to anthropologists and was customary in the Middle

Ages, from women to men as well as vice versa. See, for example, Boccaccio, *The Decameron* (London: Penguin, 1981), 288, 362 (III-7, IV-4).

13. Schelsky, *Sociologie de la sexualité*, 65–80.

14. For a concise introduction to the history of the Occitanian language, see P. Bec, *La langue occitane*, Que sais-je? no. 1059 (Paris, 1978). An interesting general study of the Occitanian region is that edited by R. Lafont, *Le sud et le nord: dialectique de la France* (Toulouse, 1971).

15. The boundaries marked the limits of the lands represented in the assemblies of the Estates of Languedoc. See P. Dognon, *Les institutions politiques et administratives du pays de Languedoc du XIIIe siècle aux Guerres de Religion* (Paris, 1895), 215–17. The best introduction to the history of the region is the *Histoire du Languedoc*, edited by P. Wolff (Toulouse, 1967). The old French province of Langedoc should not be confused with the modern administrative creation Languedoc-Roussillon, which does not include the western and northern parts of the old province and which stretches farther south. For a list of the present-day *départements* corresponding to the old province of Languedoc, see the list of archives consulted. In addition to the Languedocian towns, I refer frequently to documents from Avignon and Arles, towns on the left bank of the Rhone River, which enjoyed regular contact with Languedocian urban centers.

16. A. Fliche, "L'état toulousain," in *Histoire des institutions françaises au moyen âge*, edited by F. Lot and R. Fawtier (Paris, 1957), 1:71–99.

17. Dognon, *Institutions de Languedoc*, 57–147; P.-C. Timbal, "Les villes de consulat dans le Midi de la France," *Société Jean Bodin, La Ville* 6 (1954): 343–70; J. H. Mundy, *Liberty and Political Power in Toulouse, 1050–1230* (New York, 1954).

18. J. Strayer, *The Albigensian Crusades* (New York, 1971); Dognon, *Institutions de Languedoc*, 124–47.

19. P. Wolff, *Commerce et marchands de Toulouse (vers 1350–vers 1450)* (Paris, 1954); K. L. Reyerson, "Commerce and Society in Montpellier, 1250–1350," diss., Yale University, 1974; G. Romestan, "Draperie roussillonaise et draperie languedocienne dans la première moitié du XIVe siècle," *FHL-Perpignan* (1969): 31–60. See also the numerous articles of J. Combes, including "Les foires en Languedoc au moyen âge," *An-ESC* 13 (1958): 231–59.

20. For the economic, social, and demographic history of the region, the most important studies are those of P. Wolff, many of which have been republished in *Regards sur le Midi médiéval* (Toulouse, 1979). See also E. Le Roy Ladurie, *Les paysans de Languedoc*, 2 vols. (Paris–The Hague, 1966).

21. See especially C. Portal, "Les insurrections des Tuchins dans le pays de Langue d'oc vers 1382–84," *Annales du Midi* 4 (1892): 433 ff.

22. These problems are discussed at greater length in the epilogue to part 2.

23. See A. Gouron, "Diffusion des consulats meridionaux et expansion du droit romain aux XIIe et XIIIe siècles," *BEC* 121 (1963): 26–76; and A. Gouron, "Enseignement du droit, légistes et canonistes dans le Midi de la France à la fin du XIIIe et au début du XIVe siècle," *RMT-SHD* 5 (1966): 1–33.

24. D. Herlihy and C. Klapisch-Zuber, *Les toscans et leurs familles: une étude du catasto florentin de 1427* (Paris, 1978).

25. A succinct introduction to the literature of Occitania is found in C. Camproux, *Histoire de la littérature occitane* (Paris, 1971). The prostitute in the *fabliaux* has been studied by M.-T. Lorcin in "La prostituée des fabliaux: est-elle intégrée ou exclue?" *Sénéfiance: Cahiers du Centre universitaire d'études et de recherches médiévales d'Aix-en-Provence* 1 (1977): 106–17, and in her *Fabliaux français*, 51–67. For the Italian literature, see C. Bec, *Les marchands écrivains: affaires et humanisme à Florence, 1375–1434*, Thèse-Lettres-Paris (Paris–The Hague, 1967), 177–97.

Prologue to Part One

1. By institutionalization I mean a situation in which the public authorities take an active role in the organization of the business of prostitution, as was common in many countries of Europe in the nineteenth century and in Germany today. By tolerance I mean a neutral attitude, neither repressing prostitution nor taking an active role in its organization.

2. For a detailed discussion of these problems, see below, "Prostitution before the Twelfth Century."

3. H. Gilles, *Les coutumes de Toulouse (1286) et leur premier commentaire (1296)* (Toulouse, 1969), 228.

4. B. Schnapper, for example, assumes that, because procuring was thus punished in the early sixteenth century, prostitution was, also, in his "La répression pénale au XVIᵉ siècle, l'exemple du Parlement de Bordeaux (1510–1565)," *RMT-SHD* 8 (1971): 1–54.

5. J. Rossiaud writes that prostitution as it was practiced in the fifteenth century was "a fundamental dimension of medieval society," in his "Prostitution, jeunesse et société dans les villes du sud-est au XVᵉ siècle," *An-ESC* 31 (1976): 312, although he cautions in a later article (*Communications*, 1982, 78) that municipally owned brothels were not a feature of urban life until the late fourteenth and fifteenth centuries.

6. See n. 86, chap. 4.

7. J. Sablou, "L'origine des privilèges de la foire de Beaucaire," *FHL–Sète-Beaucaire* (1956–57): 147–65.

8. This document is studied in chap. 1 (n. 9). The source of the error lies in the work of the seventeenth-century historian G. Catel. While the document is presented accurately in his *Histoire des comtes de Toulouse* (Toulouse, 1623), 228, his summary of this and other documents concerning Toulousan prostitution in his *Mémoires de l'histoire du Languedoc* (Toulouse, 1633), 187, is misleading, attributing to them a continuity that they lack. Doms Devic and Vaissette cited Catel to prove that in this period one assigned certain streets to prostitutes (*HGL* 6:938). Recently H. Gilles has written, "La prostitution . . . a toujours fait l'objet d'une réglementation administrative. . . . A Toulouse, Raymond VII avait cantonné les prostituées dans la rue de Com-

minges" (in his "La femme délinquante dans l'histoire du droit," *Annales de l'Université des sciences sociales de Toulouse* 27 [1979]: 249). The spurious connection between the document of 1201 and the municipally owned brothel of Toulouse was first explicitly made by G. Lafaille in his *Annales de la ville de Toulouse* (Toulouse, 1687), 1:185. His inexact paraphrase of Catel's paragraph reads, "Il y avoit anciennement dans Toulouse, de même que dans plusieurs autres villes de cette province, un lieu de débauche, qui étoit non seulement toléré, mais autorisé même par les Magistrats de cette ville, laquelle en tiroit un revenu annuel. . . . Au tems de nos comtes, cette maison étoit à la rue de Comenge, d'où elle fut transférée au fauxbourg Saint Cyprien, par une ordonnance des Capitouls de l'an 1201. . . ." Lafaille's paraphrase has been cited by Rabutaux in his *De la prostitution en Europe depuis l'antiquité jusqu'à la fin du XVIe siècle* (Paris, 1865), 92, and, hence, in most subsequent general histories of prostitution. C. Roumieux has paraphrased Lafaille in his unreliable *Etude sur la prostitution à Toulouse* (Toulouse, 1914), 6.

9. AM Toulouse, AA 5, no. 371; *Ord* 20:180–83.

10. R. van Gulik has encountered a similar problem in studying prostitution in China; there, too, later texts incorrectly attribute a great antiquity to public brothels (*Vie sexuelle dans la Chine ancienne*, 95).

11. See below, "Prostitution before the Twelfth Century."

12. *PL* 179:1384–85. J. Rossiaud has interpreted this passage to mean that William founded a brothel ("Prostitution, jeunesse et société," 313 n. 6); G. Duby, on the other hand, has appropriately described this foundation as "une abbaye joyeuse de concubines," in his *Le chevalier, la femme et le prêtre: le mariage dans la France féodale* (Paris, 1981), 168.

13. Edited by J. Ramière de Fortanier in his *Chartes de franchise du Lauragais* (Paris, 1939), 701–10.

14. J. O'Faolain and L. Martines, eds., *Not in God's Image: Women in History from the Greeks to the Victorians* (New York, 1973), 291; J. H. Mundy, *Europe in the High Middle Ages 1150/1309* (London, 1973), 219.

15. See n. 87, chap. 2.

16. Sabatier, *Histoire de la législation sur les femmes publiques* (Paris, 1828), 100–103; J. Decker, *Prostitution: Regulation and Control* (Littleton, Colo., 1979), 44; J.-G. Mancini, *Prostitution et proxénétisme*, Que sais-je? no. 999 (Paris, 1972), 25.

17. P. Pansier, "Histoire des prétendus statuts de la reine Jeanne et de la réglementation de la prostitution à Avignon au moyen âge," *Janus*, 1902: 1–24; Pansier, "Les prétendus statuts de la reine Jeanne réglementant la prostitution à Avignon en 1347," *BSFHMed* 17 (1923): 157–75. The problem of the falsification of documents exists, apparently, in other fields of the history of sexuality. See Boswell, *Homosexuality*, 17–18.

18. On health problems, see the epilogue to part 1.

19. There is, to my knowledge, no adequate modern monograph on the subject. The section on Roman prostitution is disappointingly short in S. Pomeroy, *Goddesses, Whores, Wives and Slaves: Women in Classical Antiquity* (New York, 1975), 201ff. See also E. Dupouy, *La prostitution dans l'antiquité*

(Paris, 1887), 140–44; and J.-J. Servais and J.-P. Laurend, *Histoire et dossier de la prostitution* (Paris, 1965), chap. 4.

20. "Aufer meretrices de rebus humanis, turbaveris omnia libidinibus." *De ordine* II.iv.: 12 (*PL* 32: 1000).

21. J. Vives, T. M. Martínez, and G. M. Díez, eds., *Concilios visigóticos e hispano-romanos* (Madrid, 1963), 4, 9.

22. V. L. Bullough summarizes the attitude of the Church toward the prostitute in his "The Prostitute in the Middle Ages," *Studies in Medieval Culture* 10 (1977): 9–17.

23. C. Verlinden, *L'esclavage dans l'Europe médiévale* (Bruges, 1955), 1:4; Cod. Theodos. 14. 8. 2.

24. "Unusquisque ministerialis palatinus diligentissima inquisitione discutiat primo homines suos et postea pares suos, si aliquem inter eos vel apud suos ignotum hominem vel meretricem latitantem invenire possit. Et si inventus homo aliquis vel aliqua femina huiusmodi fuerit, custodiatur, ne fugere possit, usque dum nobis adnuntietur. . . . Similiter de gadalibus et meretricibus volumus, ut apud quemcumque inventae fuerint ab eis portentur usque ad mercatum, ubi ipsae flagellandae sunt . . ." A. Boretius, ed., *Capitularia regum Francorum* in *MGH Legum Sectio II* (Hanover, 1883), 1: 297–98.

25. F. L. Ganshof uses this capitulary as a typical example of reform of order in the royal palace and underlines "the very limited place which legislation occupies in the capitularies," in his *Recherches sur les capitulaires* (Paris, 1958), 72, 104.

26. Ganshof has emphasized that the capitularies are translations and that one must "make an effort to discern the realities which the author intended to render by certain terms." Ibid., 55.

27. In the primitive societies of Rwanda (east Africa), for instance, the same word—*malaya*—signifies both prostitution and adultery. Bujra, "Prostitution in Atu," 18.

28. K. A. Eckhardt, ed., *Lex Salica* (Weimar, 1953), 164–65.

29. ". . . clanculo cum meretricibus, nec palam cum ancillulis." *PL* 106: 171.

30. See E. Delaruelle, "Jonas d'Orléans et le moralisme carolingien," *Bulletin de littérature ecclésiastique* 55 (1954): 224–25.

31. See Vanderkindere, "La condition de la femme et le mariage à l'époque mérovingienne," *Bulletin de l'Académie royale de Belgique*, 3rd ser., 15 (1888): 879–80; J. McNamara and S. Wemple, "Marriage and Divorce in the Frankish Kingdom," in *Women in Medieval Society*, edited by S. M. Stuard (Philadelphia, 1976), 98–99; Duby, *Mariage dans la France féodale*, 47ff. It is well known that Charlemagne kept concubines (see Einhard, *Vita Caroli* 3: 18). For clerical opposition to Frankish concubinage, see A. Esmein, *Le mariage en droit canonique*, 2nd ed. (Paris, 1929), 2:135–36. A number of capitularies from Louis the Pious's reign and later reiterate these ecclesiastical attacks on the concubinage of married men (*Capitularia* 1: 202, 376; 2: 45, 190).

Chapter One

1. "Palam quaestum facere dicemus non tantum eam, quae in lupanario se prostituit, verum etiam si qua (ut adsolet) in taberna cauponia vel qua alia pudori suo non parcit. Palam autem sic accipimus passim, hoc est sine dilectu: non si qua adulteris vel stupratoribus se committit, sed quae vicem prostitutae sustinet. Item quod cum uno et altero pecunia accepta commiscuit, non videtur palam corpore quaestum facere." D. 23. 2. 43. The following definition is found in *Lo Codi*: ". . . femna que pareis puta, zo es comunals puta per gadaing . . ." (in the Latin version, ". . . femina illa que est publice meretrix et accepit precium pro suo corpore . . ." 4: 30). Once the Justinianic corpus was rediscovered, most medieval jurists accepted and used Ulpian's definition. The canonists, too, relied on this definition, as well as on the less complete one of Saint Jerome: "[a woman] que multorum libidini patet" (D. 34 c. 16, citing Saint Jerome's Epistle 64.7 ad Fabiolem). There was some debate among jurists as to what number constituted "many." The author of the *fuero* (custom) of Teruel (Aragon), for instance, set the threshhold at five (*El fuero de Teruel*, edited by M. Gorosch [Stockholm, 1950], 227). For Thomas of Chobham in his *Summa confessorum*, however, the important factor was gain rather than promiscuity: "Meretrices inter mercenarios computantur. Locant enim corpora sua ad turpes usus . . ." (see n. 54, chap. 1).

2. A complete study of the twelfth-century jurists' references to prostitution is clearly beyond the scope of this book. The discussion is limited to a few general remarks based on three works that were well known in the south of France: the *Exceptiones Petri*, a commentary on the Digest, probably of Occitanian origin; *Lo Codi*, an Occitanian commentary on the Code; and the *Summa Codicis* of Placentinus. The following editions have been consulted: *Exceptiones Petri*, edited by C. G. Mor in *Exceptiones legum Romanorum, Scritti giuridici pre-ireniani*, vol. 2 (Rome, 1938); *Lo Codi in der lateinischen Übersetzung des Ricardus Pisanus*, edited by H. Fitting (Halle, 1906); *Lo Codi: eine Summa Codicis in provenzalischer Sprache. Die provenzalische Fassung der Handschrift A (Sorbonne 632)*, edited by F. Detter (Zurich, 1974); Placentinus, *Summa Codicis* (Mainz, 1536; reprint, Torino, 1962). The important secondary works are: P. de Tourtoulon, *Placentin, sa vie, ses oeuvres*, Thèse-Droit-Montpellier, 1896; P. Tisset, "Placentin et son enseignement à Montpellier," *RMT-SHD* 2 (1951):67–94; A. Gouron, "Les juristes de l'école de Montpellier," *Ius Romanum Medii Aevi* IV 3a (Milan, 1970): 1–35.

3. *Lo Codi* 4: 12; Placentinus, *Summa Codicis* 4: 7. It is interesting to note that, in this passage, Placentinus makes one of his rare direct references to Montpellier (see Tourtoulon, *Placentin*, 104). Irnerius also uses the same argument in his *Summa Codicis*, edited by H. Fitting (Berlin, 1894), 77. Most medieval jurists, including the canonists, accepted this argument. See J. Brundage, "Prostitution in the Medieval Canon Law," *Signs* 1 (1976): 837.

4. *Lo Codi* 4: 30; *Exceptiones Petri* 4: 35; Placentinus, *Summa Codicis* 4: 20.

5. ". . . nobiles et honestos viros et meretrices publicas et earum filias." *Exceptiones Petri* 1:29.

6. The Code declares invalid marriage between a senator and the daughter of a brothel keeper (among other humble people), Cod. 5. 5. 7. What is noteworthy is that the author of the *Exceptiones* has transformed the parties involved in this prohibition into medieval people, thus giving the passage, integrated into his commentary on the Digest, a contemporary relevance.

7. The only contemporary copy of these customs is undated. They cannot have been written before 1205, however, as their first eighty-three articles are based on the customs of Montpellier of 1204 and on another document from Montpellier dated 1205. A. Gouron has judged them to be from just after 1209, because of internal evidence, in his "*Libertas hominum montispessulani*: rédaction et diffusion des coutumes de Montpellier," *Annales du Midi* 90 (1978): 302–4.

8. "Meretrices publice foras muros Carcassonne emittantur." The best edition is that of A. Teulet, *Layettes du Trésor des Chartes* (Paris, 1863), 1:272–81. Teulet explains that the original document is filled with scribal errors that must be corrected. In article 105, he has corrected *meretrices* for *heretices*; it is stipulated in article 84 that heretics are to be chased from the region.

9. AM Toulouse, AA 1, 27; II 61. Published by R. Limouzin-Lamothe in his *La commune de Toulouse et les sources de son histoire (1120–1249)* (Toulouse, 1932), 316–17. The document is a copy dated 1204.

10. ". . . quod nulla meretrix publica in predicta carraria nec infra muros urbis Tolose et suburbii non permaneret nec ullo modo aliquo tempore habitaret." *Suburb* here means the *bourg* of Toulouse, therefore the center of town (Mundy, *Political Power in Toulouse*, 221).

11. ". . . quod probi homines, qui tunc in predicta carraria vel infra muros urbis Tolose et suburbii steterint, illas meretrices publicas de illa carraria et de aliis carrariis, que infra muros urbis Tolose et suburbii sunt, deinde eicerent et exire facerent et quod inde non tenerentur vicario nec alicui viventi."

12. A similar policy was enforced in Italy in the thirteenth century. A statute from the town of Padua (dating from before 1236), for example, states, "Omnes publicae meretrices expellantur extra muros civitatis et extra fossas suburbiorum." A. Pertile, *Storia del diritto italiano* (Torino, 1892), 5:539–40.

13. See n. 8, prologue to part 1.

14. There is one document that might seem to contradict this conclusion. The customs of Meyrueis (Lozère), dated 1229 but surviving only in a cartulary copy from the seventeenth century (published by F. Cazalis in *Bulletin de la Société de Lozère* 13 [1862]: 262–80), include an article on prostitutes which refers to a neighborhood designated for them: "Item, meretrices debent stare extra Castrum et *debet eis locus designari extra Castrum* et si nollent exire de Castro et aliquis homo vel domina videret, vel cognosceret ipsam male regnantem poterit eam expellere de domo, et de Castro propria auctoritate et non tenetur Curiae, neque sibi si tamen Vicarius requisitus istud pre-

mitus facere noluerit" (italics mine). Another article seems to show the influence of the definition of Ulpian: "Meretrices vocantur illae quae publice peccant; si tamen mulieres caute peccant et timent verecundium, sive sunt conjugatae, sive non, non dicuntur meretrices neque debent infamari." It is unlikely that the date borne by the document is accurate. No other customs from the Gévaudan dating from the thirteenth century are known. The only study of this text is a brief one that does not deal with the problematical authenticity of the document: G. Dumas, "Les coutumes et le consulat de Meyrueis du XIIIe au XVIIe siècle," *FHL*-Mende (1955): 49–55. Only a thorough study of the whole content of this document could give a firmer idea of the date and circumstances of its composition.

15. "Statuimus quod nulla meretrix publica vel leno audeat morari in Arelate in carreria proborum hominum, et si forte invenirentur in dictis locis, quod quilibet illius contrate vel vicinie habeat potestatem expellendi de vicinia, sua auctoritate, et sine pena et contradictione curie." C. Giraud, *Essai sur l'histoire du droit français au moyen âge* (Paris, 1846), 2:205. These statutes were revised and published for the last time in late 1245 and early 1246. See Anibert, *Mémoires sur l'ancienne république d'Arles* (Yverdon, 1779), 3:259–62.

16. "We statute that public prostitutes and procuresses should in no way stay in an area or neighborhood of honest people, nor dare to wear veils; indeed, married public prostitutes shall be expelled completely from the whole city, and, if they go against this measure, be punished according to the decision of the court. Whether prostitutes dare to wear a coat, however, shall be determined by the decision of the *potestas*." "Statuimus quod publice meretrices et ruffiane seu destrales in contracta seu vicinia honestarum personarum nullatenus commorentur, nec vela defferre audeant; meretrices vero publice conjugate a tota civitate penitus expellantur, et, si contrafecerint, arbitrio curie puniantur: utrum autem meretrices publice mantellum defferre audeant, sit in arbitrio potestatis." M. A. R. de Maulde, *Coutumes et règlements de la république d'Avignon au XIIIe siècle* (Paris, 1879), 191. The last revision of these customs was made in 1246. See L.-H. Labande, *Avignon au XIIIe siècle* (Paris, 1908; reprint, Marseille, 1975), 157–65.

17. *Destral* was an Occitanian word for procuress. In 1343 a woman resident of Aix-en-Provence was fined 10 s. for having called a countess "viella destral" and her daughter "puta saguenta" (AD Bouches-du-Rhone, B 1627, Inv. Blancard). On procurers, see chap. 6.

18. The *potestas* (executive power) was to decide whether prostitutes might wear coats. Veils were not to be worn. In Arles, too, a statute forbade the wearing of veils (Giraud, *Droit français* 2:206). See n. 20, chap. 5.

19. de Maulde, *Coutumes d'Avignon*, 200. See n. 75, chap. 4.

20. ". . . ni tabernariis, vel trichariis, vel lupanaribus, vel domibus meretricum, seu albergariis." Ibid., 166.

21. Giraud, *Droit français* 2:206.

22. See L. Buisson, *König Ludwig IX und das Recht* (Freiburg, 1954).

23. An analysis of the drafting and publication of this ordinance, the pre-

paratory work to an upcoming critical edition, is found in L. Carolus-Barré, "La grande ordonnance de 1254," *Actes des Colloques de Royaumont et de Paris, 21–27 mai 1970* (Paris, 1976), 85–96. Carolus-Barré identifies the authors of this ordinance: a knight who had been on crusade with Saint Louis, a citizen of Chartres, two Franciscans, and the eminent jurist from Saint-Gilles, Gui Foucois, who was later to become Pope Clement IV (1265–68). The author states that "a perfect communion of mind existed between Saint Louis and Gui Foucois." See also Y. Dossat, "Gui Foucois, enquêteur-réformateur, archévêque et pape," *Cahiers de Fanjeaux*, Les évêques, les clercs et le roi (1250–1300), 7 (1972): 23–57.

24. "Expellantur autem publice meretrices, tam de campis, quam de villis, et factis monitionibus, seu prohibitionibus, bona earum per locorum judices capiantur, vel eorum auctoritate a quolibet occupentur, etiam usque ad tunicam vel ad pellicium. Qui vero domum publice meretrici locaverit scienter, volumus quod ipsa domus incidat domino a quo tenebitur in comissum." *Ord* 1:74. Included is the French translation. The Occitanian translation has been published by G. Mouynès in his *Inventaire des Archives de Narbonne, annexe à la série AA* (Narbonne, 1871), 87. Although seizure in feudal commission is the punishment prescribed in the original Latin text, a second version exists which stipulates that the owner, must pay the value of a year's rent of the house to the local bailiff or judge: ". . . quantum valet pensio domus uno anno, Baillivo loci, vel judici solvere teneatur." *Ord* 1:74. It is this version which appears in the contemporary French translation.

25. See the prologue to part 1.

26. See F. Olivier-Martin, "Le roi de France et les mauvaises coutumes au moyen âge," *ZSSR* (*ger. Abt.*) 58 (1938): 117–21. The distinction between good and bad customs finds its origin in canon law.

27. "Item que toutes foles femmes et ribaudes communes soient boutées et mises hors de toutes nos bonnes citez et villes especiallement qu'elles soient boutées hors des rues qui sont en cuer desdites bonnes villes, et mises hors des murs, et loing de tous lieus saints, comme églises et cimetières. Et quiconque loera maison nulle esdites citez et bonnes villes, et lieux à ce non establis, à foles fammes communes, ou les recevra en sa maison, il rendra et payera aux establis à ce garder de par nous le loyer de la maison d'un an." *Ord* 1:79.

28. The contrast between the policies on prostitution outlined in the two texts is seen in an article regulating the behavior of royal officers. In the ordinance of 1254, seneschals and other officers were ordered to abstain from swearing, gaming, "fornication and taverns" (*a fornicatione vel tabernis*); in 1256, however, in a virtually identical passage, officers are requested to stay away from "brothels and taverns" (*de bordeaux et de tavernes*). In 1254 brothels, theoretically, did not exist; in 1256 their existence was grudgingly acknowledged.

29. See N. Didier, *La garde des églises au XIIIᵉ siècle*, Thèse-Droit-Grenoble, 1927, 157–204.

30. "Coeterum notoria et manifesta prostibula, quae fidelem populum sua foeditate maculant, et plures protrahunt in perditionis interitum, penitus exterminari praecipimus, tam in villis, quam extra, et ab aliis flagitiis et flagitio-

sis hominibus, ac malefactoribus publicis, terram nostram plenius expurgari."
Ord 1:105.

31. C. Ghisalberti, "La teoria del notorio nel diritto comune," *Annali di storia del Diritto* 1 (1957):403–51; J. P. Lévy, "La hiérarchie des preuves dans le droit savant du moyen âge," *Annales de l'Université de Lyon*, 3rd ser., Droit 5 (1939):32–66.

32. Novella 14 provides severe punishments for procurers and brothel keepers (see the prologue to part 1). A viewpoint similar to that of Louis IX's letter of 1269 is seen in the *Livres de jostice et de plet*, a contemporary law treatise reflecting the influence of canon and Roman law, as well as that of the customary law of Orléans and Capetian legislation. No mention is made in this work of the punishment of prostitutes; indeed, their reinsertion into society is facilitated, following the precepts of canon law (see n. 96, chap. 4). The procurer (*maquerel de femmes*) and brothel keeper (*cil qui fet desloiaux assemblée de bordelerie*), on the other hand, are to be banished and their goods confiscated. The brothel keeper is found in a list of the infamous (*de mal renomez*). *Li livres de jostice et de plet*, edited by Rapetti (Paris, 1850), 104, 182, 279–84, 323. See also E. Chénon, "Le droit romain à la *curia regis*," in *Mélanges Fitting* (Montpellier, 1907), 1:197–212.

33. AM Arles, FF 4. See n. 36, chap. 4.

34. "Quod Robinus de Lis, qui se appellat Regem Ribaudorum, accipit de singulis meretricibus, que morantur in villa, xii denarios, et de illis que morantur in campis, vi denarios . . . predicti domini responderunt precipientes quod expellatur ribaudus, et de meretricibus servetur statutum." AM Arles, FF 4. Charles of Anjou himself apparently published an order to his officers to expel procurers from Provence. I have not been able to consult this document (reference given as *Grand coutumier de Provence* 1:1243).

35. See n. 15, chap. 1.

36. V. L. Bourilly, "Essai sur l'histoire politique de la commune de Marseille," *Annales de la Faculté des Lettres d'Aix-en-Provence* 12 (1919–20): 189–92.

37. These articles have been reprinted in H. Mireur, *La prostitution à Marseille* (Paris and Marseille, 1882), 365–67.

38. ". . . puniatur inde in tantum quantum erit loguerium illius domus annuatim . . ." Ibid., 366. See n. 27, chap. 1.

39. The statutes include a definition of the prostitute that clearly derives from Ulpian's: "Publica autem meretrix intelligitur quae publice in lupanari seu meretricali domo, vel quae se palam questum faciendo supponit, vel ad ejus mansionem duo plures vel de die vel de nocte velut ad publicam mulierem confuerint publice, animo sive causa vel gracia libidinis seu luxurie cum ea faciende." Ibid., 367.

40. Bourilly, "Histoire politique de Marseille," 189–92.

41. AM Toulouse, II 77. Published by G. Boyer in his "Remarques sur l'administration de Toulouse au temps d'Alphonse de Poitiers," *RMT-SHD* 3 (1955):6–10. The document is a copy dated 1298.

42. Saint Cyprien was not within the walls of the city in the thirteenth century (Mundy, *Political Power in Toulouse*, 8). The residents appealed to the

vicar of Alphonse, not to the consuls; the expulsion was considered a *libertas*, sold to the citizens for the price of a silver cup (*ciphum argentum*), not an enforcement of a city law. Cf. above (n. 9).

43. "... vicarius Tholose ... propter utilitatem publicam et ad evitandum pecata que ibi publice fiebant et inhoneste ... dedit et consesit talem libertatem [to the residents of the street, listed in the text] quod de cetero nulla meretrix publica audeat stare ... seu fornicari vel se permiti cognosci carnaliter ... [in Saint Cyprien] ... et si hoc predicte meretrices faciebant vel ausu temerario atemptabant, predicte persone supra nominate ... possint eam vel eas sua propria auctoritate expellere inde et denudare et ipsas ad dictum dominum vicarium vel ejus successorem vel successores adducere nudas vel indutas puniendas ad arbitrium ipsius domini vicarii vel ejus successorum ..."

44. See n. 24, chap. 1. One other document shows the attitude of the Alphonsine administration toward prostitution. In the course of an inquest carried out in Poitou in 1259, two of Alphonse's commissioners, both Dominicans, ordered the prevost of Poitiers to cease accepting money from the city's prostitutes: "Nos, de speciali verbo et mandato domini comitis, ordinavimus quod prepositus Pictavensis nullam redemtionem de cetero accipiat a stultis mulieribus seu meretricibus, sicut consuetum erat ab antiquo, ut eas *deffenderet et gariret* [crossed out and changed to *permitteret manere in villa*]." They even reimbursed a portion of the sum prevost was to receive (45 out of 360 l.)! P.-F. Fournier and P. Guébin, eds., *Enquêtes administratives d'Alphonse de Poitiers* (Paris, 1959), 84b, 113, 117b.

45. See below, p. 27.

46. See below, pp. 36–37.

47. "Meretrices publice ponantur extra muros in omnibus villis." Published by P. Timbal in his *Un conflit d'annexion au moyen âge: l'application de la coutume de Paris au pays d'albigeois* (Toulouse and Paris, 1950), 177–84.

48. See n. 8, chap. 1. Timbal limits himself to saying that this article was one of "several police measures, usual in charters of medieval customs." Ibid., 19.

49. According to Y. Bongert in her *Cours d'histoire du droit pénal* (Paris, 1973), I:174.

50. J. Le Foyer, *Exposé du droit pénal normand au XIIIᵉ siècle*, Thèse-Droit-Paris, 1931, 96–97. The *Très ancien coutumier* of Brittany has a similar measure (Bongert, *Droit pénal* I:182).

51. J. Boca, *La justice criminelle de l'échevinage d'Abbeville 1184–1516*, Thèse-Droit-Lille, 1930, 200–202. See n. 11, chap. 6.

52. See chap. 4.

53. J. Baldwin, *Masters, Princes and Merchants: The Social Views of Peter the Chanter and His Circle* (Princeton, 1970), I:133–37.

54. "Licet meretrices et histriones non suspendantur ab ingressu ecclesie, debent tamen suspendi ab acessu altari." Thomas of Chobham, *Summa Confessorum*, edited by F. Broomfield, in *Analecta Medievalia Namurcensia* 25 (Louvain and Paris, 1968):349. For his definition of the prostitute, see n. 1, chap. 1.

55. "Si publica meretrix fuerit incorrigibilis expelli debet extra castra nec scandalizet alios." *Summa* 14:15, quoted in Baldwin, *Peter the Chanter* 2:95.

56. "Inhibemus etiam ne publicae meretrices, quarum cohabitatio ex frequenti usu ad nocendum efficacior pestis est, intra civitatem vel oppida permittantur habitare, immo potius iuxta leprosorum consuetudinem sequestrentur. Quod si praemonitae secedere noluerint, per excommunicationis sententiam percellantur." G. Mansi, ed., *Sacrorum conciliorum nova et amplissima collection* (Florence, 1759–1927), 22:854.

57. In his *Policraticus*, John of Salisbury had recommended that the prince "exclude" prostitutes and *jongleurs*: "Nam de histrionibus . . . meretricibus, lenonibus . . . quae principem potius oportet exterminare, quam fovere . . . quae quidem omnes abominationes istas, non modo à principis aula excludit, sed eliminat à populo Dei" (4:4). But the emphasis of this text is on the private life of the prince, which should conform to divine law (the chapter's title is "Divinae legis autoritate constat principem legi iustitiae esse subiectum"). Even the recommendation that such people be "eliminated from the people of God" is reminiscent of Old Testament strictures rather than evocative of the practical problem of prostitution in a medieval town, so evident in the opinions of Robert of Coursson.

58. It is interesting to note that Robert made an excursion in Languedoc in 1214 (Baldwin, *Peter the Chanter* 1:21).

59. The registers of justice of the churches and monasteries of Paris contain several references to punishments inflicted, not only on those convicted of procuring or brothel keeping, but also what would appear to be simple prostitutes (*fames de chans, folles de leur cors*). L. Tanon, *Histoire de justices des églises et communautés monastiques de Paris, suivie des registres inédits de St-Maur-des-Fosses, Ste-Geneviève, St-Germain-des-Prés, et du registre de St-Martin-des-Champs* (Paris, 1883), 347–86 passim, 413–79 passim, 544. It is possible that these ecclesiastical courts were applying the canonical strictures against fornication, not punishing prostitution specifically. The term *folle de son corps* was not limited to the designation of professional prostitutes; Beaumanoir, for example, maintained that a husband had the right to punish his wife in the case that she should "faire folie de son corps." *Coutumes du Beauvaisis*, edited by A. Salmon (Chartres, 1900; reprint, Paris, 1970), 2:332.

60. *De regimine principum* 4:14; *Summa* 2:2, quest. 10, art. 11.

61. When I speak of a "positive" policy on prostitution, I do not mean to imply that the authorities encouraged prostitution, but simply that they agreed actively to organize it, defining where prostitutes should live, rather than limiting the law to the traditional "negative" policy of specifying where they should *not* live.

Chapter Two

1. AM Montpellier, Louvet 146. Edited by A. Germain, in his "Statuts inédits des Repenties du couvent de Saint-Gilles de Montpellier," *MSAMtp* 5 (1860–69):124–26.

2. The town of Montpellier was, in fact, divided in two—the smaller, east-

ern part under the lordship of the bishop of Maguelone; and the more impor-
tant, western part, a secular seigneury originally ruled by a local dynasty (the
"Guilhems," after the first name taken by its members). The king of Aragon,
Peter II, acquired this secular seigneury through marriage in 1204; in 1276
Montpellier passed to his grandson, James II (also referred to as James I of
Majorca). See A. Germain, *Histoire de la commune de Montpellier* (Mont-
pellier, 1851), 2:64–124.

3. "The legislation of the kings of France had no influence there." A.
Gouron, "La *potestas statuendi* dans le droit coutumier montpellierain du
treizième siècle," in *Atti del Convegno di Varenna (12–15 giugno 1979)*
(Milan, 1980), 114.

4. ". . . quod dicte mulieres semper et in perpetuum debeant permanere et
residenciam facere in dicta via seu carreria Ville nove que . . . appellatur Carreria Calida."

5. There would seem to have been a shift in policy on prostitution at the
court of Aragon-Majorca in this period. James II's father, James the Conqueror, had granted the residents of Biar the right to expel Saracen prostitutes
from that town ("expellere . . . omnes putas seu meretrices sarracenas") in
1258 (J. Miret y Sans, *Itinerari de Jaume I "el Conqueridor"* [Barcelona,
1918], 275–76). The Conqueror's son, Peter III of Aragon (James II's brother),
on the other hand, included Saracen prostitutes in the special tax imposed
on every Mudejar household in Valencia in 1281. R. I. Burns, *Islam under
the Crusaders: Colonial Survival in the Kingdom of Valencia* (Princeton,
1973), 96.

6. The earliest reference to a district officially reserved for prostitutes in the
published Italian documents is a text from Venice dated 1340, which records
that Rivoalti, the local red-light district, was under consular jurisdiction.
C. Calza, "Documenti sulla prostituzione in Venezia," *Giornale italiano
delle malattie veneree* 4 (1869), 1:309.

7. See n. 2, chap. 2.

8. The antiquity and international reputation of the medieval school of
medicine in Montpellier has been attributed to Arabic influence via Spanish
Jews, who "in the intellectual life of such cities as Narbonne, Béziers, Lunel
and especially Montpellier, seem to have played a prominent role." H. Wie-
ruszowski, *The Medieval University* (Princeton and New York, 1966), 78.
R. Nelli attributes much in the ideas and form of Occitanian troubadour po-
etry to Arabic influence via Spain, in his *L'érotique des troubadours* (Toulouse, 1963).

9. E. Levi-Provençal relates that, under the caliphate of Cordua in the tenth
century, prostitutes were obliged to pay a special tax, in his *Le siècle du ca-
lifat de Cordoue*, vol. 3 of his *Histoire de l'Espagne musulmanne* (Paris,
1967), 446. R. I. Burns states that "Ibn 'Abdun provides for control of this
class [of prostitutes] in twelfth-century Seville" (*Islam under the Crusaders:
Kingdom of Valencia*, 95). A. Mazahéri believes that this tax on prostitution,
contrary, of course, to the spirit of the Koran, was a development of the tenth
century, as it is attested to in Persia, Egypt, and the Iberian peninsula by the
end of the tenth century, whereas a Moslem of Siraf who had traveled to

China (where he had seen prostitutes taxed) had declared in 912, "God be thanked that . . . in Islamic countries, we do not tax such a thing." A. Maza-héri, *La vie quotidienne des musulmans au moyen âge, X^3–XIIIe siècle* (Paris, 1951), 64–65. I regret that material and linguistic problems have prevented my exploring this matter more deeply.

10. *Ord* 1:296.

11. C. Compayré, *Etudes historiques et documents inédits sur l'Albigeois* (Albi, 1841), 400. This article may have been inspired by a passage from a charter granted to Cordes by Raymond VII in 1222. See chap. 6 (n. 4).

12. See chap. 1 (n. 30).

13. See the prologue to part 1 (n. 13) and chap. 2 (n. 87).

14. "Un petit instrument . . . de l'anné mil trois cens quatre, contenant ordonnance de messeiurs les reformateurs depputez par le Roy. Par laquelle à la requision du Pere—des Cordelliers et des nobles et bourgeois de Beau-caire, les putains que residoien et faiseoien la habitation audit Beaucaire, en certaine rue lors appelée de La Laguque, sont chassées et deshabitées de la rue. Ladite ordonnance executée du mandement de lieutenant de viguyer par le soubzviguier de ladite ville." AM Beaucaire, II 2, nonfoliated (listed under index heading "Putains").

15. "Item aultres lettres royaux contenant comission au senechal de Beau-caire de faire voyder les femmes publiques des maisons lesquelles habitoient audit Alez." Dated 18 August 1312, Paris. AM Alès, iiiD 3, 212v. Indicated by A. Bardon in his *Histoire de la ville d'Alais 1250–1340* (Nîmes, 1894), 47. Both Beaucaire and Alès were firmly within the royal domain by the reign of Philip III. R. Michel, *L'administration royale dans la sénéchaussée de Beaucaire au temps de Saint Louis* (Paris, 1910), 13–19, 137–40.

16. Philip III had succeeded in establishing his right to hear appeals from Montpellier by 1281 (Germain, *Histoire de Montpellier* 2:84–89). Philip IV actually purchased the smaller eastern seigneury of Montpellieret from the bishop of Maguelone in 1292, thus establishing a foothold in the town. French royal hegemony was not complete, however, until the purchase of the western part of Montpellier from the king of Majorca in 1349.

17. On this problem, see H. de Tarde, *Conflits de pouvoir dans la séné-chaussée de Carcassonne: pouvoir royal et pouvoir seigneurial, 1270–1314*, Thèse-Droit-Montpellier, 1975.

18. "Aviatz senhors aviatzo de part de mosenher l'arsevesque de Narbona et de mosenher Aamalric vescomte et senhor de Narbona ab cosselh de pro-homes de cieutat e de borc, que totz alcaotz et tota bagassa de segle sian fora de Narbona e de sos termenis d'aqui a di ious providanamen venen, en pena de correr la viala e de bon batre." AM Narbonne, FF 602. This is largely a repetition of a Latin regulation published by the viscount and archbishop in January 1299, against which the consuls of the *Bourg* protested, because it had been published without the council of *prud'hommes* (FF 610).

19. "Quod rectores universitatis de burgo meretrices de domibus sibi con-ductis auctoritate propria valeant expellere, cum baiuli nostri super hoc suffi-cienter requisiti et promissis negligentes fuerint et remissi." AM Bourg-Saint-Andéol, AA 2. Indicated by H. Courteault in his *Bourg-Saint-Andéol*

(Paris, 1909), 229. G. Dahm cites similar documents calling for the expulsion of prostitutes from Italian cities, also dating from the early fourteenth century, in his *Das Strafrecht Italiens im ausgehenden Mittelalter* (Berlin and Leipzig, 1931), 410. For Aragon, see n. 5, chap. 2.

20. "Item queritur si conjugatus accedat ad domum ubi communiter reperiuntur mulieres pro peccunia ut puta in domo de Nag. Cagarafes in carreria Bertrandi David, credens haber rem cum soluta et erat uxorata, an committat adulterium. Respondeo non, quia locus ipsum excusat." Gilles, *Coutumes de Toulouse*, 255–56.

21. "Item mandatus dicta curia quod nulla mulier que pro pecunia se dimittat sit ausa stare infra civitatem Nemausi nec extra, nisi in postribulo publi[c]o Nemausi . . . sub pena perdendi raubam et fustigandi per villam." AM Nîmes, FF 1, no. 4. The word *postribulum* is not a scribal error; this was the current spelling, rather than the classical Latin *prostibulum*. See the prologue to part 2.

22. ". . . quod omnes mulieres vane et [illegible] dimitunt pro denario homini ab inde in anthea [illegible] et stent in hospitio Petri Rascacee scito extra Portam Stephani in carreira vocata de Naquintuna . . ." AM Uzès, BB 1, 3v. In the same year, it may be noted, the town was granted a consulate.

23. *Le Livre Vert de Lacaune*, edited by Gautran (Bergerac, 1911), 200–202. I am grateful to Jean-Marie Carbasse for calling this text to my attention.

24. The manuscript inventory of the archives of Lunel (Hérault) by Thomas Millerot includes an intriguing entry, no. 1785, dated July 1341: "Appel des consuls . . . portant défense . . . Aux putains, maquerelles et autres femmes lubriques de venir à l'auditoire [?], et ordonnant qu'il leur soit établi un bordel en lieu particulier." The original document, unfortunately, has been lost. In the deliberations of the council of Marseille dated March 16, 1339, a judge expelled *meretrices* from Bellande Street, indicating that they might live if they wished "in carreria Guarriam . . . ubi antiquo tempore teneri prostibulum est consuetum" (Mireur, *Prostitution à Marseille*, 26).

25. ". . . nos dictus Aymericus . . . damus . . . et liberaliter concedimus vobis dictis consulibus . . . ut scandala et mala plurima que acthenus in villa Narbone contigisse dicuntur et evitari debeant, quod sit et esse possit ab hinc in antea postribulum, lupanar seu carraria Calida in aliquo loco ydoneo Narbone . . . sub eisdem modis, formis, privilegiis, usibus et consuetudinibus universis sub quibus est et esse consuevit postribulum . . . in Montepessullano, ita videlicet quod in dicto postribulo . . . eligendo non possit per subvicarium vel servientes Curie nostre vel alias gentes nostras capi, de die vel de nocte, adulteria . . ." AM Narbonne, AA 7; edited by Mouynès in his *Narbonne Inv. AA*, 263–78.

26. Ibid., 265.

27. Ibid., 285.

28. Although no mention is made in the document of 1285 of such "privileges," it may be significant that the Hot Street of Montpellier was established by a decision of the bailiff, not of the king's lieutenant, who normally heard appeals and was the final arbiter in disputed matters (Germain, *Histoire de*

Montpellier 1:129ff.). The king had issued letters expelling prostitutes from various neighborhoods where they had previously been assigned, probably by the consuls, who were in charge of the police of the town. The bailiff (a resident of the town chosen with the approval of the consuls) may have been considered an appropriate arbiter in a dispute that perhaps opposed the majority of *burgenses* and the prostitutes against the royal officers, the regular clergy, and a minority of the *burgenses*.

29. For a similar correlation between the enforcement of laws on morality and the increase of political authority, see the epilogue to part 1. For the relation of this struggle to the changing morality of the day, see the epilogue to part 2.

30. See n. 9, chap. 1.

31. Gilles, *Coutumes de Toulouse*, 255–56.

32. AM Toulouse, AA 45, no. 49. The document is a royal amnesty granted to participants in riots in which the house of royal officers had been the principal target. Other places attacked and pillaged were the "domus ubi meretrices publice."

33. M. J. Chalande, "La maison publique municipale aux XVᵉ et XVIᵉ siècles à Toulouse," *Mémoire de l'Académie des sciences, inscriptions et belles lettres de Toulouse*, 10th ser., 11 (1911): 64–86.

34. The individuals paid the municipality a sum of money in exchange for the rights to all the profits they could make from the property. See chap. 3.

35. AM Toulouse, CC 2284, 29, 4, 27: "Prezas dels arendamens . . . Item del hostal delas femnas, 60 l."; "loguier del hostal delas filhas, 60 francs"; "a Johan Garnier per recubir la mayzo delas filhas, 3 l."

36. AM Toulouse, CC 1848.

37. The financial documents are laconic for the rest of the fourteenth century. The account book of 1385–87 lists among the farms "le bordel," but gives only a lump sum for all the farms (AM Toulouse, CC 1851, 131v). The brothel is not listed among the farms in the account book of 1391–92 (for an explanation of this absence, see n. 57, chap. 2), yet we find an entry detailing expenses for its repair (CC 1854, 87r: "an Guiraut Regant e an Bernat Arnaut recubeyres . . . xxvi octobre l'an desus per reparar e reciribir l'ostal del bordel . . . 6 l. 10 s.").

38. Published anonymously in the *Revue du Tarn* 8 (1890–91): 319–20. The original has apparently disappeared. For an explanation of "running the town," see n. 21, chap. 6.

39. L. de Lacger, "Castres: son affranchissement communal et ses deux enceintes successives, XIIᵉ–XIVᵉ siècles," *Revue du Tarn*, 1936: 235–47.

40. "Si fara om hostal alas femnas publicas al portal de la Tholosana. . . . Foc aponchat que om l'on compre l'ostal de Bela Sela e que aqui demoro." AM Castres, BB 5, 6v. It is interesting to note that the consuls proposed to place the prostitutes near their old neighbors, the Trinitarians. Thus, it seems that whole neighborhoods were reconstituted within the city walls.

41. "Que las putanas corrio al bordel de foras." AM Castres, BB 5, 8r.

42. "Si publicara om la ordenansa delas femnas publicas laquel es senhada per lo loctenen. del jucge. Aponchat que se publique." AM Castres, BB 5,

14r. The reference is probably to the lieutenant of the judge of criminal juris-diction, a seigneurial officer. L. Barbaza, *Annales de Castres* (Castres, 1886), 171, 198.

43. "Item que per esquerar a evitar maiors perilhs, volgro totz que las fem-nas venals que volran venir per estar en esta vila dedins la vila puescan venir a estar dedins vila en 1 hostal alor assignada en la partida que ordenaran los senhors a despens de las filhas que venran." AM Castres, BB 8, 67r.

44. No municipal deliberations have been preserved from this later period in Castres. There are several account books from the fifteenth century, but, because of the way the brothel was run, no mention is found of it in these books.

45. AD Haute Garonne, B 15, 25r.

46. See G. Prat, "Albi et la Peste Noire," *Annales du Midi* 64 (1952): 15–26; *HGL* 9:239ff.

47. L. de Lacger, *L'evêque, le roi, le clergé et la commune à Albi pendant la seconde moitié du XIVe siècle* (Albi, 1920).

48. ". . . quod dicto domino episcopo, ratione dicte sue iurisdictionis que habet in dictis civitate et pertinentiis, pertinet et pertinere debet assignare locum, carrerias et hospitia in quibus publice meretrices in dicta civitate et suburbiis comorantes habeant morare, et illas de una carreria in aliam mutare, prout necessitas et utilitas publica exigit." AM Albi, FF 38, no. 6, 23 May 1366.

49. Published document no. 1. A. Viala mentions this incident, citing the Collection Doat (BN), CIV, 40, and giving an erroneous reading of the text: ". . . les consuls ayant par esprit de rancune déplacé la maison publique près du monastère Saint Antoine." A. Viala, *Le Parlement de Toulouse et l'admin-istration royale, 1420–1525* (Albi, 1953), 1:554.

50. AM Albi, FF 44.

51. On 29 August, the carpenter Ramon Marens was paid for work done in various places, including "the passage in front of the brothel" (la passada davan lo bordel). A. Vidal, *Douze comptes consulaires d'Albi du XIVe siècle* (Toulouse, 1906), 1:325.

52. A. Vidal, "Les délibérations du conseil communal d'Albi de 1372 à 1388," *Revue des langues romanes*, 5th ser., 6 (1903):564.

53. ". . . la cort de moss. d'Albi ha requeregutz los senhors cossols que els vuelho provesir de far .1. hostal que sia bordel de foras la vila, en que estiau de dias las avols femnas, et autre hostal dins vila en que estiau la nueg . . ." Vidal, "Délibérations," 421.

54. The often close association between places of prostitution and the world of criminality in this period has been amply verified. B. Geremek, *Les mar-ginaux parisiens aux XIVe et XVe siècles* (Paris, 1976); P. Champion, "Notes pour servir à l'histoire des classes dangereuses en France," in L. Sainéan, *Les sources de l'argot ancien* (Paris, 1912), 1:341–422; J. Garnier, *Les Compa-gnons de la Coquille* (Dijon, 1842).

55. ". . . per raso del loguier del sen hostal del temp que lo avian tengut occupat las femnas publicas del bordel . . . v s." AM Albi, CC 434, 89r.

56. Besides labor, expenses included purchase of large quantities of tiles,

bricks, mortar, and wood, the total costs coming to 11 l. 9 s. 5 d. Vidal, "Comptes," 112, 115, 116, 134, 135, 141.

57. AM Albi, CC 435. See also a relevant entry in the consular account books (Vidal, "Comptes," 124). John of Clermont had been active in Toulouse, too. An account entry dated 19 September 1391 reads, ". . . per la exequcio que abia faita contra la universitat de la viela de Tholosa de mandament de mestre Johan de Clarmont comessan deputat sus lo fait dels amortozimens per l'ostal del bordel . . ." AM Toulouse, CC 1854, 6or. A document in one of the cartularies records that he had indeed confiscated much municipal property, including the brothel, pending payment (AA 6, 256r), which may explain the absence of the brothel farm from the account book of 1391–92 (see n. 37, chap. 2). *Franc-fief* was a fine on non-nobles who acquired feudal property; *amortissement* was the "price of royal dispensation empowering corporate bodies to possess property whose acquisition constituted mortmain." J. Henneman, "*Enquêteurs-réformateurs* and Fiscal Officers in Fourteenth-Century France," *Traditio* 24 (1968): 312.

58. Western Languedoc was not, of course, the only area that witnessed the creation of municipal brothels in the last third of the fourteenth century. Such a brothel was established in Tarascon in 1373 (AM Tarascon, BB 1, 25r). The municipal council of Apt assigned a street for prostitutes in 1364; the location was changed several times until 1399, when a house was bought for this purpose. The council of Sisteron bought a house to be used as a brothel in 1397. F. Sauve, *La prostitution et les moeurs à Apt et en Provence pendant le moyen âge*, vol. 3 of *Notices aptésiennes* (Paris, 1905), 9–12.

59. AM Pézenas, Cartulaire A, 131v ff.

60. AM Castelnaudary, FF 22. Few documents remain in these archives from the second half of the fifteenth century. An entry in an eighteenth-century inventory would seem to indicate that the house was still private in 1480 (II 4, 692). In the first surviving account book from the sixteenth century, that of 1505–6, the brothel is listed as farmed out by the municipality (CC 80, 4r).

61. AM Lodève, AA 3, no. 42.

62. This statement is based on the fact that the contracts for farming out the brothel appear suddenly in the middle of a series of municipal deliberations and continue regularly thereafter. AM Alès, 1D 8, 36r.

63. AM Montpellier, Grand Thalamus, 245r ff.

64. ". . . quod publice meretrices et alcavoti seu lenones extuent a villa Narbone et amodo non remanerent infra dictam villam, *nisi per unam noctem*, sub pena corporis . . ." AM Narbonne, FF 610, 27 January 1299. This regulation had been issued by the lords of the town. The phrase "nisi per unam noctem" is absent from a later text (20 July 1299, FF 602; see n. 18, chap. 2), which was issued with the agreement of the *prud'hommes*. It is difficult to imagine that the *prud'hommes* were more severe than the lords. Perhaps the exception of *semel in septimana* was implicitly understood in this and other texts proclaiming the expulsion of prostitutes from towns in the late thirteenth and fourteenth centuries. Residence in town was forbidden, but occasional activity may have been tolerated.

65. "Item que degu alcavot ni femna de segle no ause remandre per jazer al Castelnau d'una nueyt enant . . ." AM Castelnaudary, AA 1, 29r.

66. See n. 46, chap. 3.

67. "Item, quod nulla meretrix aut mulier vagabunda ruffianus seu ruffiana, sit ausus seu ausa stare vel habitare infra villam Lunelli aut ejus baroniam, nisi per unam diem et unam noctem semel in septimana dumtaxat, et hoc sub pena fustigationis ac ammissionis raube sue, nisi in postribulo extra Lunellum ordinatum." E. Bondurand, "Coutumes de Lunel, 1367," *M-ANî* 8 (1885): 54–55.

68. AM Lunel, Livre Blanc, 13v.

69. E. Bondurand, "Appel au sujet des criées de Saint-Quentin," *M-ANî* 22 (1899): 156–58.

70. Millau in Rouergue purchased a brothel in 1417 (AM Millau, CC 400, 19r). Several small municipalities in Provence acquired brothels in the fifteenth century, for example, Malaucène in 1473 and Cavaillon in 1477 (Le Pileur, *Documents*, 19–20). The public house of Saint-Flour, too, was municipalized in the fifteenth century (A. Rigaudière, *Saint-Flour, ville d'Auvergne au bas moyen âge* [Paris, 1982], 1:506). Besançon had a municipal house by 1398 (Le Pileur, *Documents*, 59), and Dijon acquired its "Maison des Fillettes" in 1436 (Garnier, *Coquille*, 2). Most German towns seem to have had municipally owned brothels by the fifteenth century. See von Posern-Klett, "Frauenhäuser in Sachsen," *Archiv für die sächsische Geschichte* 12 (1874): 63–89. The only example I have found of a fifteenth-century English municipal brothel is that of the port of Sandwich, W. Boys, *Collections for an History of Sandwich* (Canterbury, 1792), 2:680.

71. See above, pp. 27–28.

72. The king was coseigneur of Uzès, where a monopoly on prostitution had been granted by the consuls to a resident in 1326 (see n. 22, chap. 2). The "Criées du ban des murs," authorized by the royal rector of Montpellier in 1336, include a reference to the Hot Street there, which had apparently been moved from its original location to the part of town for which the king was lord by this date (AM Montpellier, EE 25, EE 26). The consuls of Narbonne made a declaration in 1337 to the seneschal of Carcassonne of their rights and privileges, including those pertaining to the Hot Street (AM Narbonne, AA 14; Mouynès, *Narbonne Inv. AA*, 285). The undated police regulation of Nîmes mentioning the *postribulum publicum* had been published by the royal court there (see n. 21, chap. 2).

73. Most of the following section is based on the article by Le Roux de Lincy, "Hugues Aubriot, prévôt de Paris sous Charles V, 1367–1381," *BEC*, 5th ser., 3 (1862): 173–213. "This active supervision, always alert, this unshakable vigor . . . had the same goal: the organization and the maintenance of public security within the town."

74. "Item, a été que toutes femmes de vie dissolue tenans bordel en la ville de Paris, aillent demeurer et tenir leurs bordeaux ès places et lieux publics à ce ordonnés et accoustumés, selon l'ordonnance de Saint Louis, c'est à sçavoir . . ." H. Sauval, *Histoire et recherches des antiquités de la ville de Paris* (Paris, 1724), 3:652.

75. For the texts, see nn. 24 and 27, chap. 1.

76. *Ord* 6:611.

77. *Ord* 5:164.

78. Under the heading "Des bordeaulx." *Le grand coutumier de France*, edited by E. Laboulaye and R. Dareste (Paris, 1868), 182.

79. *Ord* 20:182.

80. See n. 74, chap. 2.

81. ". . . Saint Louis ordonna qu'il y eut bourdel en la rue . . . de Baillehoc." M. Félibien, *Histoire de la ville de Paris* (Paris, 1725), 4:538.

82. The entry lists payment for a copy made of an order (*mandement*) of the seneschal of Carcassonne: ". . . fazent als senhors cossols que aguesso de far et baztir 1 hostal al. bordel enque estesso de filhetas fant vengro ni avero sotz grandas penas." AM Albi, CC 175, 49v. The consuls did indeed order the reconstruction of the brothel outside New Gate; the accounts for the spring of 1423 detail two pages of expenses—for wood, stone, labor, and so forth—incurred in its construction. AM Albi, CC 178, 49r: "Mesa facha per far bastir l'ostal del bordel . . ." The total expenses came to 26 l. 2 s. 8 d.

83. AM Toulouse, AA 5, no. 371, 3 February 1425. Published by Catel in *Mémoires de l'histoire du Languedoc*, 187–89; also *Ord* 13:76–77. Quotations have been taken from the document in the cartulary.

84. An entry in the consular account books records the cost of a letter requesting this permission: "feron pagar per aver una letra per far lo bordelh, ii l. xii s." AM Castelnaudary, CC 78, 8v.

85. Published document no. 2.

86. See J.-M. Carbasse, *Consulats méridionaux et justice criminelle au moyen âge*, Thèse-Droit-Montpellier, 1974, 145–48. The king of Aragon also claimed the prerogative to grant permission for establishing municipal brothels. In a letter dated 1432, Alphonse of Aragon granted the municipal authorities of Messina "licentiam et facultatem construendi et edificandi novum lupanare." A. Cutrera, *Storia della prostituzione in Sicilia* (Palermo, 1903; reprint, Palermo, 1971), 72. The king of France also accorded the right to private monopolies on prostitution, as was the case in Montpellier (1469), *Ord* 20: 180–82.

87. "Damus facultatem dictis habitatoribus, ne mulieres dissolute et impudice meretricantes per diversas domos et habitationes dicte ville exerceant earum luxuriam et libidenem in prejudicium reipublice dicte ville, exemplumque pessimum plurimarum personarum, construendi et edificandi in aliqua parte extra dictam villam, domum lupanaris, in qua dicte muliercule recipiantur, et remaneat pertineatque emolumentum dicti lupanaris eisdem habitatoribus pro reparationibus predictis fiendis." Ramière de Fortanier, *Chartes du Lauragais*, 709–10.

88. See above, p. 27.

89. The very language attests to the late date of this article. The term *domus lupanaris* (rather than *lupanar*) is a late-medieval one, as is probably *mulieres dissolute* (see the prologue to part 2). References to *res publica* were not common before the end of the fourteenth century.

Epilogue to Part One

1. "Défendons à toutes personnes de loger et recevoir en leurs maisons, plus d'une nuict, gens sans adveu et incogneus. Et leur enjoignons les dénoncer à justice à peine de prison et d'amende arbitraire. *Défendons aussi tous bordeaux*, berlans, jeux de quilles et de dez que voulons estre punis extraordinairement, sans dissimulation ou connivance des juges, à peine de privation de leurs offices." Isambert, *Recueil général des anciennes lois françaises* (Paris, 1829), 14:88. G. Picot has pointed out that this article repeats exactly article 258 of the *cahier de doléances* of the third estate, in his *Histoire des Etats Généraux* (Paris, 1872), 2:204.

2. AM Alès, 1D 15, 185r. That same year, the council of Orange voted to alienate the *maison du bordel* (Le Pileur, *Documents*, 41).

3. AM Castelnaudary, BB 4, 213r.

4. The sale must have taken place shortly thereafter, for in the session of 31 May 1558, the council decided to purchase a salt warehouse with the money acquired from the sale of the brothel and other municipal properties. AM Montpellier, Délibérations Municipales, 1557, 295r, 313v.

5. AM Toulouse, CC 1697, 26; CC 1703, 27.

6. A. W. Crosby, *The Columbian Exchange: Biological and Cultural Consequences of 1492* (Westport, Conn., 1972), 122ff.

7. Even the explanation of contagion published by Fracastorius in 1546 was slow to gain acceptance. P. Theil, "Le siècle du mal contagieux," in *Histoire culturelle de la maladie* (Toulouse, 1980), 328–33; J.-N. Biraben, *Les hommes devant la peste* (Paris, 1976), 2:18–27. I have unfortunately not been able to consult O. Temkin's study, "An Historical Analysis of the Conception of Infection," in his *The Double Face of Janus* (Baltimore, 1977), 456–71.

8. I. Bloch, *Die Prostitution* (Berlin, 1925), 2:8–16.

9. Calvin considered syphilis to be a punishment inflicted on "lechers" for their immorality. *Opera* (Brunswick, 1885), 28:404. For Calvin, as for many of his contemporaries, disease was principally a physical metaphor for a spiritual ailment. Thus, he compared lechery to an infection: "Ce mal croit, dont la ville est grandement infectée." *Opera* (Brunswick, 1879), 21:690.

10. Biraben, *Peste* 2:1–2.

11. The same article that denied access to the public house of Pamiers to syphilitics denied it also to lepers and anyone "infected with any contagious disease." Published document no. 10, §11. The author of a chronicle of the town of Orange attributed the cause of a bout of plague suffered by the town in 1545 to *une putain* operating out of a neighboring barn. *La chronique d'un notaire d'Orange, 1518–1567*, edited by L. Duhamel (Paris, 1881), 41.

12. A chronicle of the town of Delitzsch records that the brothel was closed there because of the plague in 1405 (von Posern-Klett, "Frauenhäuser in Sachsen," 68). In Millau, where quite a complete series of consular account books has survived from the fifteenth century, one sees that in plague years the municipal brothel was normally not farmed out (AM Millau, CC 400–446).

13. In 1521, a plague year, the farmer of the municipal brothel of Toulouse

claimed that she could not pay the full sum due, as, given that the plague was raging in the town, many of the women had left: "Et aussi aver regard aldit temps et al present que court de la peste, car ladite suppliante non prend negun argent, car en toute ladite maison non y a que tres filhes . . ." AM Toulouse, CC 2371, no. 510.

14. AD Haute Garonne, B 4, 27r, 393r; B 7, 65r.

15. "Illec a esté veu l'inconvenient de peste que durand l'année a esté et au moyen duquel feust commandé fermer la maison publicque des filhes apellée du Chasteau Verd . . ." (AM Toulouse, CC 1672, December 1528); ". . . que les filhes perdues du Chasteau Vert ne ailhent par la ville . . . à peine du fohet . . . c'est pour garder de pourter infection par la ville en temps de peste . . ." (AM Toulouse, BB 265, 171v). See also BB 265, 145v, 160r; BB 9, 38r, 22 April 1526.

16. AM Nîmes, LL 4, 67r, 8 October 1522; LL 5, 196v,m 17 January 1531. In 1522 the council voted to pay damages to the owner for the loss in revenues suffered; they refused to do so in 1531. It was indeed "pour doubte de gure et dangier de peste" that the house was closed in 1531, not, as A. Puech has claimed, out of fear of syphilis. A. Puech, "Documents pour servir à l'histoire de la syphilis à Nîmes," Montpellier médical, 2nd ser., 11 (1888): 397.

17. "Cum pacto et conditione quod casu quo pestis vigeat in presenti loco Castri, quod absit, in eum casum dicta domo claudetur et dicta Bernarda solvet rata pro rata." AM Castelnaudary, BB 2, 157v, 12 October 1527. See also BB 1, 32v, 26 September 1516.

18. AM Montpellier, Inv. 7, 130. The public house of Cavaillon (Vaucluse) was apparently transformed into a hospital for the poor in 1528 (Le Pileur, Documents, 37). On order of the seneschal of Beaucaire, the brothel of Nîmes was requisitioned for housing "des pouvres estrangiers et austres impotens" in 1531 (AM Nîmes, LL 5, 113v).

19. Published document no. 9. Actual sanitary inspection of prostitutes seems to have been introduced in Spain in the mid– or late sixteenth century. J. M. Guardia, "De la prostitution en Espagne," appendix in Parent-Duchatelet's De la prostitution dans la ville de Paris, 3rd ed. (Paris, 1857), 2: 778–83.

20. Bongert, Droit pénal 2:133–234.

21. Ibid., 14–20; Schnapper, "Répression pénale, Parlement de Bordeaux," 53–54.

22. A. Allard, Histoire de la justice criminelle au seizième siècle (Ghent, Paris, and Leipzig, 1868; reprint, Darmstadt, 1970), 419–26.

23. Bongert, Droit pénal 2:240–323; Bloch, Prostitution 2:260–67. This use of the strict enforcement of morals laws as an instrument of expanding power and influence recalls the policies of Louis IX, discussed in chap. 1.

24. The brothel of Vienna stopped functioning around 1540, probably as a result of these initiatives. J. Schrank, Die Geschichte der Prostitution in Wien (Vienna, 1886), 105–19.

25. The jurist Lebrun de la Rochette went so far as to claim that idleness (oisiveté) was the root of all crime (cited in Bongert, Droit pénal 2:236).

26. A précis of the demographic history of Languedoc in this period is given by E. Le Roy Ladurie in *Histoire du Languedoc*, 265–68.

27. A. G. Carmichael has found that there was, in Italy, a close association in the public mind between the poor and epidemic disease, which may have reinforced the association between prostitution and disease. In her "Epidemic Disease in Early Renaissance Florence," diss., Duke University, 1978 (*DA*).

28. For this literature, see A. Hentsch, *De la littérature didactique du moyen âge s'adressant spécialement aux femmes* (Cahors, 1903; reprint, Geneva, 1975), 154ff.

29. P. Ourliac, "L'evolution de la condition de la femme en droit français," *Annales de la Faculté de Droit de Toulouse* 14 (1966): 61–64; P. Jaubert, "Le droit des gens mariés à Bordeaux," lecture at Faculté de Droit de Montpellier, 21 April 1978. In a bull of 1520, Pope Leo X obliged the prostitutes of Rome to leave a portion of their fortune to the convent of the *convertite* (repentant women), thus limiting their capacity to make a will (Pertile, *Diritto italiano* 4: 22, 86).

30. See n. 66, chap. 4.

31. See especially the works of Rabelais, an associate of Tiraqueau in the humanist circle of Fontenay-le-Comte, and those of Joachim Du Bellay.

32. The place of women in Catholic and Protestant society of the sixteenth century is discussed by N. Z. Davis in "City Women and Religious Change," in her *Society and Culture in Early Modern France* (London, 1975), 65–96. J. Kelly-Gadol has pointed out that the increasing separation between the public and private spheres of activity in this period helped to limit women to an exclusively private role. J. Kelly-Gadol, "Notes on Women in the Renaissance," in *Conceptual Frameworks in Women's History* (Bronxville, N.Y., 1976).

33. "Cum literae afferrentur Doctori . . . in quibus scribebat Doctorem Christopherum iurisconsultum hominem esse impiissimum et Epicureum summum—probare enim simplicem fornicationem, lupanaria et alias libidines prohibitas . . . valde commotus est Doctor et dixit *Das hatt er mitt aus Italia bracht*! . . . *Ja, es ist war*, ut ille nebulo inquit: Sine peccato non est mundus; *aber* quod sic vellet colligere: Mundus non est sine peccato, ergo peccatum est concedendum, *das folget nicht*!" M. Luther, *Werke, kritische Gesamtausgabe: Tischreden* (Weimar, 1919), 5: 170–71.

34. "Mein lieber Hieronyme, Ihr sollet mit denen weder zu thun, zu schicken noch zu schaffen haben, die das gemeine Muhmenhaus wollen wieder anrichten. Leidlicher und besser wäre es gewest, man hätte den Teufel nicht ausgetrieben, denn wieder einlassen und von neuen bestätigen. Welche solche Häuser wollen wieder anrichten, die sollen zuvor Christus Namen verleugnen, und bekennen, dass sie nicht Christen, sondern Heiden seyen, die von Gott nichts wissen." *Tischreden* (Weimar, 1921), 6: 272–73.

35. Bloch, *Prostitution* 2: 54–56; von Posern-Klett, "Frauenhäuser in Sachsen," 86–88. Luther admitted the occasional necessity of a gradual adaptation to the new sexual morality, as in the case of Halle: "So duncket mich noch zur zeith, biss das Evangelium fester eingewurtzelt und das unkraut ausgerott, So sey mit dieser sachen noch ein kleine zeith geduldet zu haben. . . .

Aber so erst man gleich wol kan, ist mit ernst dazu zuthun." Luther, *Werke, kritische Gesamtausgabe: Briefwechsel* (Weimar, 1947), 10: 395-96. Luther was hostile not only to authorized brothels but also to the person of the prostitute, who should be, he felt, severely punished (Bloch, *Prostitution* 2: 53). It is significant that, as the symbol of depraved man saved by God, Luther chose the image of the prostitute taken in marriage by Christ. See H. A. Oberman, "The Shape of Late Medieval Thought: The Birthpangs of the Modern Era," *Archiv für Reformationsgeschichte* 64 (1973): 31-32.

36. "Puis qu'ainsi est donc que Dieu deteste la paillardise, que sera-ce quand les bordeaux seront permis?" Sermon, January 1556, in *Opera* 28: 111.

37. A. Biéler, *L'homme et la femme dans la morale calviniste* (Geneva, 1963), 34-54.

38. Ibid., 108, 124-26.

39. E. W. Monter, "Crime and Punishment in Calvin's Geneva, 1562," *Archiv für Reformationsgeschichte* 64 (1973): 283.

40. "[The leader of the organization] non ducet deinceps ad lupanar . . . studentes de novo advenientes . . . ymo abrogabitur funditus consuetudo illa mala et illaudata," October 1526. In May 1527 the office was abolished. A. Germain, "La Renaissance à Montpellier," *MSAMtp* 6 (1871): 138-41. The Protestant sympathies of the people responsible for these decisions are pointed out by L. Guiraud in "La réforme à Montpellier," *MSAMtp*, 2nd ser., 6 (1918): 39-45.

41. L. Romier, "Les protestants français à la veille des guerres civiles," *Revue historique* 124 (1917): 235-36. Citing a contemporary letter, Romier states that, in most of the towns where Protestants were the majority, the *filles de joie* "were expelled, and their houses, 'rented to poor craftsmen.'"

42. J. Garrisson-Estèbe, *Les protestants du Midi, 1559-98* (Toulouse, 1980), 298-99. The cutting off of ears (*essorillement*) was a common punishment in the late Middle Ages (Bongert, *Droit pénal* 1: 225-29).

43. Garrisson-Estèbe, *Protestants du Midi*, 290-300; J. Estèbe and B. Vogler, "La genèse d'une société protestante: étude comparée de quelques registres consistoriaux languedociens et palatins vers 1600," *An-ESC* 31 (1976): 381-82; Oudot de Dainville, "Le consistoire de Ganges à la fin du XVIᵉ siècle," *Revue d'histoire de l'Eglise de France* 18 (1932): 467-69, 476-77.

44. Romier, "Protestants français," 18.

45. "Lesditz Messieurs de consulz ont remonstré les grandz maulx qui sureant d'un jour a autre pour raison du lieu publique e maison de debouche où abondent plusieurs putains, ruffiens, au moyen desquels sont commis plusieurs desbauchamens de jeunes enfans, filles . . ." AM Castelnaudary, BB 4, 213r.

46. See J.-L. Flandrin, *Les amours paysannes* (Paris, 1975).

47. The Jesuits were instrumental in urging Philip IV to abolish authorized brothels in Spain in 1623 (Guardia, "Prostitution en Espagne," 763ff.). They were also responsible for the closing of the municipal brothel in Luzern in 1581 (Bloch, *Prostitution* 2:73).

48. AM Montpellier, Grand Thalamus, 245r ff.

49. AM Toulouse, BB 265, 145v.

50. AM Albi, AA 4; FF 43.

51. AM Alès, 1D 8–1D 15. See chap. 3.

52. The house was being farmed for about 1,000 l. a year. See chap. 3. Even from the period after the ordinance of Orléans, there is evidence of occasional toleration. Thus, a document from 1570 reads, ". . . attendu que, par suite des malheurs du temps la commune de Cavaillon a laissé abolir le Bordel public qui existait jadis en cette ville, les consuls veilleront à ce qu'il s'y trouve, pendant les fêtes de la Saint-Gilles deux ou trois femmes ou filles débauchées et ce pour éviter les faits de boulgrerie." Le Pileur, *Documents*, 44.

53. Published document no. 9. Already in 1430, Amadeus VIII of Savoy ordered that three-quarters of the fines levied on blasphemers, procurers, and prostitutes should go to charity (Pertile, *Diritto italiano* 5:226 n. 39).

54. See E. Rodocanachi, *Courtisanes et bouffons: étude de moeurs romaines au XVIᵉ siècle* (Paris, 1894).

55. P. Larivaille, *La vie quotidienne des courtisanes en Italie au temps de la Renaissance* (Paris, 1975).

56. See chap. 6 and the epilogue to part 2.

Prologue to Part Two

1. de Maulde, *Coutumes d'Avignon*, 166 (1246). *Lupanar* was the word used in the Justinianic corpus.

2. Such letter inversions occur in Occitanian, also, but *postribulum* seems to have been used exclusively in Latin texts in Languedoc.

3. For example, AM Castelnaudary, AA 1, 20v (1333); *Livre Vert de Lacaune*, 201 (1337); and the *Carreria Calida* (Hot Street) of Montpellier (1285) (Germain, "Statuts," 125).

4. AD Gard, IIE¹ 199, 178v (1482); IIE 18–31, 56r (Beaucaire, 1490).

5. AM Toulouse, BB 3, 57r (1419). The use of the term *domus lupanaris* in the Villefranche-de-Lauragais charter of 1280 (see n. 87, chap. 2) shows clearly that the relevant passage must have been added in the late fourteenth or the fifteenth century.

6. The word was often used in the phrases *far bordel* or *bordel se ten*, meaning to run a center of prostitution (for example, AM Beaucaire, CC 6, 126r [1520]).

7. By the 1430s the term *hostal public* had become customary in official Toulousan documents dealing with the municipal brothel.

8. AM Toulouse, CC 1868, 39r (1469–70); used frequently in the financial documents of Castelnaudary, Albi, and Toulouse beginning around 1505. In Montpellier and Tarascon, the expression *la bona carrieyra* was used already in the early fifteenth century.

9. See chap. 1.

10. One also sees the term *bagassa de segle* (*siècle*), AM Narbonne, FF

602 (1299). Cf. *fame de siècle* in the French version of Raymond Lull's *Blaquerne*, edited by A. Llinarès (Paris, 1970), 198.

11. ". . . mulier que pro pecunia se exponat . . ." AM Nîmes, FF 1, no. 21 (1353). Cf. ". . . mulieres . . . se dimitunt pro denare homini . . ." AM Uzès, BB 1, 3v (1326).

12. ". . . vana et vilis mulier . . ." AM Uzès, BB 1, 3r (1326). See also from Montpellier (1285) ". . . mulieres viles, que meretricaliter et more meretricio vivunt." Cf. the term *mala fambra* (1354), cited by J. Boswell in his *The Royal Treasure: Muslim Communities under the Crown of Aragon in the Fourteenth Century* (New Haven and London, 1977), 71.

13. *Livre Vert de Lacaune*, 201 (1337).

14. Published document no. 1; AM Castelnaudary FF 9; AM Pézenas, Cartulaire A, 88v, 131v. Cf. the Aragonese *fembra publica* (1360) (Boswell, *Royal Treasure*, 350) and the Italian term *femina mondana*, cited by R. Trexler in his "La prostitution florentine au XVᵉ siècle," *An-ESC* 36 (1981): 990.

15. See the financial documents from Toulouse and Albi; published document no. 2. The term *bone mulieres* is found in Montpellier in 1397 (Inv. 11, 71), and *filhetas du bien* in Lodève in 1441 (CC 4). For the vocabulary used in the register of the Châtelet of Paris in the late fourteenth century, see A. Porteau-Bitker, "Criminalité et délinquance féminines dans le droit pénal des XIIIᵉ et XIVᵉ siècles," *RHD* 58 (1980): 26–27.

16. For these changes, see A. Brun, *Essai historique sur l'introduction du français dans les provinces du midi de la France* (Paris, 1924).

17. These terms appear in the financial documents of Toulouse, Albi, and Montpellier in farming contracts, and in the registers of Parlement. See also in the late-medieval interpolation of the Villefranche-de-Lauragais charter, dated 1280, *mulieres dissolute* (n. 87, chap. 2).

18. "Pouvres fillettes communes," published document no. 4 (1462); "pauvra filha," AM Toulouse, CC 1356, no. 90 (1507). In addition to evoking an economic reality, the adjective *poor* was essentially pejorative in this period. See M. Mollat, "La notion de la pauvreté au moyen âge," *Revue d'histoire de l'Eglise de France* 52 (1966): 5–23. See also "pauras pecayrix," AM Albi, CC (early sixteenth century); and "filles perdues," AM Toulouse, BB 265 (1520s).

19. One could even qualify the diminutive *filheta* as affectionate, as opposed to *bagassa, -assa* being a pejorative ending in Occitanian.

20. See below, p. 72.

Chapter Three

1. Such districts existed also in Narbonne, Lacaune, Bagnols, and Castelnaudary. See chap. 2.

2. For a vivid description of the red-light district of Florence, see Trexler, "Prostitution florentine," 989–90.

3. ". . . quandam plateam cadratam quindecim cannarum, in qua platea est unus puteus et quinque camere mulierum postribullarum, cum certis arboris."

P. Pansier, *Dictionnaire des anciennes rues d'Avignon* (Avignon, 1930), 35, 206–7. Although *camera* usually meant "room," it was used also to describe small, independent structures, as is clear from an act of sale of "dua parva hospitia sive cameras" in the *lupanar* of Arles in 1517.

4. BM Arles, MS. 225, 263.

5. AM Alès, 1D 8, 36r, 71r, 154r, 205v; 1D 9, 99r, 146r, 355r.

6. AM Alès, 1D 11, 135r, 268r.

7. AM Alès, 1D 9, 355r.

8. AM Albi, AA 4.

9. AM Albi, FF 43, *cahier* dated 1535, 18v; 15r, 17r, 18r; 8r, 14r.

10. AM Montpellier, Grand Thalamus, 245r.

11. *Ord* 20: 180–83. Indeed, the municipality attempted to avoid paying the traditional 5 l. a year to the king as the private owners had done (see n. 85, chap. 6) on the grounds that the payment was for the stews, which no longer existed. The trial began shortly after the purchase of the house, though a first payment was made in the mid-twenties (Inv. 9, 112). A first decision in favor of the king was appealed to the *chambre des comptes* (123), which confirmed the decision on 12 November 1537 (". . . la ville reffuzat de payer ladite pension pour ce que audit bordeau n'a point d'estubes; toutefoys, par arrest de la chambre de comptes, a esté la ville condamnée à luy payer lesdit huits années," 126). The brothel of Nîmes included baths at the end of the fifteenth century (AD Gard, IIE¹ 206, 123v 4 July 1498).

12. ". . . est grand et espacieulx et y plusieurs estages, chambres et aultres maisons, et est tout clos . . ." Published document no. 4. High walls around the brothel were needed for the women's security, as the same text specifies. The *lupanar* of Pavia was fortified. P. Pavesi, *Il bordello di Pavia da XIV al XVII secolo* (Milan, 1897), 33. Walls were also necessary for public decency. In 1506 the consuls of Albi paid for the construction of a wall by the brothel: "pro una paret que a facha a la mayso del bordel tenen am l'ort de Jame Parayre, a causa que las filhas non podian far dedins mercat." AM Albi, FF 43.

13. AM Toulouse, DD 45, 60r, 69v, 78v.

14. ". . . una fila palina . . . per votar alas cranbas delas filhas ala requesta de una filha deleyus que avia lotat lo fuoc ala una delas cambras et avian cramada una corouda . . ." AM Toulouse, CC 2347, no. 5, February 1499.

15. ". . . las portas ou se tenen las filhetas lo jorn," AM Toulouse, CC 2367, no. 63–64 (1516); ". . . una sarralha granda per la porta dela cramba del abet et arrendeyre dela bona maiso . . ." AM Toulouse, CC 2364, no. 154 (1513).

16. In 1518 carpenters supplied the house with nineteen doors and "vint et doas sarralhes que an mesas alas portas delas crambas delas filhetas," AM Toulouse, CC 2369, no. 12; ". . . Huguet Gentieu, recubreyre de Tholose . . . a recubert, a ses despens, vingt cinq cambres au Chateau Vert . . . xv avril 1527," AM Toulouse, CC 2378, no. 26.

17. AD Gard, IIE¹ 207, 156v (see Inv.).

18. Pansier, *Rues d'Avignon*, 35, 206–7.

19. Le Pileur, *Documents*, 18–19, 34–35, 38. In 1500 the houses belonged to Joachim of Rome, a papal messenger.

20. At the beginning of the sixteenth century, Honorata Metheline sold "duas cameras . . . in lupanaria" to Trophime Jacob, and in 1517 the merchant Anthony Metheline sold to Peter Belleti, a fellow merchant, "dua parva hosptita sive cameras . . . in lupanaria." BM Arles, MS. 225, 263. These manuscripts contain summaries of medieval notarial documents made in the eighteenth century by the Arlesian priest Laurence Bonnemant.

21. AM Uzès, BB 1, 3v.

22. AM Uzès, GG 4.

23. AM Uzès, BB 1, 29v, 4 April 1357.

24. AM Foix, CC 209, 2v, 8r, 62r, 302r.

25. AM Pézenas, Cartulaire A, 88v ff. Edited by J. Azaïs in his "Documents sur les femmes de mauvaise vie," *BSABéz*, 1st ser., 2 (1837): 277–323. Shortly after the purchase, Raynauda donated the house to the Great Charity of Pézenas. See below.

26. The brothel was sold shortly after 1401 to William Andrieu. The owner owed 3 d. a year *usatge* to the lord of Fontes on this house. This payment makes it possible to distinguish this from a second, later brothel (AM Lodève, CC 1, 123v). The last reference to Andrieu is from 1423; in 1438 the same house (*1 ostal public*) was in the hands of John the Catalan. In the same *compoix*, a second brothel is also listed (*1 ostal per las publicas*), which was contiguous to the first; the proprietor was John Gues (CC 3, payment of *taille* for 1423; CC 4, 18or, 215r). Sometime between 1448 and 1452, Bernard Hughes acquired the first brothel (CC 5, list of *tailles*). It was he who donated the house to the municipality on 2 January 1455. On 13 December 1455 the town bought a second house (surely the second brothel listed in the *compoix*), probably in view of enlarging the new municipal brothel (AA 3, no. 42; no. 39). The act dated January 1455 has been partially edited by E. Martin and L. Guiraud, in *Cartulaire de Lodève* (Montpellier, 1900), 196ff. A survey of the notarial documents extant from this period has revealed no further information on this property.

27. AM Beaucaire, CC 4, 95r, 11r.

28. "Esteve Armen, sartre . . . Item, ung hostal en la guacha de hospital out se ten lo bourdel . . . vi l." AM Beaucaire, CC 6, 126r.

29. R. Trexler reports that a number of the great families of Florence owned property in the town's red-light district ("Prostitution florentine," 991). E. Pavan relates the same for Venice in the late fourteenth century, in her "Police des moeurs, société et politique à Venise à la fin du moyen âge," *Revue historique* 536 (1980): 245. In 1460 the owner of the official public house of Venice was "nobilis vir dominus" (Calza, "Prostituzione in Venezia," 319).

30. He does not give the name of the owner. A. Chassaing, ed., *Livre de Podio d'Etienne Médicis* (Le Puy, 1869), 1: 257.

31. AD Gard, IIE¹ 199, 178v, 15 October 1482. The de Fiennes were one of the most important families of Villeneuve. Research in the AM Villeneuve-lèz-Avignon has revealed no documents concerning the town brothel and its ownership.

32. AD Gard, IIE¹ 206, 110r.

33. *HGL* IX-1: 147. In 1531 the brothel belonged to John de Laye, grandson of Gabriel. AM Nîmes, LL 5, 196v.

34. *Ord* 20: 180–83.

35. ". . . la mytat d'un hostal forres la vila, so es l'abadie de la bonne carrière . . . 320 l." AM Montpellier, *compoix* of 1480, Sainte Foy, 15r. There are some documents that would seem to indicate that the brothel was municipal in the middle of the fifteenth century. In a list of revenues from municipally owned houses for 1446 is the entry ". . . Annas la Liejeyra, tavernierya del bordel, a paguat d'intrada, 15 s." A document from 1448 has the following entry: "Aven recauput de Lauzes Jacme, alias Nencho, fermyer del bordel, que monta tot son arendament, 133 l." (AM Montpellier, Inv. 9, 85). This situation must not have lasted long, however, for these are the only references in an otherwise almost complete series of consular account books.

36. AM Montpellier, Grand Thalamus, 245–46. According to P. Burlats-Brun, Montpellier was already part owner of the house. In an unpublished essay, "Courons l'aiguillette à Montpellier," he states that Pierre Brun, doctor of law, was coproprietor of the house but sold his share (2/12) to the municipality in 1513. He adds that the son of Louis de la Croix kept a small share of the brothel until February 1527, when he sold it to Arnaud Marres, who a year later sold it to the consuls. These and other facts presented in this work are based on family archives not available to the public.

37. William de la Croix was an important and trusted figure in royal administration. *HGL* IX-1: 150, 160, 169.

38. Published document no. 5.

39. See chap. 2.

40. This money was used "for the utility of the town" (*ad utilitatem dictae villae*), according to the royal safeguard of 1425 (AM Toulouse, AA 5, no. 371). There is no indication in the financial documents to justify the rumor that circulated in 1529 that the money from the brothel farm was used to pay for the consuls' robes (published document no. 9). The only example found of the consuls' earmarking the brothel farm for a specific payment is in 1460 when J. Amic was paid for repairs he had made on a bridge: 330 l. "assignada sus . . . lo emolument le l'ostal public [and other farms]" (AM Toulouse, CC 2335, no. 39). In Italy it was apparently common to earmark money made from prostitution for specific expenses. In Pavia this money was used to pay for repairs of the town fortifications and the salaries of municipal officers, and in Padua the *dazio delle meretrici* was used to finance a university chair in canon law! Pavesi, *Bordello di Pavia*, 10, 29–30.

41. M. Gramain, "Les institutions pieuses et charitables à Pézenas aux XIIe et XIVe siècles," *FHL*-Pézenas (1975): 41–48.

42. In a session dated 17 May 1481 the municipal council refused to take responsibility for the repairs of the house: "Item, que ladite maison publicque nommé le bordel, s'il a besoing de reparacion, se repara dez emoluments dudit bordel et dez lausimes des caritatz." AM Pézenas, BB 5, 24v–25v.

43. Published document no. 9. Chalande was mistaken when he claimed that the system was not actually put into effect until 1549 ("Maison publique à

Toulouse," 80). The entry for the *arrentement* of the house dated 31 December 1529 reads, "cli l., au proffit et utillité du scindic des hospitaux." AM Toulouse, CC 1673, 5, 228, 288. Every subsequent farm of the house bears the same qualification.

44. ". . . a despens de la filhas que venran." AM Castres, BB 8, 67r.

45. See n. 69, chap. 2.

46. See above, p. 35. One finds this clause in the police regulations of Saint-Privat-du-Gard dated 1450 (published by E. Bondurand in *MANî* 23 [1900]: 141–49); those of Saint-Michel-d'Euzet (Gard), 1466 (cited in Courteault, *Bourg-Saint-Andéol*, 228–29); and those of Villeneuve-lèz-Béziers, 1513 (published by J. Bédard in *BSABéz*, 3rd ser., 13 [1927]: 169–206). A number of small municipalities in Provence observed this principle, including Piolenc, 1406; Le Barroux, 1407; Barbetane, 1448; and Valréas, 1543 (Le Pileur, *Documents*, 5, 6, 10, 38).

47. For all references in the following section, see the list of farms given in appendix C unless otherwise indicated.

48. In Millau the municipal brothel was farmed for anywhere from 1 l. (AM Millau, CC 416 [1451]) to 5 l. 2 s. (CC 412 [1435]). In Saint-Flour the public house was rented for 16 s. a year in 1402 (Rigaudière, *St-Flour* 1:506).

49. The contract of 1515 shows that the consuls hoped eventually to be able to farm the house at 6 l. a year. They never attained even that modest goal.

50. All sums in this section have been converted into livres and sous, based on the table of equivalences. For the actual money paid, consult the appendix.

51. The farm of the house was paid in kind (32 *sétiers* of wheat) in 1514.

52. See the charts in appendix D.

53. *Histoire de Languedoc*, edited by Wolff, 291; G. and G. Frêche, *Les prix des grains à Toulouse (1486–1868)* (Paris, 1967).

54. It is possible that these totals were merely theoretical goals never actually paid in full. Such disparities between apparent and real profits did exist in Castelnaudary. For Toulouse, however, this is difficult to verify after 1529, when the revenues of the brothel were transferred from the general coffers to those of the hospitals.

55. See especially the case of Alès.

56. This surely explains why the sum due was paid in kind in 1514 (see n. 51, chap. 3).

57. Published document no. 7.

58. "Illec est venue Pierre du Val, arrentier de Chasteau Vert, qui a dit que le tresorier de la ville l'a faict mettre en prison pour ce que ne bayloict cautions, disçant que pour le present n'en pourroit trouver. . . . Lors a esté appoincté par lesdictz messieurs que ledict arrentier bailhera cautions entre cy et ladicte feste de l'Epiphanie dudict arrentement . . ." AM Toulouse, CC 1671, 8, 22 December 1528.

59. In Albi and Toulouse, for example, the municipality paid directly the workmen who did these repairs. In Tarascon in the early fifteenth century, on the other hand, sums previously expended by the farmer were reimbursed by the authorities (AM Tarascon, CC 125–30). In Saint-Flour the consuls even

went so far as to supply the bed linen of the brothel! Rigaudière, *St-Flour* 1:506.

60. "... Perreta tenebitur facere reparationes necessarias in dicta domo et dictus Massoti tenebitur reparare *las gotieyras* suis sumptibus ..."

61. "... tenir belles et plaisantes filhes putains pour à cause d'entretenir ledit bordel." The Alès historian A. Bardon claimed to have found in the contract of 1511 a requirement to keep "pensionnaires agréables et agousteuses." There is no such clause in this contract; Bardon probably misread a passage concerning the more banal subject of gutter upkeep: "Item, plus teneatur et debeat dictam domum perseverare agoltoris."

62. The former have been discussed above, p. 41; for the latter, see below, pp. 84–85.

63. Several of the farmers are listed in the *compoix* of 1518. Glaudius Pelhis, weaver, who farmed the brothel in 1510 and again in 1515, had a house rated at 19 l. and a vineyard. Aubert Perret, carder, who was to farm the brothel in 1524, had half a house at 14 l. and a garden and shares of various vineyards. G. Richart, hat maker, had a house at 24 l., gardens, a vineyard, and an oat field.

64. The consular account books of Beaucaire mention an *abadessa* in July 1493, an *abbé* in July 1496, and again an *abaesse* in July 1497 (AM Beaucaire, CC 226, 21v, 90r, 107v).

65. The man who farmed the brothel of Pézenas in 1455 was apparently taking over from an *abbatissa*.

66. L. Ménard, *Histoire de Nismes*, 7 vols. (Paris, 1750–58), 4:80. The terms *abbot* and *abbess* were used frequently to indicate the farmer or manager of Languedocian public houses. Such a parody of religious terminology was not limited to brothels, however; the leaders of Languedocian youth organizations were also referred to as "abbots." See J. Rossiaud, "Fraternités de jeunesse dans les villes du sud-est à la fin du moyen âge," *Cahiers d'histoire*, 1976: 67–102.

67. Published document no. 3. This is perhaps the same J. Sudre who cofarmed the house with Johaneta Delascura in 1431.

68. He was obliged to pay a fine following a brawl with Anthony Peyrot in the *bon hostal*. AM Castelnaudary, CC 81, 4r (1506–7). Maria Lanas had taken on the brothel farm for four years in 1505–6.

69. The consuls enjoined her to "put an adequate man there" (y mectre home suffisant). AM Toulouse, CC 1671, 102, 104, 26 August and 2 September 1529. She was perhaps unable to find a partner, for in December 1529 the house was farmed out to Domenge de la Font.

70. In Toulouse, J. Eymeric, farmer in 1511–12 and 1514–15, was followed in that position by his wife, Johana Dangiera, from 1516 to 1522. In Montpellier, Mia Vincens, widow of Antoine Gerbaut, who had farmed the brothel in 1539 and 1541, took the farm in 1542. The public house of Sandwich was also run by a man and wife, John and Jane Waldrand, in 1494 (Boys, *History of Sandwich* 2:630). The farmer Germanus Andree, however, abandoned the farm of Alès in 1518 when he married: "se in matrimonium collocaverit ... propter honestatem dicti matrimonii, nolit hanc domum neque gubernationem illius amplius tenere ..." This may indeed be an indica-

tion of increased moral sensitivity, but it could also be a pretext for backing out of what seems to have been a rather unprofitable venture.

71. Rossiaud, "Prostitution, jeunesse et société," 313 n. 6.

72. Recent research in the AM Tarascon has revealed a tendency toward "masculinization" of the office of brothel farmer in that town, too, from the fourteenth to the fifteenth century.

73. "Item, quod domus lupanaris pertinet ville et quolibet anno solet arendari per filias competenti precio . . ." AM Toulouse, BB 3, 57r (1419). The passage relates that this year a man bid, also, pushing up the price of the farm. Three or four of the women decided to rent another house in the town "in qua morantur et faciunt earum peccatum."

74. AM Toulouse, AA 5, no. 31. All-female management seems to have been characteristic of the brothels of Foix, Pézenas, and Lodève at the end of the fourteenth century (see above).

75. AD Haute Garonne, B 1988, 233v, 29 July 1460. See below, pp. 92–93.

76. Published document no. 4. An entry in the accounts for 1459–60 reads, "Pagat al clerc de M. Pelan Fort per far una requesta per las femas del hostal public . . . contra la vila, ii s. vi d." AM Toulouse, CC 2334, no. 68.

77. ". . . l'en doit exterper et mectre annéant toutes choses provocans à luxure, et non pas les norrir, et porter soubz umbre et couleur de arrendement de grosses sommes de deniers à appliquer."

78. ". . . les roigne et taille tout ainsi que bon lui semble." "Car ung ruffien, entre telles pouvres et miserables femmes est comme ung reynart entre les gelines, *tanquam fera pessima.*"

79. ". . . puet chacun sçavoir, que si au temps passé la matière fust venue en jugement comme maintenant, *non fuisset tolleratum.*"

80. Each woman was to contribute five sous a week to a common fund to be used for the repair of the house, bedrooms, beds, and for other things necessary to the running of the brothel, supervised by a *maistre des heures* appointed by the king and checked by a merchant of Toulouse. An abbess, the oldest of the women, was to be in charge of the house on a daily basis, and to consult with the "master of hours" monthly concerning the necessary repairs.

81. See the epilogue to part 1.

Chapter Four

1. Even M. Perry, working on the early modern period, has encountered a similar dearth of information on prostitutes, in her " 'Lost Women' in Early Modern Seville," *Feminist Studies* 4 (1978): 195–214.

2. To give just a few examples: The two prostitutes cited in the document recording the creation of the red-light district of Montpellier in 1285 were from Béziers and Le Puy (Germain, "Statuts," 126), and two of the four prostitutes listed in the royal safeguard granted to the Toulousan brothel in 1425 were definitely "foreigners" (appendix B). "La Picarda" is mentioned in AM Toulouse, CC 2345, no. 65 (1511). One-third of the Dijonese prostitutes studied by J. Rossiaud were from the region surrounding the city and another third from farther away ("Prostitution, jeunesse et société," 321). The majority

of Florentine prostitutes studied by R. Trexler were not born in that city ("Prostitution florentine," 985–87). For the municipal brothel of Leipzig, G. Wustmann has found no mention in the archives of a prostitute born in that city. G. Wustmann, "Frauenhäuser in Leipzig im Mittelalter," *Archiv für Kulturgeschichte* 5 (1907): 472.

3. See chap. 3.

4. See appendix B.

5. Ibid.

6. Three women were from municipalities in southwestern France; one was a Moor.

7. One may note that in the list of 1521 the place names are indicated in order to distinguish between women bearing the same first name.

8. A document from Montpellier reinforces this impression of prostitutes as foreigners. In a will dated 1357, the merchant Berenger of Meyrueis left a great fortune to the sisters of Saint Gilles in Montpellier, formerly a community of repentant women, including penitent prostitutes, on condition that the community be reformed and drawn more strictly under episcopal control. The conditions for admittance give a negative of the image of the prostitute. Postulants were to be virgins; they were to be in sound mind and body (cf. appendix B, Toulouse); they were to have been born in legitimate wedlock; they were to be natives of Montpellier and the surrounding area. AD Hérault, G 1375.

9. Servais and Laurend, *Histoire et dossier de la prostitution*, chap. 11.

10. Three-quarters of sixty-one women studied came from craftsmen or peasant families; the husbands of those who were married were mainly journeymen and manual workers. Rossiaud, "Prostitution, jeunesse et société," 303, 321.

11. P. Montanari, *Documenti su la popolazione di Bologna alla fine del trecento* (Bologna, 1966), 96–97. The *catasto* of 1371 is incomplete.

12. A. Fabretti, *Prostituzione in Perugia* (Torino, 1890), 87–89. The food and clothing are valued at 10 to 20 florins per year.

13. See below, p. 83.

14. There are some references to "vagabond women" (see n. 69, chap. 2), but this is hardly conclusive evidence, as a person who "vagabonded" was not necessarily a poor person but essentially a mobile one.

15. See the prologue to part 2.

16. See nn. 66 and 67, chap. 6.

17. Dowries for poor women had been a popular form of charity in the thirteenth and fourteenth centuries. P. Pansier, *L'oeuvre des repenties à Avignon du XIIIᵉ au XVIIIᵉ siècles* (Paris, 1910), 15–24; M.-S. de Nucé de Lamothe, "Piété et charité publique à Toulouse d'après les testaments," *Annales du Midi* 76 (1964): 5–39. The latter stresses the virtual disappearance of this form of charity from fifteenth-century wills, prior to the revival of popularity in the sixteenth century.

18. In the testament of the canon John Chavarrot of the collegial church of Saint Julien in Tournon, for instance, he made this aim a condition for the legacy to the *paupera filia* Catherine Chabanat: ". . . sub conditione quod

ipsa Catherina sit et permaneat filia honesta et pervenit ad matrimonium; alioquin, casu quo ipsa Catherina vitam inhonestam et lubricam duceret, ipsam donationem noluit habere locum." AD Ardèche, G 174, 19 May 1508. Dowries were provided for women wishing to leave—or avoid entering—the *postribulum* of Avignon, in the fifteenth and sixteenth centuries. Pansier, *Repenties à Avignon*, 18–19.

19. Méray, *Libres prêcheurs* 2:242–44.

20. In 1492 Claudia Fabresse, *filia publica* and native of Nîmes, instituted as her heir James Torrelli, alias Cassolet, her *fidelis amicus* (procurer), and left small sums for masses and to her husband, Peter Chabandi and her brother, Bernard Fabri, notary public, both living in Vézenobre. Le Pileur, *Documents*, 139–41. See also AD Gard, IIE¹ 18–31, 56r.

21. AM Toulouse, CC 2356, no. 90.

22. AM Foix, CC 209 (116), 2v, 8r, 62r, 302r.

23. AM Lodève, CC 1, 123v.

24. AM Pézenas, Cartulaire A, 88v, 131v.

25. "Johanna, relicta Arnaudi Denat, filiaque Bernardi Live de Sancto Felice, etatis . . . xxii anni, et ultra modicca bona possidens, mulier publica." AM Castelnaudary, FF 10, 28 October 1406.

26. BM Arles, MS. 225, 263.

27. AM Montpellier, Inv. 11, 71. In Pavia at the same time, it was a prostitute, Anastasia of Venice, who farmed the brothel for 200 florins a year (Pavesi, *Bordello di Pavia*, 33).

28. L. Barthelemy, *La prostitution à Marseille* (Marseille, 1883), 7.

29. AD Pyrénées-Orientales, B 240, 182r.

30. *Ord* 7:327 (see n. 29, chap. 5).

31. ". . . dictas mulieres quae . . . habitabunt in dicto hospitio cum earum bonis, rebusque universis ac familiaribus in eodem hospitio commorantibus." *Ord* 13:76–77. A *familiarus* could be a domestic servant as well as a family member.

32. Edited by G. Brucker, in his *The Society of Renaissance Florence: A Documentary Study* (New York and London, 1971), 191–92 (dated 1398).

33. See chap. 1, and B. Schnapper, "*Testes inhabiles*: les témoins reprochables dans l'ancien droit pénal," *Tijdschrift voor Rechtsgeschiedenis* 33 (1965): 580.

34. William del Gam, a royal sergeant, objected to the testimony of Raymunda Bodina: ". . . quod dicta Raymunda est . . . vilis mulier et meretrix, et meretricaliter vivens. . . . moratur palam et publice in lupanar cum aliis meretricibus vilibus, et permisit se carnaliter cognoscere cum pecunia eidem data a quibuscumque volentibus eam cognoscere . . ." (Carbasse, *Consulats et justice criminelle*, 406). His close paraphrase of Ulpian's definition of the prostitute indicates a familiarity with Roman law.

35. In this the canonists concurred (Brundage, "Prostitution in Medieval Canon Law," 837, 839). "Honest" women could accuse freely.

36. "Quod meretrices et persone infamate accusant, et recipiuntur earum accusationes, quod fieri non deberet." AM Arles, FF 4. See chap. 1.

37. The *Exceptiones Petri* declared invalid marriages between "nobiles et

honestos viros et meretrices publicas et earum filias" (1 : 29). A statute of Avignon ordered that all married prostitutes be expelled from the whole city (de Maulde, *Coutumes d'Avignon*, 191). The Church, while encouraging men to marry reformed prostitutes (see n. 96, chap. 4), was hostile to the marriage of practicing prostitutes (C. 32 q. 1 c. 10). See Brundage, "Prostitution in Medieval Canon Law," 843.

38. Such an article is found in a charter from Tournon (Ardèche) of 1292 (Francus, "Chartes de Tournon," *Revue du Vivarais* 13 [1905]: 398). Similarly, an article from a charter of 1211 allows an honest man to slap a woman who had run after him: "Si alet folia prohome, lo prohome le donra duas gautadas . . ." (373). This latter provision appears to be unique in Occitanian customs.

39. The ordinances are dated 1208, 1311, and 1314. Courteault, *Bourg-Saint-Andéol*, 229.

40. A custom from Apt dated 1252 reads, "Que si deguna putan o home vil . . . disien paraulas coutumeliosas o fasien deguna injuria a degun bon home o bona famna e de bona condition e aquell o aquella *moderamens* en prenie veniansa, *sensa effusion de sanc e extraxion del cotell*, que per aquella veniansa la cort non pot ni deu ren demandar ni exhigir daquellos, ni far enquesta." A register of justice from the same town shows a man exonerated for beating such a "base" person who had insulted his wife (Sauve, *Prostitution à Apt*, 20–21). Similar provisions are found in a charter from La Mure (Isère) dated 1309 and in one from Pont-de-Beauvoisin (Isère) dated 1288 (FCM).

41. Dahm, *Strafrecht Italiens*, 108–9.

42. AM Toulouse, AA 1, 27; Giraud, *Droit français* 2:205; AM Bourg-Saint-Andéol, AA 2. See chaps. 1 and 2. There are similar provisions in Italian urban statutes. (Dahm, *Strafrecht Italiens*, 412).

43. Giraud, *Droit français* 2:206.

44. Principally through the so-called police regulations (see chap. 5).

45. This was also the punishment prescribed in the royal ordinance of 1254 (see n. 24, chap. 1). The confiscation of clothing may have been inspired by sumptuary strictures but was also used to sanction other infringements. The dress was not only an item of value, and therefore its confiscation the equivalent of a fine, but a tool of the trade whose loss hurt the prostitute's business.

46. For example: in the undated police regulation from Nîmes, the Uzès deliberation from 1326, and a statute of Lunel from 1367 (see n. 21, chap. 5, for references). Flogging was a common punishment for minor crimes from the thirteenth century onward, used especially against members of the lower classes who had little money to pay fines (Bongert, *Droit pénal* 1 : 236–40). I have found no example in the Languedocian texts of an order to mark offending prostitutes with a hot iron, as was decided in Florence in 1318 and again in 1350. R. Davidsohn, *Storia di Firenze* (Florence, 1962), 7:616; J. Galligo, "Documenti riguardanti la prostituzione di Firenze," *Giornale italiano delle malattie veneree* 4 (1869): 1 : 125.

47. See chap. 6.

48. AM Foix, BB 201 (323), 47v, 28 March 1402. Edited by A. Dufau de Maluquer, in his *Le pays de Foix sous Gaston Phoebus* (Foix, 1901), 204–5.

A summary of the cases in this register is given by G. de Llobet in his *Foix médiéval* (St-Girons, 1975), 216–20.

49. AM Foix, BB 201 (323), 65v, 12 June 1402.

50. AM Castelnaudary, FF 10, 28 October 1406. The outcome of the trial is not recorded. An introduction to this register and to the procedure observed is given by J.-M. Carbasse in his "La justice criminelle à Castelnaudary au XIVe siècle," *FHL*-Lauragais (1981): 139–48.

51. Rossiaud, "Prostitution, jeunesse et société," 322–23. There is nevertheless evidence in the fifteenth century of unwillingness to allow married women in the *postribulum*, although the measures seem to have been aimed more at formerly honest women who abandoned their husbands and sought refuge in the brothel rather than at the common prostitutes who married. J. Girard and P. Pansier have published a decision of the temporal court of Avignon to send a married woman found in the *postribulum* back to her husband in Beaucaire, in their *La cour temporelle d'Avignon* (Paris and Avignon, 1909), 196–98. The regulations of the public house of Nürnberg (1500) forbade the manager to keep "einlich frawen, die eynen eeman hat, oder die hie burgers kindt sey" (J. Baader, ed., *Nürnberger Polizeiordnungen* [Stuttgart, 1861], 117). In Genoa in 1469, the manager of the brothel could not keep "aliquam mulierem habentem maritum que non sit publica et venalis meretrix" (R. Granara, *Prostituzione in Genova* [Genoa, 1863], 85). Married prostitutes were not rare, however. See Brucker, *Society in Renaissance Florence*, 191–95; Montanari, *Populazione di Bologna*, 96–97.

52. See nn. 20 and 28, chap. 4. It should be noted, however, that notarial acts made by prostitutes have been found principally in the lower Rhone River valley and surrounding area (Tarascon, Beaucaire, Arles, Marseille).

53. See chap. 3.

54. Cod. 9. 9. 20–22. There is no reason to suppose that punishment of the rapist of the prostitute might find a precedent in Germanic law, given its hostility to "immoral" women.

55. Gratian considers only violence to a virgin to constitute *stuprum*, in C. 36 q. 1 c.2. J. Brundage's only reference to the problem is a summary of a case of the attempted rape of a prostitute in Mantua reported by Alberto dei Gandini, who states that a famous jurist consulted in the matter concluded that the man could not be punished, given the profession of the woman ("Prostitution in Medieval Canon Law," 840). But see Dahm, *Strafrecht Italiens*, 435; P. Hinschius, *Kirchenrecht in Deutschland* (Berlin, 1895), 5:824.

56. J.-L.-A. Huillard-Bréholles, *Historia diplomatica Friderici secundi* (Paris, 1854), IV-1:23–24.

57. Among the Italian towns that did not recognize the rape of the prostitute as a crime were Bologna (1250) and Parma (1347); often, however, as in Rome (1363), Perugia (1342), and Pisa (1286), such a rapist was sentenced to pay a fine. Dahm, *Strafrecht Italiens*, 436; Pertile, *Diritto italiano* 5:532. Similarly in Germany, some towns (e.g., Ems, 1212), explicitly exonerated the rapist of the prostitute, whereas others (e.g., Augsburg, 1276) provided for punishment (R. His, *Strafrecht des deutschen Mittelalters* [Weimar, 1920; reprint, Darmstadt, 1964], 2:152; von Posern-Klett, "Frauenhäuser," 76).

The rapist of the prostitute is exonerated in the customs of Valencia (*Fori Antiqui Valentiae*, edited by M. D. Serrano, vol. 22 of *Textos Escuela de estudios medievales* [Madrid and Valencia, 1950–67], 230).

58. "Si mulier aliqua communis conqueratur se vi oppressam etiam non audiatur" (1192 and 1221). "Si mulier aliqua communis conqueratur se vi oppressam et probaverit eidem sicut alli etiam honeste justitia impendatur" (1244) (Schrank, *Prostitution in Wien*, 51–53). The change may have been due to the growing influence of Roman law (that is to say, Justinianic legislation) in Vienna in this period. See H. Baltl, "Einflüsse des römischen Rechts in Osterreich," *Ius Romanum Medii Aevi* V-7-9 (1962): 28–31.

59. This would seem to be true in the north as well as in the south. The customal of Normandy (c. 1200) stipulates that such a rapist should be punished by the authorities and pay damages to the victim (Le Foyer, *Droit pénal normand*, 96). The Breton customal establishes that such a rape should be punished "like other crimes" (cited in Bongert, *Droit pénal* 1:182).

60. Carbasse, *Consulats et justice criminelle*, 335; Bongert, *Droit pénal* 1:182.

61. The relevant statutes are, in chronological order: Pexiora (Aude), 1194, 1 s.; Fumel (Lot-et-Garonne), 1265, 20 s.; Tournon (Ardèche), 1292, 7 s.; St-Jean-de-Bournay (Isère), 1292, 100 s.; Auch (Gers), 1301, 65 s.; Aspres-sur-Buëch (Hᵗᵉˢ Alpes), 1302, 15 s.; Caussade (Tarn-et-Garonne), 1306, 5 s.; Tarascon (Bouches-du-Rhone), 1348, 2 s. 6 d. (FCM and Carbasse, *Consulats et justice criminelle*, 336). The fines imposed in the Italian cities seem generally to have been higher (e.g., Pisa, 1286, 10 to 40 s.; Vallassina, 1343, 60 s. and, 1388, 10 l.). Dahm, *Strafrecht Italiens*, 436.

62. See nn. 49 and 50, chap. 4. The register of the Châtelet of Paris records the execution in 1391 of a man who had raped a prostitute (cited in Bongert, *Droit pénal* 1:182). The woman in question had decided to repent, which probably accounts for the severity of the punishment.

63. Sauve, *Prostitution à Apt*, 21–22.

64. *Ord* 6:481 (Troyes, 1380), 656 (Paris, 1382); 9:133 (Amiens, 1406). Other persons fearing prosecution on such charges invested in a royal letter of remission, like that granted in 1390 to some young men who had forced (but also paid) a *fille de joie* on pilgrimage. R. Vaultier, *Le folklore pendant la Guerre de Cent Ans* (Paris, 1965), 122. As late as 1524 several *compagnons de guerre* thought it prudent to obtain such a letter, even though they denied the charges. C. Samaran, ed., *La Gascogne dans les registres du Trésor des Chartes* (Paris, 1966), 198.

65. See n. 43, epilogue to part 2.

66. The criminalist Damhoudère gave the following reason for this repudiation, in his *Pratique criminelle* (1555): "Mais pour ravir ou efforcher femmes legières qui sont exposées au commun ou au bourdeau, n'est aulcune punition car il faut qu'elles soient à tous habandonnez, sans nulluy contredire ou escondir estans en estat." Even if a virgin dressed as a prostitute were raped in a brothel, the violator would be excused (cited in Le Foyer, *Droit pénal normand*, 96). Relying on this text for evidence, B. Geremek has mistakenly pre-

sumed that the rape of prostitutes went unpunished in the Middle Ages, using this as a justification for classifying prostitutes as marginal people (Geremek, *Marginaux parisiens*, 267).

67. See, for example, the banality of divorce procedure in fifteenth-century Avignon, despite canonical strictures. P. Ourliac, "Notes sur le mariage à Avignon au XVᵉ siècle," *RMT-SHD* I (1948): 55–61.

68. B. Schnapper has noted that, in general, jurists became more lenient about allowing suspect persons to testify in criminal trials in the fifteenth and sixteenth centuries, a tendency that he attributes to a growing desire for more effective repression of crime, in his "*Testes inhabiles,*" 575–616.

69. The fine imposed on the rapist of the prostitute in Tarascon (1348) is explicitly intended to be an upper limit (". . . et nichil ulterius exigatur"). A similar ceiling was fixed on fines punishing blasphemy in Apt (1352). Giraud, *Droit français* 2:145.

70. For example: "Les filles publiques formèrent une corporation qui avait ses règlements, ses coutumes ou privileges." Sabatier, *Histoire de la législation sur les femmes publiques*, 89 (paraphrasing Sauval, *Histoire de Paris* 3:617).

71. I have relied to a great extent in this section on M. Kriegel, *Les juifs à la fin du Moyen Age dans l'Europe méditerranéenne* (Paris, 1979). For discussion and bibliography on both Jews and usury, see also Mundy, *Europe in the High Middle Ages*, 81–108, 174–88, and passim.

72. *Summa* 2:ii, 10, 11.

73. Text published in E. Rodocanachi, *Les juifs et le Saint Siège* (Paris, 1891), 315–19.

74. For example, the charter dated 1288, which records that the seigneur of Buis-les-Baronnies (Drôme) reserved for himself the right to determine places of residence for *meretrices publice* and *usurarii* (FCM).

75. "Item statuimus quod Judei vel meretrices non audeant tangere manu panem vel fructus qui exponuntur venales; quod si fecerent, tunc emere illud quod tetigerint teneantur" (de Maulde, *Coutumes d'Avignon*, 200). A similar statute from Salon dated 1293 includes lepers (Giraud, *Droit français* 2:251). Kriegel says that the archbishop of Arles, lord of Salon, intervened in favor of the Jews to limit the products mentioned to bread and fruit, allowing them to touch meat and fish. Kriegel also lists comparable regulations in other Mediterranean towns (Kriegel, *Juifs*, 40ff.). Similar prohibitions aimed only at prostitutes are found in the regulations of Saint-Félix-de-Lauragais in 1463 (Ramière de Fortanier, *Chartes du Lauragais*, 607–26) and in those of Toulon dated 1393 (O. Teissier, "Criées publiques au moyen âge," *Bulletin de la Société d'études scientifiques et archéologiques de Draguignan* 4 [1863–63]: 421–22). Another such measure directed at *meretrices* and lepers is found in the Bagnols regulation of 1358 (E. Bondurand, "Statuts de Bagnols-sur-Cèze," *MANî* 12 [1889]: 31–66).

76. Mireur, *Prostitution à Marseille*, 366–67. Kriegel notes a similar regulation in Tortosa (Spanish Catalonia), in his "Un trait de psychologie sociale dans les pays méditerranéens au bas moyen âge: le juif comme intouchable,"

AnESC 31 (1976): 326–30. Boswell indicates that both prostitutes and Jews were barred from practicing agriculture in Solsona (Aragon) in the fifteenth century (*Royal Treasure*, 349).

77. Kriegel, *Juifs*, 22. See chap. 5.

78. M. Riquet, "St. Louis et les juifs," *Actes des Colloques de Royaumont et de Paris*, 21–27 mai 1970 (Paris, 1976), 345–50. J. Cohen demonstrates that this double policy of attack and proselytizing, a departure from Augustinian toleration, was characteristic of the Mendicants, in his *The Friars and the Jews: The Evolution of Medieval Anti-Judaism* (Ithaca, 1982). I have only been able to consult the dissertation abstract of the original thesis (Cornell University, 1978).

79. See n. 99, chap. 4. Yet, although Jews and prostitutes were often treated in similar ways, these two groups were nonetheless not supposed to mix, as the Marseille statute requiring separate bath days for Jews and prostitutes shows. It would also appear that Christian prostitutes were not to accept Jews (or Saracens) as clients (Boswell, *Royal Treasure*, 349; S. Kahn, "Documents sur les juifs de Montpellier au moyen âge," *Revue des études juives* 28 [1894]: 134–35; see n. 64, chap. 5).

80. J. Le Goff has pointed out that more and more professions were becoming socially acceptable in the later Middle Ages. J. Le Goff, "Métiers licites et métiers illicites dans l'occident médiéval," in his *Pour un autre Moyen Age* (Paris, 1977), 99.

81. Larivaille, *Vie quotidienne des courtisanes*, 171–72. For a similar incident, see Trexler, "Prostitution florentine," 100.

82. Reported in S. Chojnacki, "Crime, Punishment and the Trecento Venetian State," in *Violence and Civil Disorder in Italian Cities, 1200–1500*, edited by L. Martines (Berkeley, Los Angeles, and London, 1972), 211.

83. Le Pileur, *Documents*, 136.

84. Ménard, *Histoire de Nismes* 3:341–42. The consul in question was the owner of the house, Gabriel de Laye.

85. For example, AM Montpellier, Grand Thalamus, passim.

86. The first archival references to this custom of prostitutes' races are from the 1490s. A payment was made to the subvicar on 21 July 1493 "per aver vaccat ala fiera de la Magdalena du cors, sault et luchas, tant de homes coma de las filhetas" (AM Beaucaire, CC 226, 21v). An ordinance on the fair dated 1499 describes this custom: "Item, l'on fait asçavoir aux belles fillettes que se vouldront despourter à courir après les cours et sault desditz hommes, comme est de bonne coustume, que se ayent à trouver au lieu acoustumé, car à la mieulx courante seront delivres ung per de chausses et ung per de sollies, comme est acoustumé" (HH 13). See also n. 7, prologue to part 1.

87. Anibert, *Mémoires sur Arles* 2:364.

88. Fabretti, *Prostituzione in Perugia*, 93.

89. von Posern-Klett, "Frauenhäuser," 80–81.

90. B. Guenée and F. Lehoux, *Les entrées royales françaises de 1328 à 1515* (Paris, 1968); see also N. Coulet, "Les entrées solennelles en Provence au XIVᵉ siècle," *Ethnologie française* 7 (1977): 63–82.

91. ". . . lui faisant la reverence et balhant fleurs" (Duhamel, *Chronique d'Orange*, 36).

92. AD Bouches-du-Rhone, B 1724, Inv. Blancard.

93. Bec, *Marchands écrivains*, 57–64; Lorcin, "Prostituée des fabliaux." One may also note that the butcher's guild of Paris in 1381 forbade its members to marry prostitutes without first obtaining permission from guild officers (*Ord* 6:595).

94. When asked how long a woman might work as a prostitute, Lozana, the courtesan heroine of the romance by the same name of Francisco Delicado (written in 1524), responds, "From twelve to forty." J. Rossiaud has shown that most active prostitutes in Dijon were in their teens or twenties ("Prostitution, jeunesse et société," 303, 321).

95. Bullough, "Prostitute in the Middle Ages."

96. "Inter opera caritatis . . . non minimum est errantem ab erroris sui semita revocare ac presertim mulieres voluptuose viventes et admittentes indifferenter quoslibet ad commercium carnis, ut caste vivant, ad legitime thori consortium invitare. Hoc igitur attendentes presentium auctoritate statuimus, ut omnibus qui publicas mulieres de lupanari extraxerint et duxerint in uxores, quod agunt, in remissionem proficiat peccatorum." *PL* 214:102, 29 April 1198.

97. A. Charasson, *Un curé plébéien au XIIe siècle: Foulques de Neuilly* (Paris, 1905), 62–65; M. R. Gutsch, "A Twelfth-Century Preacher: Fulk of Neuilly," in *The Crusades and Other Historical Essays Presented to Dana C. Munro*, edited by L. J. Paetow (New York, 1928; reprint, New York, 1968), 83–206. Fulk may well have been influenced by the ideas of Innocent III, as it was he who assumed the mission of preaching the Fourth Crusade, originally conferred by this pope on his aging master.

98. A. Simon, *L'ordre des Pénitentes de Sainte Marie-Madeleine en Allemagne au XIIIe siècle*, Thèse-Théologie-Fribourg (Suisse, 1918), 5.

99. Ibid.; Joinville, *Vie de Saint Louis*, edited by N. de Wailly (Paris, 1968), 258.

100. Simon, *Pénitentes*, 15.

101. The special relation between these German communities and the pope is discussed by P. Hofmeister in his "Die Exemption des Magdalenerinnen ordens," *ZSSR* (*kan. Abtg.*) 66 (1948): 305–29.

102. Pope Alexander IV (1254–61) was an important supporter of communities of repentant sisters in Italy. Rome, Bologna, and Viterbo had such houses by the mid–thirteenth century. Simon, *Pénitentes*, 7–8.

103. J. Mundy, "Charity and Social Work in Toulouse, 1100–1250," *Traditio* 22 (1966): 206. P. Wolff states that Saint Dominic himself had founded such a community in Toulouse in 1215, in his *Histoire de Toulouse* (Toulouse, 1974), 120. A second community seems to have been founded by a Franciscan in the early fourteenth century. These sisters followed the Augustinian rule and were referred to as the canonesses of Saint Sernin (Simon, *Pénitentes*, 6).

104. Simon, *Pénitentes*, 6.

105. Pansier, *Repenties à Avignon*, 20–22.

106. A legacy to this community is found in a will dated 1321. J. Caille, *Hôpitaux et charité publique à Narbonne au moyen âge* (Toulouse, 1978), 43, 46, 53, 119–21; Pansier, *Repenties à Avignon*, 13.

107. According to a letter of Clement V of 30 June 1309, cited in Simon, *Pénitentes*, 7.

108. R. Bouges, *Histoire ecclésiastique de Carcassonne* (Paris, 1741), 227–28. In Raymond Lull's *Blaquerne*, it is a "bourjois" who founds a house for penitent prostitutes (198).

109. E. Desplanque, *Les infâmes dans l'ancien droit roussillonnais* (Perpignan, 1893), 108.

110. AM Montpellier, EE 299, Inv. 12.

111. See n. 115, chap. 4.

112. AM Montpellier, EE 840.

113. AM Montpellier, EE 335. A will of 24 November 1326 refers to "black" repentant sisters and "white" repentant sisters (EE 348), and one dated 17 July 1334 identifies the black sisters as those of Saint Catherine and the white as those of the Courreau (EE 534). Not until 13 October 1343 does one find the name Saint Mary Magdalene attached to the white repentant sisters (EE 383). For the close association between the communities of repentant sisters and the spread of the cult of Saint Mary Magdalene in fourteenth-century Occitania, see V. Saxer, *Le culte de Marie Madeleine en occident*, Thèse-Théologie-Strasbourg, 1953 (Auxerre and Paris, 1959), 249–50.

114. Municipal financial documents refer to alms given to these communities throughout this period (AM Montpellier, Inv. 9, 196). The merger is related in the town chronicle, the *Petit Thalamus*: "Item, un dimergue xx d'octobre, las Sorres repentidas negras de Sancta Katarina se ajusteron am las repentidas blancas de Sancta Magdalena." *Le Petit Thalamus* (Montpellier, 1840), 412.

115. A. Germain, "Statuts inédits des repenties du couvent de St. Gilles de Montpellier," *MSAMtp* 5 (1860–69): 123–42. As the title indicates, Germain mistakenly believed that the sisters of Saint Gilles were still a community of repentant sisters having taken Saint Catherine as a second patron; he was misled principally by a will of 1357 that "reforms" the sisters of Saint Gilles (see n. 8, chap. 4) and by lack of access to documents that have since been classified. Similar errors plague L. Guiraud's study of the repentant sisters in her *La paroisse de St. Denis de Montpellier* (Montpellier, 1887), 47–53, leading her even to doubt the authenticity of the passage of the *Petit Thalamus* (see n. 114, chap. 4), which is, of course, perfectly correct.

116. Pansier, *Repenties à Avignon*, 106–45.

117. ". . . mulieres peccatrices juvenes que sint infra etatem vigniti quinque annorum . . ."

118. In Avignon this recital of prayers was assigned only to those sisters who could not follow the service because they were illiterate. Apparently, in Montpellier few, if any, of the sisters were literate.

119. See below, p. 81.

120. An example of this aspect of a halfway house is the rule for the repen-

tant sisters of Abbeville dated 1480: "lesdittes soeurs pourront se leur volonté si tourne et ossi se ch'est du gré de la maistresse et des gouverneurs de eslire aultre estat honneste et salutaire comme le sainct estat de mariage . . ." Louandre, "Statuts des Soeurs de la Magdeleine d'Abbeville," *Mémoirs de la Société d'émulation d'Abbeville*, 1834–35, 124. This community, like Montpellier, was under municipal surveillance. It was open to *pecheresses publiques* without a strict age limit and was only semicloistered. The repentant sisters of Vienna, too, could leave to marry (Schrank, *Prostitution in Wien*, 81). The low level of religious life in such an institution appears in the documentation on the convent of the Magdalene in Perpignan. There, no attempt was made to cloister the women, and escapes were frequent. Inventories list fine linen, furs, and jewels among the sisters' possessions. The women—even those holding offices of responsibility—used vulgar language, quarreled and assaulted other sisters (Otis, "Notes on Prostitution and Repentance in Late Medieval Perpignan" in J. Kirshner and S. Wemple, eds., *Women of the Medieval World* [Oxford, 1985]; Desplanque, *Infâmes*, 112–13).

121. The consuls of Marseille purchased a house for the residence of the repentant sisters there in 1380 (Mireur, *Prostitution à Marseille*, 27). In Pavia the construction of a residence for repentant sisters in 1399 was a joint effort of the municipal authorities and the duke, much of the money coming from the revenues of the *postribulo*; the sisters were placed under the safeguard of the duke, and aggressors were threatened with the death penalty (Pavesi, *Bordello di Pavia*, 38–41). Duke Albert III of Austria granted a *Freiheitsbrief* to the penitents of Vienna in 1384, placing them under the patronage of the municipal authorities (Schrank, *Prostitution in Wien*, 80–81).

122. The few texts that survive from the fifteenth century attest to the decadence of the institution, as in Avignon, where the community had shrunk from forty sisters in the late fourteenth century to two in 1489, before a modest revival in the early sixteenth century (Pansier, *Repenties à Avignon*).

123. A miniature illustrating this important event adorns the town chronicle. E. Roschach, "Les douze livres de l'histoire de Toulouse, MS. 1295–1787, étude critique," in *Toulouse—Histoire Archéologie*, etc. (Toulouse, 1887).

124. AM Toulouse, CC 1576, 56r; CC 2369, no. 96 (repairs); CC 2352; CC 2378, no. 281, 282 (contributions). Since only one community is mentioned in these documents, it seems that the others referred to in the thirteenth and fourteenth centuries had disappeared or had been reformed in 1516.

125. Published document no. 8. Outside Languedoc there is similar evidence of an upsurge of interest in repentance. It was toward the end of the fifteenth century that the city of Cologne acquired a house for repentant women (J. Kemp, *Die Wohlfahrtspflege des kölner Rates*, Diss.-Phil.-Bonn, 1904, 40–41). The *échevins* of Amiens rented a house for the use of penitent prostitutes in 1491 and bought one for this purpose in 1503 (J.-C. Delannoy, *Pécheresses et repenties à Amiens* [Amiens, 1943]). In Avignon the municipal authorities increasingly took the responsibility for repairs and other expenses of the repentant sisters in this period (Pansier, *Repenties à Avignon*, chap. 8). The municipal council of Besançon granted a subsidy to a poor young pros-

titute wanting to return to her family in the Savoy in 1534 (Le Pileur, *Documents*, 105). A new house for reformed prostitutes in Paris, the Filles Pénitentes, was established by John Tisserand in 1492 and confirmed by letters of Charles VIII in 1496 (Sabatier, *Histoire de la législation sur les femmes publiques*, 126–27). It is recorded that a preacher succeeded in converting a large number of Roman prostitutes to the religious life in 1508 (A. Bertolotti, *Repressioni straordinarie alla prostituzione in Roma nel secolo XVI* [Rome, 1887], 8). In Sicily communities for repentant sisters were founded in Palermo in 1512 and in Messina in 1542 (Cutrera, *Prostituzione in Sicilia*, 89).

126. This work did not always go smoothly, however, as the following text testifies: "Item comme bien sçavez et est notoire il a quatre ans on emirre que furent depputées et mises certaines repenties à l'ospital de Sainct Jacques du bout du pont, lesquelles de commancement faisoient grand service aux pauvres malades dudict hospital, et les tractoient tres bien, et estoient norries et bien acoustées aux despens dudict hospital, et le monastere desdictes repenties en estoit grandement deschargé. Mais il est advenu que durant nostre administracion, il n'en y avoit que une nommée Seur Johanne, laquelle aussi a esté reprochée de plusieurs insolences, et en y a informacions aussi que Salamonis vostre notaire vous dira. Si elles vouloient fer comme au commencement, vous en y retourneres mectre *in competenti numero* si bon vous semble, à tout le moins donneres ordre que les pauvres mallades dudict hospital soyent bien traictez, car c'est l'une des choses principalles que vous avez à faire et en estez chargez." AM Toulouse, BB 265, 109r (1522). Some of the sisters of Abbeville also worked in the hospitals (Louandre, "Statuts des Soeurs de la Magdeleine d'Abbeville," 124). Starting in the 1490s the Soeurs Noires de la Madeleine of Lille nursed plague victims and other hospital ill (Scrive-Bertin, "L'hygiène publique à Lille," *Bulletin de la Commission historique du département du Nord* 17 [1886]: 402).

127. ". . . mise ou couvent des seurs repenties de Thoulouse pour illec servir perpetuellement à dieu et audit couvent . . . avec defense de ne jamais sortir . . . sur peine d'estre pendue et estranglée." AD Haute Garonne, B 17, 245r. Given this custom, one understands easily why in years of poverty the repentant sisters of Toulouse sent requests for alms, not only to the bishop of Toulouse and to the consuls, but also to the Parlement of Toulouse, requesting of them "quelque somme d'argent sur les emandes et condempnacions que on esté et seront faictes par icelle" (AM Toulouse, CC 2352 [1522]). The service they provided as a prison for female criminals entitled them to a claim on the fruits of justice. B. Schnapper cites a case of a woman sentenced to imprisonment in a convent of repentant women by the Parlement of Bordeaux in 1565. Because such an institution lacked, she was placed in a hospital to serve the poor (Schnapper, "Répression pénale, Parlement de Bordeaux," 33). Sherril Cohen has found a similar tendency in such institutions in Florence in preparing a thesis, to be defended soon at Princeton, entitled "The *Convertite* and the *Malmaritate*: Women's Institutions, Prostitution and the Family in Counter-Reformation Florence." Trexler notes that Florentine women convicted of sexual offenses were confined to the convent of the *Convertite* in the early sixteenth century (Trexler, "Prostitution florentine," 1002, 1013).

128. On these later institutions, see Delamarre, *Traité de Police* I : 527–32. H. Gilles has noted, "C'est par l'intermédiaire des femmes que la privation de la liberté a fait son entrée dans notre appareil répressif" (in his "Femme délinquante," 255). See also M. Foucault, *Surveiller et punir* (Paris, 1975).

Chapter Five

1. See also the epilogue to part 2.

2. To give just a few examples: The red-light district of Montpellier was established in the suburb Villanova, then transferred to another suburb along the road to Lattes in the early fourteenth century. The brothel of Pézenas was outside the walls from the fourteenth to the sixteenth century (AM Pézenas, Cartulaire A, 88v; *compoix* of 1509, cited in J. Combes, "Aspects économiques et sociaux de Pézenas médiéval," *FHL*-Pézenas [1975]: 20). The house of prostitution of Lodève was in Lo Barri, a suburb southwest of the town center, in the fifteenth and sixteenth centuries (AM Lodève, CC 1, 123v). In 1498 the brothel of Nîmes was outside the walls, located, appropriately enough, in the suburb of Saint Mary Magdalene (AD Gard, IIE¹ 206, 110r).

3. ". . . de toute ancienneté, est de coustume en notre païs de Languedoc, et especiallement ès bonnes villes dudit païs, estre establie une maison et demourance au dehors desdites villes pour l'habitacion et residence des filles communes . . ." *Ord* 20 : 180–83. The king of France ordered the brothel of Castelnaudary to be placed "hors de la ville" in 1445 (published document no. 2). The relevant passage of the charter of Villefranche-de-Lauragais refers to a house "in aliqua parte extra dictam villam" (Ramière de Fortanier, *Chartes du Lauragais*, 710).

4. See also the case of Albi, chap. 2.

5. AM Uzès, BB 1, 3v, 29v.

6. The *Libre de memorias* of Jacme Mascaro has this entry for 1348: ". . . et 1 cavalier seu sen anet deportar al borc del Rey foras los murs; et anet en una carieyra pres del bordel . . ." (published anonymously in *BSABéz*, 1st ser., 1 (1836): 74). One of the proclamations of the seneschal of Carcassonne in April 1436 was, "Item, de habitationibus mulierum publicarum quas infra presentem villam faciunt quod detur provisio" (F. Guibal, "Registre de la maison consulaire de Béziers, 1435–36," *BSABéz*, 1st ser., 1 [1836]: 272).

7. Gilles, *Coutumes de Toulouse*, 256; J. Coppolani, "Les noms anciens des voies publiques de Toulouse," *Mémoires de la Société archéologique du Midi de la France* 35 (1970): 91–99.

8. See L. Guiraud, *Recherches topographiques sur Montpellier* (Montpellier, 1895), 133. This quarter seems to have been one of the least densely settled within the walls.

9. It has generally been assumed that throughout the fifteenth century the brothel of Toulouse was located outside the city walls (Chalande, "Maison publique à Toulouse," 69–71). The royal safeguard of 1425 indicates that the house at that time was located "infra civitatem Tolosae et ante clausuras civitatis," which is ambiguous, since it could mean either inside the agglomeration but outside the walls or within the walls (AM Toulouse, AA 5, no.

371). The leases of the garden of this brothel, once the structure itself had been demolished during reconstruction of the city walls in the 1520s, state clearly, however, that the garden was located *infra muros* (". . . plathea sita infra muros presentis civitatis Tholose. Et illa plathea solebat esse ortus domus publice sive lupanaris prope portam de la Crosas. . . ," AM Toulouse, DD 45, 69v, 78v). It does not seem likely that the brothel was moved between 1425 and the 1520s, because the municipal archives, extremely rich in documentation on the public house, show no sign of a change in location. The brothel would seem to have been within the walls in the fifteenth century.

10. The brothel of Le Puy was moved from the very center, near the cathedral, to a location on the edge of town (but within the walls) in 1516. *Livre de Podio* 1:288. There may even have been a trend favoring bringing brothels within the town walls in the sixteenth century (all three sites proposed for the new brothel in Toulouse in the 1520s were within the walls), possibly with the same goal as in the fourteenth century—to assure better police of the brothel. In Toulouse one site was advocated because it was "près de justice [the town hall]" (see below).

11. Trexler, 990. The brothel of Leipzig had been located in the very center of town until, on complaint of the Dominican prior in the fifteenth century, it was moved to a suburb (Wustmann, "Frauenhäuser in Leipzig," 471).

12. See n. 1, chap. 2.

13. See published document no. 1. The consuls of Albi had considered moving the brothel in the early fifteenth century because of complaints: ". . . quar aqui era en loc trop public et en la passa de las gens . . ." AM Albi, BB 18, 92v.

14. See the royal ordinance of 1256 and the statutes of Marseille, nn. 27 and 37, chap. 1. In Aix-en-Provence in 1329, the radius from the church within which no prostitute could exercise her profession was the distance traveled by an arrow shot from a crossbow (Barthélemy, *Prostitution à Marseille*, 5). Similar provisions appear in the Italian statutes. In Florence no prostitute could work within approximately one hundred meters of a church (Pertile, *Diritto italiano* 5:540).

15. In 1489 the convent of the Carmes in Arles complained of the proximity of the *luoc public*; by 1497 the municipality had constructed a house for the women in another neighborhood (BM Arles, MS. 225, 265). The Franciscans of Avignon complained of the conversion of a house in their neighborhood into a *lupanar* in 1466 (Le Pileur, *Documents*, 16–17). The Parlement of Toulouse obliged the consuls of Castres to move the *maison des filles de vie* farther from the local Franciscan convent in 1511, on pain of a 100 marc fine (AD Haute Garonne, B 15, 25r). The king of Aragon closed a house used by prostitutes in the vicinity of a Dominican convent of Barcelona on the Dominicans' request in 1363 (A. Lopez de Meneses, *Documentos acerca de la pesta negra en los dominios de la Corona de Aragon* [Saragossa, 1956], 438–41). Proximity of prostitution to a church could be justified, however, as in this gem of casuistry presented to the Parlement of Paris by the lawyer for prostitutes threatened with expulsion from a street near a church in Paris: "Et

est expedient que le bordiau soit près de l'église, car combien que telles femmes pechent, elles ne sont pas du tout damnées, et est expedient qu'elles voisent aucunes fois à l'église, ce qu'elles font plustost quand elles sont près que se elles estoient loing" (Félibien, *Histoire de Paris* 4:538).

16. AM Toulouse, BB 9, 38r–41v; FF 609/1; AD Haute Garonne, B21, 244r.

17. Rossiaud notes a complaint about the proximity of the brothel to schools in Dijon in 1426 ("Prostitution, jeunesse et société," 315). The prostitutes of Venice were prohibited from living near the school Saint Gothard in 1460 (Calza, "Prostituzione in Venezia," 367). The consuls of Montpellier protested to the Parlement of Toulouse in 1498 that one of the illicit stews in that town was near the university (published document no. 5). One may wonder whether this new interest in keeping prostitutes away from schools may not have reflected a change in the conception of childhood and adolescence in this period. A regulation from Ulm dated 1527 forbade the brothel manager to let twelve- to fourteen-year-old boys enter the house (von Posern-Klett, "Frauenhäuser in Sachsen," 70). In 1556 Calvin complained about "tant de paillardes qui debochent tant de ieunes enfans" (*Opera* 21:639). The consuls of Castelnaudary urged the closing of the public house there in 1555 because of "plusieurs desbauchamens de jeunes enfans" (AM Castelnaudary, BB 4, 213r). E. Garin notes that the fifteenth-century humanist schoolmasters stressed the necessity of setting a good moral example for young children, whose good education was of the highest interest to the state. E. Garin, *La pédagogie de la Renaissance* (Bari, 1957; Fr. trans., Paris, 1968), 117, 127, 137.

18. In the first vote on 29 April 1526, out of eight council members described as *bourgeois*, seven voted against the Saint Paul site and only one for it. Only two *licenciés* opposed the site, whereas three *licenciés* and all four *docteurs* on the council voted for it. Also in favor of Saint Paul was the royal counselor Vabres. The royal counselor Reynier had suggested that the municipality no longer farm the house. Thus, *la chose publique* seems to have found its most reliable defenders among those council members with university degrees and royal officers.

19. J. Rossiaud does not, it seems to me, sufficiently appreciate the immense logistic problem posed in such a situation when he claims that the consuls of most medieval towns were "lukewarm" in their respect of certain principles concerning the location of brothels (in "Prostitution, jeunesse et société," 292, 315).

20. Giraud, *Droit français* 2:205; de Maulde, *Coutumes d'Avignon*, 191.

21. To simplify notation, a list is given here of all major late-medieval Languedocian police regulations, including articles on prostitution, and their references, in alphabetical order of the towns. The reader is asked to consult this list for all otherwise unidentified references. Alès, 1454 (AM Alès, 1S 18, no. 37); Bagnols-sur-Cèze, 1300 (P. Béraud, *Histoire de Bagnols* [Nîmes, 1941], Pièce Justificative); Bagnols, 1358 (Bondurand, "Statuts de Bagnols, 1358 et 1380," *MANî* 12 [1889]: 45–49); Beaucaire, 1373 (A. Eysette, *His-*

toire de Beaucaire [Beaucaire, 1888], 2:284); Castelnaudary, 1333 (AM Castelnaudary, AA 1, 10r–41r; Ramière de Fortanier, *Chartes du Lauragais*, 305–25); Castres, 1373 ("Réglements de police municipale de Castres," *Revue du Tarn* 8 [1890–91]: 319–20); Lunel, 1367 (AM Lunel, Livre Blanc, 13v–15v; Bondurand, "Les coutumes de Lunel, 1367," *MANî* 8 [1885]: 54–78); Nîmes, undated (AM Nîmes, FF 1, no. 2); Nîmes, 1350 and 1353 (AM Nîmes, FF 1, no. 18 and 21; Ménard, *Histoire de Nismes* 2:138, 153); Saint-Félix-de-Lauragais, 1463 (Ramière de Fortanier, *Chartes du Lauragais*, 623–24).

22. ". . . vestes longuas per terram trahentes." AM Pézenas, 791.

23. Civil and ecclesiastical officers often cooperated in enforcing such legislation. See H. Kantorowicz, "*De ornatu mulierum*: A Consilium of Antonius de Rosellis with an Introduction on Fifteenth-Century Sumptuary Legislation," *Rechtshistorische Studien*, edited by H. Coing and G. Immel (Karlsruhe, 1970), 341–76.

24. Similar sumptuary legislation was actively enforced in Leipzig in the 1470s, when prostitutes were fined for having worn silk, silver, and coral (Wustmann, "Frauenhäuser in Leipzig," 475).

25. U. Robert, *Signes d'infamie* (Paris, 1891), 175–89. Robert points out that many authors have confused measures prohibiting the wearing of veils with those requiring a sign, thus reading back these late-medieval provisions to the thirteenth century. Kriegel, *Jews*, 22ff. For another police regulation concerning both prostitutes and Jews—statutes forbidding them to touch food displayed on the market—see n. 75, chap. 4.

26. "Item, que deguna aul femna no ause star ni anar per lo Castelnau sino porta 1 cordo de fil cint sobre la rauba . . . e si es trobada en malvestat, hom ley scintar malgre son grat." The document is a late-fourteenth-century copy.

27. "Item, ut tales viles mulieres propter ornamenta que portant discernantur alterius, quod in rauba quam portabunt desuper fiat una manica alterius panni et alterius coloris . . ."

28. All towns and regions of western Europe seem to have required prostitutes to wear distinguishing signs or clothing, although the sign or clothing varied greatly from town to town. G. Brucker has published court records relating the prosecution of a public woman in Florence for failure to wear the distinctive apparel required there, "gloves on her hands and a bell on her head" (*Society in Renaissance Florence*, 191–95).

29. ". . . pour cause de certains chaperons et cordons blans, à quoy elles sont astraintes porter par icelle ordenances . . . avons octroyé . . . que doresenavant elles ne leurs successeurs en ladicte Abbaye portent et puisse porter et vestir telles robes et chapperons et de telles couleur comme elles vouldront vestir et porter, parmi ce qu'elles seront tenues de porter entour l'un de leurs bras une Ensigne ou difference d'un jaretier en lisière de drap d'autre couleur que la robe . . ." *Ord* 7:327.

30. Rossiaud, "Prostitution, jeunesse et société," 304.

31. For regulations concerning residence, see chap. 6, and for those on circulation during Holy Week, see below.

32. "Quod aliqua vilis meretrix postribuli non sit ausa accedere seu ire per

civitatem Nemausi simul cum alia, sed tantum sola" (1350). "... non vadant per ipsam civitatem Nemausi, sole nec sociate" (1353).

33. Prostitutes in Barcelona were fined if caught working after curfew (Boswell, *Royal Treasure*, 70–71).

34. AM Toulouse, BB 265, passim; FF 171.

35. *Petit Thalamus*, 139.

36. "... que les filles de la bonne mayson facent residence, mangent et beuvent en ycelle et non ... aller vagant par les tavernes ..." AM Toulouse, BB 265, 30r (1513).

37. "Quant à l'eglise, sont lesdites ribauldes derriere et segreguées des autres femmes de bien." AM Pézenas, Cartulaire A, 21v.

38. AD Bouches-du-Rhone, B 1917, Inv. Blancard.

39. AM Castelnaudary, FF 9 (unfoliated), 25 December 1390. In 1459 two Leipzig prostitutes were banished from that city for a similar offense (Wustmann, "Frauenhäuser in Leipzig," 474).

40. "Item, quod nulla mulier publica sit ausa cantare vel corizare de nocte per carrerias, neque corizare de die, nisi in earum carreria, excepto tempore nundinarum Balneolarum, quo tempore eis liceat corizare ..."

41. *Government* had a much broader meaning in the Middle Ages than today; it was used to describe the proper ordering of an institution or even an individual, as well as a political body.

42. Published document no. 10. The dates 1491–94 are suggested by F. Baby in his chapter of the collective work *Histoire de Pamiers* (Pamiers, 1981), 207. Number references given in parentheses correspond to the articles of this document. See the table of money equivalences.

43. The following is a list of these regulations, which the reader is asked to consult for all further references: Sandwich, 1494 (Boys, *History of Sandwich* 2:680); Ulm, 1430 (H. Lippert, *Die Prostitution in Hamburg* [Hamburg, 1848], 3–5); Strasbourg, 1500 (J. Brucker, ed., *Strassburger Zunft- und Polizeiverordnungen* [Strasbourg, 1889], 468–69); Nürnberg, undated (Baader, *Nürnberger Polizeiordnungen*, 117–21); Perugia, 1388 (Fabretti, *Prostituzione in Perugia*, 12–26); Pavia, 1405 (Pavesi, *Bordello di Pavia*, 34–36); Foligno, 1446 (in Fabretti, *Perugia*, 90–92); Genoa, 1459 (Granara, *Prostituzione in Genova*, 82–87); Venice, 1460 (Calza, "Prostituzione in Venezia," 319–20, 365–68).

44. "... qu'il ait à tenir ladite maison proveue de vin, de pain et de autres causes necessaires, aux pris et taux qui ont estez faiz autrefoys tant par nous que noz predecesseurs, c'est assavoir, trois dobles pour checun jour tout compris ..." AM Toulouse, BB 265, 45r (1513). A more flexible plan was recommended in 1517. The farmer was "chargé à tenir provision ausdites garces avecques leur argent à taulx reasonable segond le merché des vivres et à votre tauxation." BB 265, 80r.

45. In Sandwich, Strasbourg, and Nürnberg the women paid on a weekly basis; and in Venice, once a month. In Genoa prostitutes were specifically exempted from payment when ill, and in Pavia in 1405 the amount the prostitute paid the farmer depended on her physical appearance: beautiful women (*pulcriores et formosiores*) owed only half as much as plain women!

46. Louis XI's letter of 1469 states that brothels were intended "pour l'habitacion et residence des filles communes, tant de celles qui y font residence que autres passans et frequentans ledit pays." *Ord* 20: 180.

47. ". . . so offt sie mit einichem man leiplicher werck pfligt."

48. The *slaffgelt* amounted to three pennies in Nürnberg and a *kreuzer* in Ulm, where the man was to pay a penny if he used a light. The prostitute in Ulm kept all that she earned at night, except the *slaffgelt*; two-thirds of what she earned in the daytime went into a kitty for common purposes, and the remaining third went toward her payments due to the manager.

49. In Ulm municipal officers made regular inspections of the brothel, reading the house ordinances aloud to the women on these occasions, presumably to inform them of their rights as well as their obligations.

50. This practice recalls the provisions for expeditive or "popular" justice against prostitutes in certain thirteenth- and early-fourteenth-century customs. See above, p. 67.

51. For notarial records of such debts, see n. 12, chap. 4. The notable exception in Italy was Venice, where, in 1438 and again in 1460, municipal legislation prohibited contracting debts with prostitutes and accepting such women as pledges on debts (Calza, "Prostituzione in Venezia," 317–18, 366).

52. The regulations of Ulm allowed the manager to accept a woman as a pawn for a debt owed by her parents or husband, as long as she agreed to the arrangement. The statutes of Nürnberg forbade the buying of women not already prostitutes and prohibited the manager from preventing the departure of an endebted prostitute. For a similar concern with protecting the prostitute from exploitation, see the regulations of the public houses of Grenada (1539) and of Seville (1553), summarized by Guardia in his "Prostitution en Espagne," 778–83.

53. Published document no. 4.

54. ". . . que les filhes perdues du Chasteau Vert ne ailhent par la ville . . . à peine du fohet, sinon les dimenches et festes pour oÿr messe, que ailhent toutes ensemble et toutes aussi après retourner en ladite maison . . ." AM Toulouse, BB 265, 171v, 172r (1528).

55. For an explanation of "running the town," see n. 21, chap. 6. The consuls of Toulouse had defended the necessity of maintaining the brothel farmer by emphasizing his importance as a "bouncer," in the case before Parlement in 1462. Published document no. 4.

56. The brothel manager of Pavia was allowed an armed guard of six men!

57. An entry in the account books, dated 16 June 1507, reads, "a Mestre Peyre Mest, de las hobras per aver mesa la dagua de Pr Francoh de Sanct Pastor aldit pal davant lo bon hostal, per so quel avia picada una filha del bon hostal . . . 1 s. 3 d." AM Castelnaudary, CC 81, 9r. This *pal* apparently served to display various insignias, including the fleur-de-lis; an entry dated 12 June records that John Loyso was paid 4 s. "per so quel a faycta una flor dalis per mectre en hun pal davant la mayso del public." Ibid.

58. Published document no. 4; see chap. 2.

59. See appendix C.

60. Rossiaud, "Prostitution, jeunesse et société," 321.

61. ". . . ordonnances et appointemens sur le fait et gouvernement de ladite maison et étuves." *Ord* 20: 180–83.

62. Published document no. 4; see n. 80, chap. 3.

63. External police agents, moreover, like brothel managers, often received payments from the prostitutes. The king himself received a 5 l. annual payment from the brothel owners whose monopoly he guaranteed in Montpellier (*Ord* 20:180). In Paris it was a royal court officer, the *roi des ribauds*, who collected 5 s. a year from the prostitutes in the early fifteenth century (A. Terroine, "Le roi des ribauds de l'Hôtel du roi et les prostituées parisiennes," *RHD*, 4th ser., 56 [1978]: 253–67). In Bordeaux the prostitutes paid the prevost 15 s. a year in 1455 (H. Barckhausen, ed., *Livres des Coutumes*, vol. 5 of *Archives de Bordeaux* [Bordeaux, 1890], 663). In 1428 the town executioner of Pamiers had the right to levy 6 d. a week on every *filha publica* (M. Lahondès, *Annales de Pamiers* [Toulouse and Pamiers, 1882], 1:478). In Amiens the same officer received 4 d. a week (A. Dubois, *Justice et bourreaux à Amiens dans les XVᵉ et XVIᵉ siècles* [Amiens, 1860], 6).

64. Le Pileur, *Documents*, 15–16. The punishment for a Jew caught with a *meretrix* in Venice was a 500 l. fine and six months in prison, according to a text dated 1424 (Calza, "Prostituzione in Venezia," 318). A Jew who entered the Nürnberg brothel in 1406 was banished (von Posern-Klett, "Frauenhäuser in Sachsen," 69).

65. von Posern-Klett, "Frauenhäuser in Sachsen," 70.

66. Le Pileur, *Documents*, 7.

67. von Posern-Klett, "Frauenhäuser in Sachsen," 70; Schrank, *Prostitution in Wien*, 106.

68. As no mention is made of Castel Joyos, the women may have been clandestine prostitutes. They were obliged to run the town and were banished; the man was fined 4 écus. AM Pamiers, FF 20, 62v.

69. She was sentenced to run the town. AM Pamiers 20, 30r.

70. "In domo postribuli o lupanaris . . . ogni persona cuiusvis gradus, sexus vel conditionis, anche ecclesiastica et . . . secularis matrimonio coniuncta, possit et valeat licite accedere et conversari causa stuphandi, bibendique, et comendendi ac dormiendi tam de die quam de nocte, tam cum mulieribus ibi existentibus, et tam honestis quam inhonestis conducendis." Pertile, *Diritto italiano* 5:541.

71. Published document no. 7. See chap. 6.

72. "Item, plus fuit de pacto quod dictus Albi renderius non permictat intro nec extra propter dictam domum ludere nec tenere ullum ludum tempore divini officii, sub pena carceris per mensem cum pane et aqua." AM Alès, 1D 11, 135r (1533).

73. AM Pamiers, FF 20, passim.

74. J.-L. Flandrin has published the first volume of a projected three-volume study of this subject, *Un temps pour embrasser: aux origines de la morale sexuelle occidentale (VIᵉ–XIᵉ siècle)* (Paris, 1983), in which he points out that, while abstinence from intercourse was recommended for a number of holy days in the liturgical year, the period of Lent received the greatest atten-

tion in the medieval penitentials (135–143). See also T. Tentler, *Sin and Confession on the Eve of the Reformation* (Princeton, 1977), 213–16. Such abstinence was practiced as well as preached; in 1404, for example, the merchant G. Dati vowed to keep chaste on Fridays "in memory of the passion of our Lord" (G. Brucker, ed., *Two Memoirs of Renaissance Florence* [New York, 1967], 124). This custom is spoofed in a story of the *Decameron*, in which an impotent husband attempts to justify his reluctance to pay the conjugal debt by arguing that "there was not a single day that was not the feast of one or more Saints, out of respect for whom . . . man and woman should abstain from sexual union" (Boccaccio, *Decameron*, 221–22 [II-10]).

75. "Item, quod quelibet mulier que se dimittat pro pecunia non sit ausa septimana sancta veniente intrare civitatem Nemausi nec accedere per eandem, sub pena perdendi raubam." AM Nîmes FF 1, no. 2. A city law of Augsburg dated 1276 prohibited prostitutes from staying in the town during Holy Week (Schrank, *Prostitution in Wien*, 54).

76. ". . . quod quacumque vana et vilis mulier exuet ab inde in anthea a civitate Ucece et tenemento eiusdem et quod non esset ausa redire in dicta civitate et tenemento eiusdem usque post festum proximum Pasce per unum mensem, et hoc sub pena viginti solidarum tur. et sue raubam . . ." AM Uzès, BB 1, 3r.

77. "Item, quod nulla vilis mulier que pro peccunia publice se exponat sit ausa ire per carrerias civitatis Nemausi quamdiu ediffica protenduntur in ipsa civitate Nemausi, quantum durabit septimana sancta, nisi hoc esset causa orandi et causa confitendi, et quod tunc et alias incedat sole et absque alia socia vel socio, et hoc sub pena viginti solidorum tur. et amitendi raubam." AM Nîmes, FF 1, no. 21.

78. The text, badly water-damaged, reads, ". . . servientes et bannerios duci . . . hospitalis pauperum Ucece et ibidem ista septimana . . . predicti consules preceperunt dictis meretricibus quod de hac septimana non essent ause exire de dicto hospitale quam ipsi consules eis et cuilibet ipsarum provident in cibo et potum et de aliis eis necessariis . . ." AM Uzès, BB 1, 30r.

79. Calza, "Prostituzione in Venezia," 319.

80. Pertile, *Diritto italiano* 5:541.

81. Dufau de Maluquer, *Le pays de Foix sous Gaston Phoebus*, 204–5.

82. AM Perpignan, BB 7, 307v.

83. ". . . alas pauras pecayrix del bon hostal d'albi . . . affin quels estesso de fayre pecat per la semana sancta." AM Albi, CC 219.

84. AM Albi, CC 224, 226, 250, 255.

85. For all references, see appendix E.

86. "Et so essy que la sepmana de davant Pasques et la sepmana apres Pasques ala honor de Dieu et de ladicta fete de Pasques non ahan a tenir las filhas publicas aldit hostal . . . ahan a tenir a ung autre hostal honestament sans menar vida dissoluda ny amettre peccat. Et que puescan anar al sermo et alas gleysas . . ."

87. Published document no. 6b.

88. Published document no. 6c.

89. Anthony Nanvielas claims to have led the women to sermons through-

out Lent (published document no. 6c). In 1527 Hugh Combas reported that his services began the third Sunday in Lent.

90. In 1511 and 1517 they went to the Franciscan church, in 1514 to the chapel of Saint Felix in the Daurade, and in 1526 to the Dominicans.

91. In 1520 the sergeant claimed he was obliged to get up at one in the morning and again at seven for this purpose. In 1527 the women went to church in the morning and after dinner.

92. ". . . par le vouleur de Dieu une desdites filhes c'est convertie et par vousdit mendement fust mise à la mayson dudit suppliant et bailhie en garde jusques à tant que pour vous sera mise au couvent de les Repenties . . ."

93. See n. 123, chap. 4.

94. Published document no. 8. Similar waves of repentance affected Roman prostitutes in 1508 and later (Rodocanachi, *Courtisanes et bouffons*, 61).

95. Larivaille, *Vie quotidienne des courtisanes*, 161–62. Attendance at these sermons became obligatory (with soldiers guarding the doors of the church) under the Counter-Reformation popes, who issued a series of repressive measures against prostitutes (Rodocanachi, *Courtisanes et bouffons*, 97–103). Not all public women responded positively to this forced penitence, as in the case of the prostitute who answered back to the preacher, "che l'uffitio suo era di declarare lo evangelico, et non biasimar la vita loro." Bertolotti, *Repressioni alla prostituzione in Roma*, 11.

Chapter Six

1. The most common vernacular terms for procurer were *roffia* or *roffiana*, of Italian origin; *macarel* or *macarella*, of Netherlandish origin, probably via French; and in western Languedoc, *alcavot* from the Arabic *al gawwad*, via Catalan. L. Alibert, *Dictionnaire occitan-français* (Toulouse, 1977).

2. AM Narbonne, FF 1107. Inclusion of *lenocinium* in lists of cases of high justice seems to begin only in this period. None of the texts on high justice from the feudal period cited by Y. Bongert refer to *lenocinium* (Y. Bongert, *Recherches sur les cours laiques du Xe au XIIIe siècle* [Paris, 1949], 126–27).

3. ". . . quod erat accusatus quod quandam pupillam piuzellam vendiderat pro defflorando." AM Narbonne, AA 20, cited in Mouynès, *Narbonne Inv. AA*, 5.

4. ". . . homocidium vel lenoscinium . . . vel alia crimina hiis consimilia."

5. ". . . si aliquis in domo propria lenoscinia commiserit, domus cedat nobis in comissum, si vero non esset propria sed conducta vel aliter concessa, sic committens in viginti lib. tur. nobis teneatur." C. Compayré, *Etudes sur l'Albigeois*, 399–400.

6. See chap. 1.

7. See n. 21, prologue to part 1. See Burchard of Worms, *Decretum* 19:5 (*PL* 140:975); Brundage, "Prostitution in Medieval Canon Law," 835.

8. See the prologue to part 1.

9. *Las Siete Partidas del Rey Don Alfonso el Sabio*, 5 vols. (Paris, 1843–44) 4:638–40 (title XXII).

10. See n. 32, chap. 1.

11. Bongert, *Droit Pénal* 1:174; Boca, *Justice criminelle d'Abbeville*, 200–202; P. Desportes, *Reims et les rémois aux XIIIe et XIVe siècles* (Paris, 1979), 492–93.

12. As in the case of two procuresses banished from the town of Sens in 1342. H. Furgeot, *Inv. des Actes du Parlement de Paris* (Paris, 1920), 1:427.

13. See nn. 8 and 9, chap. 1.

14. Giraud, *Droit français* 2:205; de Maulde, *Coutumes d'Avignon*, 191. Italian statutes from this period also acknowledged procurers (Pertile, *Diritto italiano* 5:539–40).

15. AM Narbonne, FF 610. A vernacular text refers to "totz alcaotz e tota bagassa" (FF 602).

16. "Et expellendi homines et mulieres lenones, questuarios, meretrices et suspectos vehementer de premissis, de boniis viis, locis et carreriis honestis et non suspectis dicte ville." AM Narbonne, AA 36, cited in Mouynès, *Narbonne Inv. AA*, 291.

17. AM Castelnaudary, AA 1, 10r–41r.

18. AM Lunel, Livre Blanc, 13v.

19. ". . . ribaldi, lenones et malivole, non verentes deum, neque iustitiam . . ." AA 5, no. 371.

20. ". . . roffianatges . . . tenan avols femnas tant en bordels publics quant autrament secretament." AM Narbonne, FF 77.

21. ". . . corran la viala totz nuts, et seran batutz en tir la sanc, et estaran al pillori, et tota rigor de iusticia lor sera administrada sens deguna misericordia." AM Narbonne, FF 77. "Running the town" was a form of punishment in which the convicted person was to run along a given course in the town, sometimes only partially clothed and sometimes being beaten. It was a common punishment for adultery and other morals offenses. R. Aubenas, *Cours d'histoire du droit privé* (Aix-en-Provence, 1958), 6:52–61.

22. AM Toulouse, AA 5, no. 372.

23. AD Haute Garonne, B 1899, 145r.

24. "Item, cum lenones sint totaliter Deo ingrati, et habominabiles, et pariter sacre regie majestati, et debent esse unicuique, et tales quod non debent substineri, sed totaliter cassari secundum Deum et justiciam, mediante miserabili et habominiabili vita quam tenent et substenent, ob quod evenerunt et intervenerunt murtres, furta, latrocinia et diversa alia maleficia, fuit per dictum consilium ordinatum, ad honorem et laudem Dei, et utilitatem regie majestatis, et pro bono statu ejusdem, et presentis universitatis, quod ab inde omnes lenones cassentur a civitate presenti penitusque et omnino . . ." BM Arles, MS. 225, 265 (taken from AM Arles, BB 2, 93v). This prohibition was repeated in 1481.

25. AM Toulouse, AA 5, no. 70.

26. "Item, quod omnes lenones seu ruffiani et ruffianes a ruffianagiis de cetero abstineant abinde inantea aut exeant dictam civitatem Avenionensem infra decem dies proximos, ad quam redire non audeant sub pena libr. CC . . ." Le Pileur, *Documents*, 14.

27. Published documents no. 7 and no. 10.

28. Pavesi, *Bordello di Pavia*, 25–27 (1378, 1387, 1390). In Foligno the brothel farmer was called frankly *leno* (Fabretti, *Prostituzione in Perugia*, 90–92).

29. Dahm, *Strafrecht Italiens*, 436.

30. In 1423 the punishment prescribed was a 25 l. fine and a month in prison; in 1460 the fine had been increased to 100 l. and the prison term to six months; and in 1492 the term was extended to a year in prison, followed by banishment. Calza, "Prostituzione in Venezia," 313, 368; 2:119–21.

31. Neither Pertile nor Dahm attempts a synthesis.

32. Granara, *Prostituzione in Genova*, 85–86.

33. Fabretti, *Prostituzione in Perugia*, 54–58, 75–76.

34. I. Galligo, *Trattato sulle malattie veneree* (Florence, 1864), 774. R. Trexler discusses this confraternity and cites notarized contracts concluded between prostitute and procurer ("Prostitution florentine," 1000–1001).

35. A man who had induced married women to prostitution was executed in 1379. In 1417 a man who had pandered his wife was fined 1000 lire, whipped, and imprisoned for two years, and his wife was whipped and imprisoned a month. Brucker, *Society in Renaissance Florence*, 196–201.

36. S. di Giacomo, *La prostituzione in Napoli* (Naples, 1899), 72–76; Cutrera, *Prostituzione in Sicilia*, 85–88, 108–11.

37. Procuring was theoretically illegal in Roussillon, but it was, in fact, often tolerated, as is shown by a contract of *alcaboteria* concluded between a woman, native of Toulouse, and a student of Perpignan in 1395 (Desplanque, *Infames*, 7–8). Even in Beaucaire, the word *amicus* in the wills of prostitutes is a thinly veiled euphemism for procurer. See n. 20, chap. 4.

38. The Parlement of Toulouse complained of this, accusing in particular the officiality that released without punishment clerics who had procured: "Il n'y a ruffien ne mauvais garson qui n'ait son ydolle et son soutenance de quelcun plus grand . . . Ce jour la court a fait venir en icelle les capitoulx et assesseurs de Thoulouse, et leur a remontré les maulx que l'un fait chacun jour en cest ville dont ne se fait aucune justice ne punicion, par quoi lesditz maulx pululent et multiplient . . . La plupart desditz ruffians et delinquans sont clercz . . . on les baille à l'église et dedans deux jours après, ils vont par la ville comme devant, et ne s'en fait aucune punicion . . ." AD Haute Garonne, B 1, 244r.

39. AD Haute Garonne, B 1, 115v, 188v, 192r, 193r, 198v, 279r; B 1985, 9v; B 1988, 163v, 233v, 255v. Case and references cited in Viala, *Parlement de Toulouse* 1:554.

40. " . . . 24 exces, crimes et delitz. . . . il a mis sa vie entierement au fait de ruffianarie, batemens de gens et roberies."

41. AD Haute Garonne, B 4, 50r.

42. The court refrained from inflicting a more severe punishment due to Roy's advanced age and in consideration of his wife and children. AD Haute Garonne, B 4, 335v.

43. " . . . rufianages et vies dissolues, blasfemes et autres exces." AD Haute Garonne, B 8, 395r, 6 September 1491.

44. Ménard, *Histoire de Nîmes*, vol. 3.

45. E. de Balincourt, *Le budget de la viguerie d'Aiguesmortes en 1460* (Nîmes, 1886), 16.

46. AM Toulouse, CC 2344, no. 2.

47. AM Toulouse, CC 2351, no. 90.

48. AM Toulouse, CC 2354, no. 152.

49. AM Toulouse, FF 660, 11v.

50. AM Toulouse, CC 2371, no. 496.

51. Places of residence are specified in all police regulations concerning prostitutes of the fourteenth and fifteenth centuries, whether they refer to a *postribulum* (Nîmes and Beaucaire), a suburb (Bela Cela in Castres), or a "place assigned or to be assigned" (*loco deputato seu deputando*; Saint Félix). The punishment was usually a small fine, although in Alès in 1454 a prostitute keeping "a public or private brothel unless in the accustomed place" (*bordel public ho privat sinon el luoc acostumat*) was subject to a fine of 10 l. (AM Alès, 1S 18, no. 37). In Saint Félix in 1463, punishment of offenders was left up to the court (Ramière de Fortanier, *Chartes du Lauragais*, 624).

52. Sometimes running was an alternative to the fine, but this was a common provision of many municipal laws, intended to be inflicted only if the person in question was unable to pay the fine.

53. AM Narbonne, FF 77.

54. BM Arles, MS. 225, 264–65.

55. AD Haute Garonne, B 1899, 155r.

56. In Besançon in 1468, each of these women was to pay a florin for the privilege of residing outside the brothel and to wear a sign (Le Pileur, *Documents*, 11–12, 72–73).

57. "Idem, verres de fere touchant tant de cantonières que sont dans la ville et fere que la justice les fasse mener au bordeau" (Livres de mémoyres du notaire du consulat, 1491–1519, AM Montpellier, Inv. 11, 94). In Saint-Flour in 1443, twelve sergeants were sent out by the consuls to round up illicit prostitutes (Rigaudière, *St-Flour* 1:506).

58. Desplanque, *Infames*, 104; Granara, *Prostituzione in Genova*, 83.

59. Rossiaud, "Prostitution, jeunesse et société," 308, 324.

60. See n. 56, epilogue to part 2.

61. De Balincourt, *Budget de la viguerie d'Aiguesmortes*, 16.

62. AM Toulouse, CC 2351, no. 90.

63. AM Toulouse, FF 660, 8r; CC 1582, 48r.

64. AM Toulouse, CC 2365, no. 279.

65. AM Toulouse, CC 2371, no. 496.

66. ". . . garsa . . . demorana an ung hostal que y tenan bel bordel . . . per se que era pauvra filha amarida." AM Toulouse, CC 2354, no. 152.

67. ". . . per ce qu'esta pouvres." AM Toulouse, CC 2371, no. 496.

68. Published document no. 10.

69. Published document no. 7.

70. AM Toulouse, CC 2365, no. 26.

71. "Johana de Chanya et Johana dela Clavaria, filles del bon hostal . . .

Jehanne de Serre, palharde du public." AM Toulouse, CC 2371, no. 45bis, 496. A list of prisoners of 1503–4 includes "Revel Vena del bordel" (CC 2354, no. 152).

72. Both cases cited are from AM Toulouse, FF 171, which is nonfoliated. My thanks go to Barbara Beckerman Davis, who kindly brought them to my attention.

73. ". . . où faisoit surdorer girofflées et dans les feohes d'icelles escripre les noms et surnoms de leurs roffiens aussi en lettre d'or, qu'est ung cas pendable."

74. ". . . qu'elle sera delivrée entre les mains de l'executor de la haulte justice, qui luy faira fere le courtz acoustumé, icelle fustigeant, jusques à effuzion du sang, et ce faict, sera renvoyée au public, inhibition et deffence, à poine d'estre pandue et estranglée, ne vaguer par ville."

75. AM Lunel, Livre Blanc, 13v.

76. "Negun no las ause reculhir dins son hostal per maniar ni per beure, ni per far ab lor neguna malvestat." "Règlements de Castres," 320.

77. For example, in the statutes of Villeneuve-lèz-Béziers dated 1513: "Que negun no aja a reculhir ni tener neguna famma publiqua en son houstal de una nuyt en lay, sus pena de 60 s. t." Bédard, "Statuts de Villeneuve-lèz-Béziers," 197.

78. *Ord* 20:180–83.

79. AD Haute Garonne, B 1, 247r.

80. "Maistre Jehan Olivier, notaire, loue une maison au près de la Place Mage . . . en laquelle il tient continuellement trois ou quatre paillardes et femmes dissolues et bordeau public à tous allans et venans, au mauvais exemple de la chose publicque . . . Il bon plaise commander et enjoindre sur telle peine que semblera à la court aux capitolz et autres officiers deladite ville de Thoulouse, qu'ilz aient à faire entretenir, garder et observer le contenu desditz articles et arrest, et en ce faisant qu'ilz ayent à donner ordre et police à tout en faisant punicion des coulpables telle que sera à faire par raison." AM Toulouse, AA 3, no. 305. The court of Provence was also active in prosecuting such offenses; in 1406 a man renting houses illegally to prostitutes in Marseille was sentenced to pay a 100 s. fine, as was each of the prostitutes. AD Bouches-du-Rhone, B 1943, Inv. Blancard.

81. "Les bains sont les centres d'une prostitution notoire et permanente, mais aussi des maisons de rendez-vous et des lieux de maquerellage." Rossiaud, "Prostitution, jeunesse et société," 291.

82. As we have seen, this was not the case in Moncalieri, where "honest" and "dishonest" bathers mixed in the municipal brothel *cum* stews. Pertile, *Diritto italiano* 5:541.

83. Le Pileur, *Documents*, 6–9.

84. "Cum pacto expresso quod non erit phas neque licitum eidem Coline tenere mulieres lubricas et publicas ac inhonestas in dictis stuphis Sancti Antonii, ymo bene in illis de burgati Magdalene." AD Gard, IIE[1] 206, 123v, 4 July 1498.

85. ". . . lesdits supplians ont fait construire et ediffier à leurs propres coustz et despens certaines estuves et baings pour lesdites filles . . . afin d'es-

chever que elles n'allassent estuver ne baigner en ladite ville ne ailleurs pour les inconveniens qui se pourroient en suir . . ." *Ord* 20: 181.

86. Published document no. 5. The Parlement of Toulouse had sentenced a dishonest Toulousan bath keeper to running the town and banishment in 1477. See n. 42, chap. 6.

87. AM Montpellier, Liber preceptorum 1498–99, Inv. 8, 130.

88. Rossiaud, "Prostitution, jeunesse et société," 291, 308–9. It is obvious that in the larger towns policing all of the baths was a difficult task. In Besançon the municipal authorities wavered between different policies concerning morality in the stews. A law of 1457 prohibited dishonesty in bathhouses. Almost yearly, stiff fines were imposed on a recalcitrant stew keeper from 1458 to 1464. In 1465–66 a similar prohibition was followed by an acknowledgment of prostitutes in stews and a tax on them, a measure that was revoked two days later when another prohibition was issued. This tax seems to have been restored and levied until 1495, when an ordinance provided for two honest houses and one dishonest one. Sometime before 1514 a total prohibition was once again put into effect. Offenders were fined and sometimes banished (Le Pileur, *Documents*, 67–100 passim).

89. These concerns are seen in the complaint against a dishonest bathhouse in Lyon (the property of the archbishop!), filed in 1478 by a coalition of offended neighbors and royal counselors. Although the defense protested that the house was not scandalous, since no married people frequented it, the plaintiffs, while not denying that claim, cited the unseemly behavior of women and clients and attributed to them the responsibility for numerous thefts and an attempted rape. They accused the stews of being "prejudiciables au roy et aladite ville . . . il seroit facile en temps de guerre . . . de conspirer et machiner contre le roi et les habitants de ladite ville"; all prostitutes, they said, should be limited to "certains lieux publics et deputez à tenir les femmes publiques." The outcome of the trial is not known, although other documents would seem to indicate that the plaintiffs were not successful. J. Lacassagne and A. Picornot, "Vieilles étuves de Lyon: un curieux procès au XVe siècle relatif aux étuves de la Pêcherie (1478–83)," *Albums du Crocodile*, 1943 (nonpaginated).

Epilogue to Part Two

1. "Au XVe siècle . . . la prostitution officielle ou tolérée par les pouvoirs apparait donc comme un produit naturel des structures démographiques, d'un ordre et d'une morale." "Prostitution, jeunesse et société," 310.

2. Toulouse, for example, had a population of approximately 25,000 in the fifteenth century (more in the sixteenth century). The descriptions of the brothel at the end of the fifteenth century and the lists of women residing there give an idea of how many prostitutes were working in the authorized house: from a low of 25 up to 54 (1532) women (see appendix E). To give a comparison, there are about 30 prostitutes in contemporary Montpellier, a town of 200,000 people, including many unmarried men (students, immigrant workers, etc.). There were proportionally at least seven times as many prostitutes

in medieval Toulouse as in twentieth-century Montpellier! (Statistics for Montpellier are based on testimony of "Dora," in a public debate on prostitution held 20 October 1981 at the Centre Lacordaire, Montpellier.)

3. Statistics from this period are, of course, rare. Herlihy and Klapisch-Zuber have shown a drop in marrying age, especially for men, in Tuscany in the fourteenth century (*Toscans*, 204–9). A chronicle of the monks of Saint-Denis states that, after an attack of plague, "the remaining men and women married at will" (quoted in *Toscans*, 195).

4. No proof is presented of the logical step from dissuading from homosexuality to consequently increasing the desire to legitimately procreate. "Prostitution florentine," 984, 1007 n. 6.

5. Herlihy and Klapisch-Zuber, *Toscans*, 328.

6. Ibid., 342; Biraben, *Peste* 1:167.

7. See n. 3, epilogue to part 2; see also Biraben, *Peste* 1:167.

8. See above, pp. 65–66.

9. See above, p. 37.

10. See above, pp. 33–34.

11. A forty-year-old worker testified, "Quod ipsi tuchini erant mali regiminis et vite dissolute et male iudici quia plures ipsorum vidit tam in tavernis quam in postribulo et lupanari." A draper's son had seen them "tam in tavernis quam in postribulo sive lupanari, ducentes vitam dissolutam . . . meretrices per villam ducendo [leading prostitutes about the town]." AM Bagnol-sur-Cèze, FF 11.

12. The expression is Le Goff's, in his "Métiers licites et illicites," 99. See G. Ouy, "L'humanisme et les mutations politiques et sociales en France au XIVᵉ et au XVᵉ siècles," *L'humanisme français au début de la Renaissance* (Paris, 1973), 27–44.

13. Verlinden, *Esclavage* 1:748–803.

14. For the frequent use of slaves as concubines, see J. Heers, *Esclaves et domestiques au moyen-âge dans le monde méditerranéen* (Paris, 1981), 214–24.

15. An explicit avowal of pecuniary motivation is found in Perugia, where the *gabella bordelli* was sold in 1359 "because the city needs money" to pay its officers. Fabretti, *Prostituzione in Perugia*, 8.

16. See published document no. 4, and chap. 3.

17. For example: "pro majori dampno evitando" (St-Quentin, 1377); "a evitar maiors perilhs" (Castres, 1398); "ne maius malum subsequatur" (Toulouse, 1462).

18. See Boswell, *Homosexuality*, 269–302.

19. "Tolle meretrices de mundo et replebis ipsum sodomia." *De regimine principum* 4:14. A similar idea is expressed in a statute from the town of Lucca (Pertile, *Diritto italiano* 3:129 n. 72). E. Pavan has found no text explicitly connecting the policy on prostitution with that on homosexuality, in her "Police des moeurs à Venise." The only explicit reference from southern France is late: in 1570 the consuls of Cavaillon justified their hiring of a few prostitutes during a fair by saying that they sought to avoid "buggery" (*boulgrerie*) (Le Pileur, *Documents*, 44).

20. See also J. Rossiaud, "Fraternités de jeunesse."

21. ". . . magis comode et cum minori scandalo et detrimento hujus ville . . ." (Germain, "Statuts," 124).

22. AM Albi, FF 38, no. 6 (1366).

23. "En faveur de la chose publique" (Toulouse, 1462); AM Toulouse, AA 3, no. 305 (1498), etc.

24. "In prejudicium reipublice . . . ville." (Villefranche-de-Lauragais, fifteenth century). The same reasoning, of course, could justify repression. In Toulouse in 1271, the brutal repression of prostitution *extra muros* was done "for public utility and to avoid sin" (*propter utilitatem publicam et ad evitandum pecata*). The same, of course, is true for the sixteenth century.

25. See J. Le Goff's analysis of the connection between this acceptance of previously scorned trades in the interest of "common utility," growing public administration, and the reasoning of Aristotelian philosophy, in his "Métiers licites et illicites," 99.

26. See n. 17, chap. 5.

27. ". . . multe bone et probe mulieres facte fuerunt meretrices." AM Montpellier, EE 732, Inv. 12, 144.

28. Published document no. 5a.

29. ". . . le mal exemple que prennent les femmes de bien de la ville à tels paillardes." Livres de mémoyres du notaire du consulat, 1491–1519, AM Montpellier, Inv. 11, 94.

30. See above, p. 81.

31. See N. Z. Davis, "Women on Top," in her *Society and Culture in Early Modern France*, 124–25.

32. "Una feda morbosa enficisca tot lo tropel." *Livre Vert de Lacaune*, 201.

33. See above, p. 71.

34. See the histories of Paris by Sauval and Félibien, and the history of Nîmes by Ménard. A. Biéler, in his work on Calvin's sexual morality, refers to the fifteenth century as a period of "dépravation morale . . . et dévergondage généralisé" (*Homme et femme dans la morale calviniste*, 9). R. Aubenas has seen this period as one of the decline of morals (*Cours d'histoire du droit privé* 6:55), and P. Wolff has used the term *relachement moral* in discussing the fifteenth century ("Relachement moral et superstitions populaires à Toulouse au milieu du XVᵉ siècle," *RMT-SHD* 9 [1971]: 791–98).

35. J. Rossiaud has criticized the conventional equivalence noted above between institutionalized prostitution and growing decadence of the late Middle Ages, only to state that this phenomenon was "a fundamental dimension of medieval society," offering no explanation for these historians' "intuition" of a moral change in the fifteenth century, which is, I believe, basically correct.

36. "Simplex fornicatio est coitus illicitus soluti cum soluta, vel econtrario," according to Peter the Chanter in his *Verbum Abbreviatum*, c. 136 (*PL* 205:332). Gratian does not use this term in his definition of sexual offenses (C. 36 q. 1 c.2), although it appears in the *Glossa Ordinaria* (D. 81 c.6v *removeantur*).

37. See Esmein, *Mariage en droit canonique*.

38. C. 32 q. 7, and P. Lombard, *Sententiae* 4:35. According to Aubenas, the council of Bourges had admitted divorce for adultery in 1031 (*Cours d'histoire du droit privé* 6:45).

39. G. Duby states that the last church council to invoke the canon of the Council of Toledo (398) tolerating concubinage was that held in Rome in 1069 (*Le mariage dans la France féodale*, 129).

40. O. Pontal, *Les statuts synodaux français du XIIIe siècle* (Paris, 1971), 204–11.

41. L. de Lacger, "Statuts synodaux d'Albi du XIIIe siècle," *RHD* 6 (1927): 418–66. Béziers 1342 and Nîmes 1252 in E. Martène and U. Durand, *Thesaurus novus anecdotorum* (Paris, 1717) 4:643, 1030.

42. This point of view is clearly presented in the commentary on the Sixth Commandment in the council of Béziers in 1342. In the direction for confession published by the council of Nîmes in 1252, the article concerning sexual sins advised the confessor to ask whether the man had sinned "cum corrupta." Thus, a man sinned in having intercourse not only with an unmarried woman, but also with a prostitute or other "fallen" woman. Profiting from prostitution, moreover, was considered one of the businesses that could not be conducted without mortal sin: "negocia de sui natura illicita et inhonesta, ut usura, symonia, meretricium, lenocinium et simila, que absque mortali peccato exerceri non possunt" (J. Berthelé, ed., *Les instructions de G. Durand le Spéculateur* [Montpellier, 1900–1907], 37). Yet the Church occasionally profited from prostitution. At the Council of Vienne, William Durand the Younger demanded that houses of prostitution be placed far from the papal palace and that the pope and his officers receive no money from prostitutes (Le Pileur, *Documents*, 3). This "tribute" paid by prostitutes to papal officers was acknowledged by the municipal authorities of Avignon in 1337 (BM Avignon, MS. 2480, 46v, cited by G. Cartoux in his *Condition des courtisanes à Avignon* [Lyon, 1925], 14). This practice was abolished by Pope Innocent VI in a bull dated 29 July 1353 (E. Deprez, ed., *Lettres closes d'Innocent VI* [Paris, 1909], 1927–28). Pope Alexander VI rented out several houses of prostitution in 1496 (Rodocanachi, *Courtisanes et bouffons*, 192).

43. J. Duvernoy, ed., *Les registres d'inquisition de Jacques Fournier, 1318–1325* (Toulouse, 1965) 3:299. Another man who fell into the same trap decided to remain silent once his error had been pointed out to him (2:246–47). It is Duvernoy who describes this ploy as a "trap" (*piège*), in his notes to the French translation of the register (Paris, The Hague, and New York, 1978), 2:720. See also E. Le Roy Ladurie, *Montaillou, village occitan 1294–1324* (Paris, 1975), 217–19, 242–54.

44. Carbasse, *Consulats et justice criminelle*, 301–3. In the ecclesiastical seigneury of Aspres-sur-Buëch, in Savoy, a married man who had intercourse with an unmarried woman paid the same fine as a man who had intercourse with a married woman, but the offense, instead of being called *adulterium*, was known as *meretricium* (FCM).

45. Thus, the author of the first commentary on the customs of Toulouse

states, "Item queritur si conjugatus accedat ad solutam an comittat adulterium. Respondeo non per legem [C. 9. 9. 1.)." Gilles, *Coutumes de Toulouse*, 255.

46. See chap. 2. J.-M. Carbasse has noted that punishment for adultery became lighter from the twelfth to the fourteenth century. The customs fixed maximal punishments and imposed strict rules of evidence. This may have been another aspect of the counterattack on the king's and local lord's attempts to introduce the canonical definition of adultery. Even punishments for adulterous women were relatively light. In 1320 an adulterous woman in Pézenas was fined and warned not to misbehave in the future (AM Pézenas, 791). A Toulousan resident protested against the public punishment of his wife for adultery in 1398 (Aubenas, *Cours d'histoire du droit privé* 6:59). One may speculate that it was perhaps the increasing difficulty in obtaining a divorce that led to the moderation of these punishments for women. Exemplary punishment of an adulterous wife was "interesting" for the offended husband only so long as he could repudiate her and take another wife; once he was obliged to keep her, severe punishment became a humiliation for him as well as for her, one might imagine.

47. Giraud, *Droit français* 2:205. This provision may reflect the views of the powerful ecclesiastic lord of Arles more than those of the residents.

48. Gilles, *Coutumes de Toulouse*, 30, 213. The author of this commentary has been identified as Arnaud d'Arpadella, doctor of law, probably professor at the law school of Toulouse and royal advocate in the seneschalsy of Toulouse, obviously an eminent person. J. Strayer, *Les gens de justice du Languedoc sous Philippe le Bel* (Toulouse, 1970), 18, 195. See also Le Roy Ladurie, *Montaillou*, 242–54.

49. Aubenas states that concubinage existed legally in Corsica, Spain, and the Béarn (*Cours d'histoire du droit privé* 6:24–27). Statutes of some Italian towns specify clearly that concubinage was allowed (Lucca, 1308; Florence, 1415; Mantua, 1303; Lodi, 1390); in Tivoli (1305) it was limited to relationships with women of an inferior class (Pertile, *Diritto italiano* 3:370–72; Dahm, *Strafrecht Italiens*, 428). A short study of the institution in the Pyrenees is given by G. Bascle de Lagrèze in his *Les Massipia* (Bordeaux, 1851), including an edited notarial act of concubinage dated 1452.

50. See chap. 1.

51. Azaïs, "Documents sur les filles de mauvaise vie," 265–76.

52. F. Pasquier, *Cartulaire de Mirepoix* (Toulouse, 1921), 2:465–68.

53. Cited in Courteault, *Bourg-Saint-Andéol*, 228–29.

54. AM Alès, 1S 18, no. 37.

55. Le Pileur, *Documents*, 13. A police regulation from Barbetane dated 1448 specifies that this prohibition applied to married men (*homo uxoratus*) (Ibid., 10).

56. AD Haute Garonne, B 5, 478r, 29 January 1481; 585r, 9 July 1481. There are numerous cases of people brought before the Parlement on morals charges in the late fifteenth century, many accused generally of leading a *vie dissolue*.

57. AM Castelnaudary, FF 22, 22 March 1510.

58. Sauve, *Prostitution à Apt*, 33.

59. Aubenas cites the legislation of Amadeus VIII of Savoy (1430) calling for prison sentences for men and the whip for women found in concubinage, and a Catalonian law of 1451 forbidding married men to keep concubines (*Cours d'histoire du droit privé* 6: 30, 61).

60. P. Ourliac, "Notes sur le mariage à Avignon." See also L.-H. Labande, "Autour du mariage: moeurs avignonnaises des XIVᵉ et XVᵉ siècles," *Mémoires de l'Académie de Vaucluse* 13 (1894): 63–79.

61. Le Pileur, *Documents*, 6–7.

62. Published document no. 2. This phrase is written over an erasure mark. One wonders what slip of the pen the scribe might have been correcting!

63. "[In bathhouses] les hommes non mariés ont bien acoustumé de mener femmes non mariées pour eulx en aider et servir . . ." Lacassagne and Picornot, "Vieilles étuves de Lyon."

64. See chap. 6.

65. ". . . adulterare cum aliquo homino, nec homo cum ea, sub pena xxv s." Le Pileur, *Documents*, 33.

66. See n. 68, chap. 5. In Amiens in 1476, several married men were sentenced to *amende honorable* for having been caught with prostitutes (Dubois, *Justice et bourreaux à Amiens*, 16).

67. See N. Grévy-Pons, *Célibat et nature, une controverse médiévale* (Paris, 1975).

68. See n. 11, epilogue to part 2. Carbasse notes that in the late fourteenth century, frequenters of brothels (*meretricatores*) were not supposed to testify in Castelnaudary, although prostitutes there could bring accusations and, in the same period in Foix, could testify (Carbasse, "Justice criminelle à Castelnaudary au XIVᵉ siècle," 143, 148).

69. D. Herlihy, "Some Psychological and Social Roots of Violence in the Tuscan Cities," in *Violence and Disorder in Italian Cities*, 137.

70. Ibid. See also Bec, *Marchands écrivains*, 57, 105; Garin, *Pédagogie de la Renaissance*, 127, 137; and A. Coville, *La vie intellectuelle dans les domaines d'Anjou-Provence de 1380 à 1435* (Paris, 1941), 307.

71. For the Calvinist view of marriage, see Biéler, *L'homme et la femme dans la morale calviniste*. For the legislation of the Council of Trent concerning marriage, see Esmein, *Mariage en droit canonique*, vol. 2.

72. Grévy-Pons has edited a short treatise (in her *Célibat et nature*) written by a pious Languedocian layman early in the fifteenth century, in which it is proposed that priests be allowed to marry, a project which, while hardly representative of mainstream thinking, seems not to have placed the author's orthodoxy in doubt. See also Natalis de Wailly, "Memoire sur Sumaria Brevis," *Académie des inscriptions et belles lettres* 18 (1855). By the end of the fifteenth century, even municipal authorities were capable of taking initiatives against what they considered to be priestly misconduct. The council of Beaucaire took an initiative against some "immoral" priests: ". . . male et inhoneste se habent circa servicium domini, et pocius manutenent meretrices et mulieres inhonestas . . . Fuit conclusum . . . quod consules accedant ad dominum Arelatensem archiepiscopum seu eius vicarium Arelatensem, ad

finem sibi remonstrandi et notifficandi malum regimen et vitam inhonestam dictorum servitorum dicte ecclesie beate Marie de Pomere et quod placeat dicto domino vicario venire ad presentem villam ad finem se informandi et inhonestam vitam pugniendi." AM Beaucaire, BB 2, 107v, 19 January 1494. These would seem to be the same priests to whom some prostitutes left legacies in their wills (see n. 20, chap. 4). A priest caught with a prostitute in Alès in 1542 was ordered to beg pardon on his knees before the consuls for having injured the honor of the town (AD Gard, MS. A. Bardon, 589). The royal order to the judge of Castelnaudary urging stiff penalties for married men keeping concubines prescribed the same punishment for *gens d'église* found living with loose women (AM Castelnaudary, FF 22, 22 March 1510).

73. Estèbe and Vogler, "Registres consistoriaux," 381–82. See the epilogue to part 1.

74. Thus, Benedicti, in his *Somme des péchés* (1584) wrote, "Ceux qui ont apprins de faire l'amour aus putains, seront encore plus enflambez et hardis à faire le mesme à l'endroit des sages et honestes femmes." Quoted in Flandrin, *Amours paysannes*, 80–81.

75. L. Otis, "Une contribution à l'étude du blasphème au bas moyen âge," *Atti del Convegno di Varenna (giugno 1979)* (Milan, 1980), 213–23.

76. The Onestà was instituted in Florence in 1403 (Trexler, "Prostitution florentine," 983). See also A. Staehelin, "Sittenzucht und Sittengerichtsbarkeit in Basel," *ZSSR* (*ger. Abt.*) 85 (1968): 78–103. For the contemporary debate, see E. Schur and H. Bedau, *Victimless Crimes* (Englewood Cliffs, N.J., 1974).

77. It is interesting to note that the proposals made by the "puritanical" Counter-Reformation popes concerning prostitution in Rome were virtually identical to the measures taken by the Languedocian municipalities in the fifteenth century—to outlaw procuring and to limit prostitutes to one section of town, which was to be fortified and to be closed during Lent. Rodocanachi, *Courtisanes et bouffons*, 74–120.

78. In fact, prostitution was in a sense imposed, whereas before it had merely been tolerated. Thus, in Amiens, when the heir of the owner of houses in the street traditionally reserved for prostitutes decided that he preferred other tenants, the prostitutes filed a complaint with the town council, which passed a resolution obliging the new owner to continue renting to prostitutes: ". . . consideré que de tout temps lesdites filles ont demouré en ladite rue, messeigneurs ont ordonné qu'elles demourent ou lieu où elles sont acoustumé de demourer comme elles souloient" (Dubois, *Justice et bourreaux à Amiens*, 14–15).

🦋 Essay on Bibliography and Sources

Books and Articles

The books consulted in preparing this essay fall roughly into three categories: those monographs dealing with individual towns and regions, books dealing with certain important themes in medieval history, and those books and articles dealing specifically with prostitution. Of the first category little need be said; the best guide to this literature for France is the *Bibliographie des villes de France* by P. Dollinger and P. Wolff (Paris, 1967). The thematic literature is too vast to be discussed thoroughly here, as it includes books on such varied topics as church history; customary,[1] Roman, and canon law; royal legislation, criminal law, and justice; disease and public health; and intellectual and social history in general. It is sufficient here, I think, to call special attention to those books dealing with the history of sexuality. Although they concentrate on the early modern and modern periods, they are indispensable to a historian of any period for their insight into methodological problems and concepts. Particularly interesting are the first volume of *L'histoire de la sexualité* of M. Foucault (Paris, 1976) and the work of J.-L. Flandrin: his *Les amours paysannes* (Paris, 1975) and a recent collection of his numerous articles under the title *Le sexe et l'occident* (Paris, 1981).[2]

Vital to this essay, of course, are those works dealing specifically with prostitution, which can be subdivided into three categories: the popular general histories of prostitution, documents concerning prostitution published in the nineteenth century in numerous local and regional periodicals, and contemporary analyses of prostitution, consisting of articles published in the last decade.

The first general histories of prostitution were written in the early and mid-nineteenth century, a response to the contemporary concern with the rise of prostitution concurrent with the growing industrialization and urbanization of western Europe in that period. First published in 1827, *Histoire de la législation sur les femmes publiques* by the jurist Sabatier is based to a great extent on the relevant pages in the five-volume *Traité de police* by Delamare (Paris, 1722), which summarize the initiatives taken against prostitution over the centuries. The main interest of *De la prostitution en Europe de l'antiquité jusqu'à la fin du XVIe siècle* by the *littérateur* Rabutaux (Paris, 1851) is the author's republication of many previously edited primary sources dealing with prostitution. Perhaps the best known of these early histories is *Histoire de la prostitution chez tous les peuples du monde depuis l'antiquité la plus reculée jusqu'à nos jours* by Pierre Dufour, published from 1851 to 1853.[3] A six-volume enterprise, this work includes many references to printed sources and more analysis, albeit polemical, than the books by Sabatier and Rabutaux. Most later histories of prostitution have been based on one or more of these three works.[4] The most accessible recent history of prostitution in English is that of V. Bullough, *The History of Prostitution* (New York, 1964). The same author has also published *A Bibliography of Prostitution* (New York and London, 1977), which is far from complete for the Middle Ages. There is, of course, a whole mass of pulp histories of prostitution or sexuality, most of which provide a mishmash of misinformation.[5] Not all, however, can be peremptorily dismissed; E. J. Burford's *The Orrible Synne: A Look at London Lechery* (London, 1973), for instance, despite its unpromising title and manifestly scabrous orientation, provides a surprisingly useful compendium of published primary-source references to prostitution in England.

A number of documents concerning prostitution appeared in various regional journals and books in the nineteenth and early twentieth centuries, published as curiosities by local amateur historians, often medical doctors with an interest in the history of venereal disease. For the south of France, the most important are the documents concerning the brothel of Pézenas published by J. Azaïs in 1837 (*BSABéz*), those on prostitution in Marseille published by the doctors H. Mireur and L. Barthélemy in 1882 and 1883 respectively, and the mass of documents from Provence and Besançon published by L. Le Pileur in 1908. A more scholarly study of the public house of Toulouse by M. J. Chalande apperaed in 1911 (in the *Mémoires de l'Académie des sciences, inscriptions et belles-lettres de Toulouse*). Similar local documents have been published in Germany and Italy. The books by H. Lippert on Hamburg (1848) and by the doctor J. Schrank on Vienna (1886) are noteworthy; for Italy, the most important works are the publication of documents concerning Venice, by C. Calza (1869), and Perugia, by A. Fabretti (1890). These older works continue to be essential, as the recent histories of prostitution, relying almost exclusively on the very old ones cited above, have by and large not taken these documents into account.

Several studies dealing with medieval prostitution have been published in recent years, and frequent reference is made to them throughout this essay. B. Geremek has included a chapter on the world of prostitution in his study of marginal people in late-medieval Paris, published in Polish in 1971 and translated into French in 1976. J. Rossiaud has discussed institutionalized prostitution in his study of sexual mores, violence, and rape in fifteenth-century society (*AnESC*, 1976; see also *Communications*, 1982). Recently (*AnESC*, 1981), R. Trexler has presented a very complete study of a fifteenth-century police register concerning the prostitutes of Florence.[6] The recent studies of prostitution in the early modern and modern period are too numerous to mention here.

The bibliography is a selective one, concentrating on those works cited most frequently throughout the book and those having a direct and significant relevance to the history of prostitution. Those books including editions of primary sources are marked with an asterisk. This system has been preferred to the traditional division of the bibliography into primary and secondary sources, because some of the most important and interesting documents in print are those that have been edited in the footnotes or *pièces justificatives* of secondary works.

Manuscript Sources

Although many theoretical works—canon and Roman law collections, church councils, theological tracts, works of literature—have been consulted and cited in this essay, they have been used largely as a complement to the principal body of documentation. The documentary core of the book is archival material, and the most important archives consulted are those of the urban communities of Languedoc.[7]

An important chronological division must be kept in mind when dealing with these municipal archives. The documents on prostitution from the period before 1350 are scant, consisting essentially of customs or statutes (AA), police regulations (AA, BB, or FF), and charters from cartularies (AA), many of which have been published.[8] Thus, the documentary basis is less firm than for the period after 1350, when the sources become more plentiful.

In studying these late-medieval sources, a distinction must be made between documents dealing with a system of publicly owned houses and those dealing with privately owned centers of prostitution. The "public" system has left a great number and variety of sources: privileges (AA), deliberations of the town councils and other administrative documents (BB), account books of the municipality (CC), documents concerning municipal property (DD), and cases of civil justice (FF). The sources are rarer and more scattered for towns in which a system of private houses prevailed. Some of the series mentioned above are relevant (especially BB and FF), since the town council usually retained a supervisory role. One may consult, in addition, the *compoix* (assessment of real estate for tax purposes) and the *tailles* (lists of those who paid taxes), both found in the series CC. The notarial registers in the departmental archives (IIE) include rentals and sales of brothels, and wills and other civil acts made by prostitutes.

This distinction between sources for the public and for the private systems points up a difficult methodological problem confronting the researcher. For the private system, the sources, not being in one archival series or type of document, are scattered. As it would be impossible to examine all documents thoroughly in order to extract the few references to prostitution, a selection must be made of the documents having the greatest concentration of information (and the information of the greatest interest); others must be consulted by following up a reference indicated elsewhere. For example, almost all the notarial documents cited in this book have been found by following up references in descriptive inventories or other published works. It would be folly to try to go through all medieval Languedocian notarial registers seeking the occasional mention of prostitution! The deliberations and account books of towns having municipal brothels, on the other hand, because they contain numerous references to prostitution, have generally been systematically studied, page by page, to find all relevant information. This book, as a result, is somewhat "biased" toward towns in which the municipality owned the local center of prostitution, as material is more plentiful and accessible there than in towns where prostitution remained a private affair.

For information concerning the prosecution of procurers and illicit prostitutes, the records of the Parlement of Toulouse have been consulted (in addition to the municipal series FF).[9] The rare records of episcopal jurisdiction (G) preserved in Languedocian departmental archives include few references to prostitution, but the series H, on the other hand, has been useful for studying the religious houses founded for repentant women.

In the national archives, the records of the Parlement of Paris (X) apparently contain little information about prostitution, either in Languedoc or in the rest of France.[10] The royal letters of amnesty (JJ) are a more fruitful source of information on prostitution, although the references to Languedocian brothels seem to be rare.[11]

The documents included in the list of archives consulted are only those that have disclosed useful information on prostitution, the numerous other documents consulted without success having been omitted from the list.

Notes

1. Often for Occitanian customary law, I refer in this book to the Fonds des coutumes méridionales (FCM), a collection of photocopies of the law codes of Occitanian towns, mainly from editions in obscure local periodicals. A list of these customs and the sources from which they have been taken is given in J.-M. Carbasse, "Bibliographie de coutumes méridionales (Catalogue des textes édités)," *RMT-SHD* 10 (1979): 7–89.

2. An overview of this literature is presented in E. Ross and R. Rapp, "Sex and Society: A Research Note from Social History and Anthropology," *Comparative Studies in Society and History* 23 (1981): 51–72.

3. The name Pierre Dufour is a pseudonym. The work has generally been attributed to Paul Lacroix, a prolific *littérateur*, although the latter always denied this attribution.

4. I have not been able to consult the classic history of prostitution in English, written by W. W. Sanger in 1858. Perhaps the most serious history to date is a German work in two volumes, *Die Prostitution*, written by the medical doctor Iwan Bloch and published in 1912 and 1925. I have, unfortunately, been able to consult only the second volume, dealing with the early modern period.

5. Such is the case of G. L. Simons, *A Place for Pleasure: The History of the Brothel* (London, 1975). Reay Tannahill (*Sex in History*, New York, 1980) seems to take a perverse pleasure in concocting the most absurd untruth: "Temple prostitution came to Europe. There was a church brothel in Avignon where the girls spent part of their time in prayer and religious duties, and the rest of the time servicing customers." This is, of course, a fallacious fusion of the very strict convent for repentant women in Avignon (see chap. 4) and the mythical brothel of Queen Jeanne (see the prologue to part 1).

6. Also to be noted is the article by J. Brundage on prostitution in medieval canon law (*Signs*, 1976). If few references are made to E. Pavan's 1980 article in the *Revue historique* on prostitution and homosexuality in Venice, it is because the section on prostitution is based to a great extent on the documents published by C. Calza in 1869, which I had already incorporated into the body of my thesis.

7. The rarity of references to the towns of Béziers, Carcassonne, and Le Puy is explained by the poor state of conservation of the medieval archives for these towns. The only important Languedocian urban center with well-preserved archives not to yield a document concerning prostitution is Limoux. One could speculate that the local brothel was private, since the preservation of documents concerning such private houses is often a matter of chance. See the following discussion.

8. Double letters indicate categories of classification in municipal archives; single letters indicate categories in departmental archives. The most important categories are the following:

AA: political documents
BB: administration
CC: finances

DD: municipal property
EE: military and defense
FF: police and justice
GG: charity
HH: commerce
II: inventories
B: justice and administration
IIE: notaries
G: secular clergy
H: regular clergy

The archives of some towns were classified before the above standardized system was adopted and hence have systems of their own; this is true of Montpellier, Nîmes, Pézenas, and Alès.

9. I have not gone through all the registers of the Parlement of Toulouse but, rather, have followed up references from the inventories and from A. Viala, *Le parlement de Toulouse et l'administration royale laïque, 1420–1525* (Albi, 1953). Despite the importance of this institution, such an approach seems justifiable for three reasons: (1) The state of the inventories is so lamentable, and the material so vast, that any researcher covering a long period of time must face the same problem. (2) The Parlement did not often hear small cases such as those concerning prostitutes, which were usually decided in local courts. (3) The registers for the late medieval period are incomplete; in addition, most of the important cases concerning municipalities are found in the archives of the town in question. Thus, the most interesting parliamentary case presented in this book (Toulouse, 1462, published document no. 4) was found in the municipal archives of Toulouse.

10. I am grateful to Mme Metman and Mlle Langlois of the CNRS, who kindly consulted the file of cases of the Parlement of Paris that they are compiling with the other members of the team of M. Timbal and advised me that cases concerning prostitution were virtually nonexistent.

11. The papers of Douët d'Arcq include a kind of inventory of the series JJ that is extremely helpful (AN, AB XIX 204$^\wedge$–206).

℘ Manuscript Sources

The municipal archives marked with an asterisk are housed in the appropriate departmental archives.

Ardèche
  AM Bourg-Saint-Andéol
    AA 2 (privileges)
Ariège
  *AM Foix
    BB 201 (testimony in municipal court)
    CC 209 (*compoix*)
  AM Pamiers
    BB 11 (register of regulations)
    FF 20 (police register)
Aude
  *AM Castelnaudary
    AA 1 (statutes)
    BB 1–4 (council deliberations)
    CC 78–81 (account books)
    FF 4–13 (testimony in municipal court)
    II 3–4 (inventories)
  AM Narbonne
    FF 77, 602, 610 (police regulations)
Gard
  AD Gard
    IIE¹ 134, 199, 206, 207, 222; IIE 18–31

AM Alès
  1D 8–12 (council deliberations)
  3D 3 (inventory)
  G 5 (*compoix*)
  1S 16, 18 (police regulations)
*AM Bagnols-sur-Cèze
  FF 11–11bis (testimony in trial of Tuchins)
AM Beaucaire
  BB 1–5 (council deliberations)
    100 (police regulations)
  CC 4–6 (*compoix*); 225–27 (account books)
  HH 13 (fair regulations)
  II 2 (inventory)
*AM Nîmes
  FF 1, 31 (police regulations)
  LL 4–5 (council deliberations)
AM Uzès
  BB 1–3 (council deliberations)
  GG 4
Haute Garonne
  AD Haute Garonne
    B 1, 4–8, 10, 11, 17, 21; 1899, 1985, 1988, 1997, 2010 (registers
      of the Parlement of Toulouse)
  AM Toulouse
    AA 1, 3, 5, 6, 17, 18, 45 (cartularies)
    BB 1–9 (council deliberations)
      72 (consistory register)
      265 (advice of outgoing to incoming consuls)
    CC 1576, 1579–82; 166–97 (control of accounting)
      1843–86 (account books); 2284
      2322–83, 2394, 2402 (*pièces à l'appui des comptes*)
      2832, 2833
    DD 10, 37, 45
    FF 117 (case from the Parlement of Toulouse)
      171 (register of royal justice)
      609/1 (report of committee of Parlement of Toulouse)
      660 (list of prisoners)
Hérault
  AD Hérault
    IIE 39/155, 95/998
    G 1375
  *AM Lodève
    AA 3

BB 3 (council deliberations)
CC 1–5 (*compoix* and *tailles*)
AM Lunel
  AA 1 (cartulary)
AM Montpellier
  Louvet 146, 147
  Grand Thalamus
  Deliberations of 1557
  Compoix
AM Pézenas
  140 (police regulations)
  791
  Cartulaire A; Cartulaire B
  1774–77 [BB 1–4] (council deliberations)
Haute Loire
  AD Haute Loire
    G 104 (register of episcopal court)
Lozère
  AD Lozère
    G 943 (register of episcopal court)
Tarn
  *AM Albi
    AA 4 (cartulary)
    BB 16–19, 22 (council deliberations)
    CC 175, 178, 202, 217, 226, 252, 434, 435 (account books)
  FF 38, 43
  AM Castres
    BB 1–8 (council deliberations)
  AM Gaillac
    BB 4 (council deliberations)
Archives Nationales
  AB XIX 204ᵃ–206 (papers of Douët d'Arcq)
  JJ 181 (royal letters of remission)

⚘ Bibliography

The reader may also with to consult the list of late-medieval Languedocian police regulations given in chap. 5, n. 21.

Asterisks indicate books that include editions of primary sources.

Aubenas, R. *Autour des deux passions de l'homme: la femme (en marge du mariage légitime) et l'argent (son trafic).* Vol. 6 of *Cours d'histoire du droit privé.* Aix-en-Provence, 1958.

*Azais, J. "Documents inédits du XIVe siècle sur les filles ou femmes de mauvaise vie." *BSABéz*, 1st ser., 2 (1837): 255–323.

*Baader, Joseph, ed. *Nürnberger Polizeiordnungen.* Bibliothek des litterarischen Vereins in Stuttgart, 63. Stuttgart, 1861.

*Barthélemy, L. *La prostitution à Marseille pendant le moyen-âge: rapport au comité médical sur la partie historique de l'ouvrage de M. le docteur Mireur intitulé La prostitution à Marseille. Documents nouveaux.* Marseille, 1883.

Bayle, Gustave. "Notes pour l'histoire de la prostitution au moyen âge dans les provinces méridionales de la France." *Mémoires de l'Académie de Vaucluse* 6 (1887): 233–45.

*Bertolotti, A. *Repressioni straordinarie alla prostituzione in Roma nel secolo XVI.* Rome, 1887.

Biéler, André. *L'homme et la femme dans la morale calviniste: la doctrine réformée sur l'amour, le mariage, le célibat, le divorce, l'adultère et la prostitution, considérée dans son cadre historique.* Geneva, 1963.

Bloch, Iwan. *Die Prostitution.* 2 vols. Berlin, 1912–25.

*Bondurand, E. "Appel au sujet des criées de Saint-Quentin." *MANî* 22 (1899): 153–58.

Bongert, Yvonne. *Cours d'histoire du droit pénal.* 2 vols. Paris, 1973.

*Boswell, John. *The Royal Treasure: Muslim Communities under the Crown of Aragon in the Fourteenth Century.* New Haven, 1977.

*Boyer, Georges. "Remarques sur l'administration de Toulouse au temps d'Alphonse de Poitiers." *RMT-SHD* 3 (1955): 6–10.

*Boys, W. *Collections for an History of Sandwich.* 2 vols. Canterbury, 1792.

*Brucker, Gene, ed. *The Society of Renaissance Florence: A Documentary Study.* New York and London, 1971.

*Brucker, J., ed. *Strassburger Zunft- und Polizei- Verordnungen des 14. und 15. Jahrhunderts, aus den Originalen des Stadtarchivs.* Strassburg, 1889.

Brundage, James A. "Prostitution in the Medieval Canon Law." *Signs: Journal of Women in Culture and Society* 1 (1976): 825–45.

Bullough, Vern L., et al. *A Bibliography of Prostitution.* New York and London, 1977.

———. *The History of Prostitution.* New York, 1964.

———. "The Prostitute in the Middle Ages." *Studies in Medieval Culture* 10 (1977), 9–17.

Burford, E. J. *The Orrible Synne: A Look at London Lechery from Roman to Cromwellian Times.* London, 1973.

*Calza, Carlo. "Documenti inediti sulla prostituzione tratti dagli Archivii della Repubblica Veneta." Parts 1, 2. *Giornale italiano delle malattie veneree e della pelle* 5 (1869): 305–20, 365–72; 119–25, 247–55, 316–19.

*Carbasse, Jean-Marie. *Consulats méridionaux et justice criminelle au moyen âge.* Thèse-Droit-Montpellier, 1974.

*Carboneres, Manuel. *Picaronas y alcahuetes ó la mancebía de Valencia, apuntes para la historia de la prostitución desde principios del siglo xiv hasta poco antes de la abolición de los fueros, con profusión de notas y copias de varios documentos oficiales.* Valencia, 1876.

Cartoux, Georges. *Condition des courtisanes à Avignon du XIIe au XIXe siècle.* Lyon, 1925.

*Catel, Guillaume. *Mémoires de l'histoire de Languedoc.* Toulouse, 1633.

Chalande, M. J. "La maison publique municipale aux XVe et XVIe siècles à Toulouse." *Mémoires e l'Académie des sciences, inscriptions et belles lettres de Toulouse.* 10th ser., 11 (1911): 65–86.

Charasson, A. *Un curé plébéien au XIIe siècle: Foulques, curé de Neuilly-sur-Marne (1191–1202).* Paris, 1905.

*Compayré, Clément. *Etudes historiques et documents inédits sur l'Albigeois, le Castrais et Lavaur.* Albi, 1841.

*Courteault, Henri. *Le Bourg-Saint-Andéol: essai sur la constitution et l'état social d'une ville du Midi de la France au moyen âge.* Paris, 1909.

*Cutrera, Antonio. *Storia della prostituzione in Sicilia: monografia storico-giuridica.* Palermo, 1903. Reprint. In *Classici della Cultura Siciliana,* edited by Antonio Buttitta. Palermo, 1971.

Dahm, Georg. *Das Strafrecht Italiens im ausgehenden Mittelalter (vornehmlich XIV Jhdt.).* Berlin and Leipzig, 1931.

Delamare, *Traité de la police.* 5 vols. Paris, 1722.

*Delannoy, J. C. *Pécheresses et repenties: notes pour servir à l'histoire de la prostitution à Amiens du XIVe au XIXe siècle.* Amiens, 1943.

*Desplanque, Emil. *Les infâmes dans l'ancien droit roussillonnais*. Perpignan, 1893.

Devic, Cl., and J. Vaissete. *Histoire générale de Languedoc*. 15 vols. Toulouse and Paris, 1872–92.

Duby, Georges. *Le chevalier, la femme et le prêtre. Le mariage dans la France féodale*. Paris, 1981.

*Dufau de Maluquer, A. de. *Le pays de Foix sous Gaston Phoebus: rôle des feux du comte de Foix en 1390*. Foix, 1901.

Dufour, Pierre. *Histoire de la prostitution chez tous les peuples du monde depuis l'antiquité la plus reculée jusqu'à nos jours*. 6 vols. Paris, 1851–53.

*Duvernoy, Jean. *Les registres d'inquisition de Jacques Fournier, 1318–1325*. 3 vols. Bibliothèque méridionale, 2nd ser., 41. Toulouse, 1965.

Esmein, A., and R. Genestal. *Le mariage en droit canonique*. 2nd ed. 2 vols. Paris, 1929.

*Fabretti, Ariodante. *La prostituzione in Perugia nei secoli XIV, XV e XVI: documenti editi*. 2nd ed. Torino, 1890.

*Felibien, Michel. *Histoire de la ville de Paris*. 5 vols. Paris, 1725.

Flandrin, Jean-Louis. *Le sexe et l'occident*. Paris, 1981.

*Galligo, J. "Circa ad alcuni antichi e singolari documenti inediti riguardanti la prostituzione tratti dal' Archivo centrale di stato de Firenze." Part 1. *Giornale italiano delle malattie veneree e della pelle* 4 (1869): 123–28, 185–92, 247–53.

Geremek, Bronislaw. *Les marginaux parisiens aux XIVe et XVe siècles*. Paris, 1976.

*Germain, A. "Statuts inédits des repenties du convent de Saint-Gilles de Montpellier." *MSAMtp* 5 (1860–69): 123–42.

*Giacomo, Salvatore di. *La prostituzione in Napoli nei secoli XV, XVI e XVII*. Naples, 1899.

*Gilles, Henri. *Les coutumes de Toulouse (1286) et leu premier commentaire (1296)*. Toulouse, 1969.

*Giraud, Charles. *Essai sur l'histoire du droit français au moyen âge*. 2 vols. Paris, 1846.

*Granara, Romolo. *Di alcune metamorfosi della sifilide: nozioni storiche sulla prostituzione in Genova, coll' aggiunta de considerazioni e proposte politico-mediche*. Genoa, 1863.

Guardia, J. M. "De la prostitution en Espagne." Appendix in vol. 2 of Parent-Duchatelet, *De la prostitution dans la ville de Paris*. 3rd ed. Paris, 1857.

Gutsch, Milton R. "A Twelfth-Century Preacher: Fulk of Neuilly." In *The Crusades and Other Historical Essays Presented to Dana C. Munro by His Former Students*, edited by Louis J. Paetow. New York, 1928. Reprint. New York, 1968, 183–206.

Hartung, Wolfgang. *Die Spielleute: eine Randgruppe in der Gesellschaft des Mittelalters*. Vierteljahrschrift für Sozial- und Wirtschaftsgeschichte, Beihefte 72. Wiesbaden, 1982.

Herlihy, David, and Christiane Klapisch-Zuber. *Les toscans et leurs familles: une étude du catasto florentin de 1427*. Paris, 1978.

His, Rudolph. *Das Strafrecht des deutschen Mittelalters.* 2 vols. Weimar, 1920. Reprint. Darmstadt, 1964.

*Kemp, Jacob. *Die Wohlfahrtspflege des kölner Rates in dem Jahrhundert nach der grossen Zunftrevolution.* Diss.-Phil.-Bonn, 1904.

*Lacassagne, Jean, and Alice Picornot. "Vieilles étuves de Lyon et d'ailleurs: un curieux procès au XVᵉ siècle relatif aux étuves de la Pêcherie (1478–1483)." *Albums du Crocodile,* 1943.

Larivaille, Paul. *La vie quotidienne des courtisanes en Italie au temps de la Renaissance (Rome et Venise, XV–XVI siècles).* Paris, 1975.

*Laurière, Eusèbe-Jacques de; ed. *Ordonnances des roys de France de la troisième race.* 21 vols. Paris, 1723–1849.

Le Foyer, Jean. *Exposé du droit pénal normand au XIIIᵉ siècle.* Thèse-Droit-Paris, 1931.

Le Goff, Jacques. "Métiers licites et métiers illicites dans l'occident médiéval." In his *Pour un autre moyen âge: temps, travail et culture en occident, 18 essais.* Paris, 1977, 91–107.

*Le Pileur, Louis. *La prostitution du XIIIᵉ au XVIIᵉ siècle. Documents tirés des archives d'Avignon, du comtat Venaissin, de la principauté d'Orange et de la ville libre impériale de Besançon.* Paris, 1908.

*Le Roux de Lincy. "Hugues Aubriot, prévôt de Paris sous Charles V, 1367–1381." *BEC,* 5th ser., 3 (1862): 173–213.

*Limouzin-Lamothe, R. *La commune de Toulouse et les sources de son histoire (1120–1249): étude historique et critique suivie de l'édition du cartulaire du consulat.* Bibliothèque méridionale, 2nd ser., 26. Toulouse, 1932.

*Lippert, H. *Die Prostitution in Hamburg.* Hamburg, 1848.

Li livres de jostice et de plet. Edited by Rapetti. Collection des documents inédits sur l'histoire de la France, 1st ser., Histoire politique. Paris, 1850.

Livre Vert de Lacaune. Edited by Gautran. Bergerac, 1911.

Lorcin, Marie-Thérèse. *Façons de sentir et de penser: les fabliaux français.* Paris, 1979.

———. "La prostituée des fabliaux, est-elle intégrée ou exclue?" *Senefiance* (Cahiers du Centre universitaire d'études et de recherches médiévales d'Aix-en-Provence) 1 (1977): 107–17.

*Louandre. "Statuts des Soeurs de la Magdeleine d'Abbeville." *Mémoires de la Société d'émulation d'Abbeville,* 1834–35: 117–42.

Mancini, Jean-Gabriel. *Prostitution et proxénétisme.* Que sais-je? 999. Paris, 1972.

*Maulde, M. A. R. de. *Coutumes et règlements de la république d'Avignon au XIIIᵉ siècle.* Anciens textes de droit français. Paris, 1879.

Mazahéri, A. *La vie quotidienne des musulmans au moyen âge, X–XIII siècles.* Paris, 1951.

*Ménard, Léon. *Histoire civile, ecclésiastique et littéraire de la ville de Nismes, avec les preuves.* 7 vols. Paris, 1750–58.

Méray, Antony. *La vie au temps des libres prêcheurs, ou les devanciers de Luther et de Rabelais: croyances, usages et moeurs intimes des XIVᵉ, XVᵉ et XVIᵉ siècles.* 2nd ed. 2 vols. Paris, 1878.

*Mireur, Hippolyte. *La prostitution à Marseille*. Paris and Marseille, 1882.

*Möring, W. *Die Wohlfahrtspolitik des hamburger Rates im Mittelalter*. Berlin and Leipzig, 1913.

*Mouynès, Germain. *Ville de Narbonne: Inventaire des archives communales antérieures à 1790. Annexes de la série AA*. Narbonne, 1871.

*Pansier, Pierre. *L'oeuvre des repenties à Avignon du XIIIe au XVIIIe siècle*. Paris, 1910.

————. "Les prétendus statuts de la reine Jeanne règlementant la prostitution à Avignon en 1347." *BSFHMed* 17 (1923): 157–75.

Pavan, Elisabeth. "Police des moeurs, société et politique à Venise à la fin du moyen âge." *Revue historique* 536 (1980): 241–88.

*Pavesi, Pietro. *Il bordello di Pavia da XIV al XVII secolo ed i soccorsi di S. Simone e S. Margherita*. Milan, 1897.

Perry, Mary Elizabeth. " 'Lost Women' in Early Modern Seville: The Politics of Prostitution." *Feminist Studies* 4 (1978); 195–214.

Pertile, Antonio. *Storia del diritto italiano dalla caduta dell' impero romano alla codificazione*. 6 vols. Torino, Rome, Naples, and Milan, 1892.

Le Petit Thalamus. Edited by F. Pégat, E. Thomas, and Desmazes. Société archéologique de Montpellier. Montpellier, 1840.

Porteau-Bitker, A. "Criminalité et délinquance féminines dans le droit pénal des XIIIe et XIVe siècles." *RHD* 58 (1980): 13–56.

Posern-Klett, von. "Frauenhäuser und freie Frauen in Sachsen." *Archiv für sächsische Geschichte* 12 (1874): 63–89.

*Rabutaux, *De la prostitution en Europe depuis l'antiquité jusqu'à la fin du XVIe siècle*. Paris, 1865.

*Ramière de Fortanier, J. *Chartes de franchises du Lauragais*. Paris, 1939.

Rigaudière, Albert. *Saint-Flour, ville d'Auvergne au bas moyen âge: étude d'histoire administrative et financière*. 2 vols. Paris, 1982.

Robert, Ulysse. *Les signes d'infamie au moyen âge: juifs, sarrasins, hérétiques, lépreux, cagots et filles publiques*. Paris, 1891.

Rodocanachi, E. *Courtisanes et bouffons: étude de moeurs romaines au XVIe siècle*. Paris, 1894.

Rossiaud, Jacques. "Prostitution, jeunesse et société dans les villes du sud-est au XVe siècle." *An-ESC* 31 (1976): 289–325.

————. "Prostitution, sexualité, société dans les villes françaises au XVe siècle." *Communications: Ecole des hautes études en sciences sociales, Centre d'études transdisciplinaires* 35 (1982): 68–83.

Sabatier. *Histoire de la législation sur les femmes publiques et les lieux de débauche*. Paris, 1828.

Salusbury, G. T. *Street Life in Medieval England*. 2nd ed. Oxford, 1948.

*Sauval, Henri. *Histoire et recherches des antiquités de la ville de Paris*. 3 vols. Paris, 1724.

*Sauve, Fernand. *La prostitution et les moeurs à Apt et en Provence pendant le moyen âge*. Vol. 3 of *Notices aptésiennes: études et documents historiques*. Paris, 1905.

*Schrank, Josef. *Die Geschichte der Prostitution in Wien*. Vol. 1 of *Die Pros-*

titution in Wien in historischer, administrativer und hygienischer Beziehung. Vienna, 1886.

Servais, Jean-Jacques, and Jean-Pierre Laurend. *Histoire et dossier de la prostitution.* Paris, 1965.

Simon, André. *L'Ordre des Pénitentes de Sainte Marie-Madeleine en Allemagne au XIIIe siècle.* Thèse-Théologie-Fribourg (Suisse), 1918.

*Terroine, Anne. "Le roi de ribauds de l'Hôtel du roi et les prostituées parisiennes." *RHD*, 4th ser., 56 (1978): 253–67.

*Thomas of Chobham. *Summa Confessorum.* Edited by F. Broomfield. Analecta Mediaevalia Namurcensia, 25. Louvain and Paris, 1968.

Trexler, Richard C. "La prostitution florentine au XVe siècle: patronages et clientèles." *An-ESC* 36 (1981): 983–1015.

Vaultier, Roger. *Le folklore pendant la Guerre de Cent Ans d'après les lettres de rémission du Trésor des Chartes.* Paris, 1965.

Viala, André. *Le Parlement de Toulouse et l'administration royale laïque, 1420–1525.* 2 vols. Albi, 1953.

*Vidal, Auguste. "Les délibérations du conseil communal d'Albi de 1372 à 1388." *Revue des langues romanes*, 5th ser., 6 (1903): 33–73; 7 (1904): 75–90, 348–73, 535–64; 8 (1905): 240–79, 420–70.

*———. "Douze comptes consulaires d'Albi du XIVe siècle." 2 vols. Toulouse, 1906–11.

Wolff, Philippe, ed. *Histoire du Languedoc.* Toulouse, 1967.

Wustmann, Gustav. "Frauenhäuser und freie Frauen in Leipzig im Mittelalter." *Archiv für Kultur-Geschichte* 5 (1907): 469–82.

ꙮ Index

Index

Index

Index